A detailed history of
BRITISH RAILWAYS STANDARD STEAM LOCOMOTIVES

Volume Three: The Tank Engine Classes

THE RAILWAY CORRESPONDENCE AND TRAVEL SOCIETY
1997

Cover photo: 80154 Stands in steam outside Brighton Works when new 13 April 1957. This was the last locomotive of its class and the last steam engine built at Brighton. This was the only member of the class to carry the second lion and wheel totem from new.

A SECTION OF COLOUR ILLUSTRATIONS IS PRESENTED ON PAGES 81-88

© RCTS 1997

Second Impression 2007

www.rcts.org.uk

ISBN 090 1115 77 0

Published by the Railway Correspondence and Travel Society
70 Heathfields, Downend, Bristol, BS16 6HS, England.

COVER DESIGN by JOHN HOLDROYD

Printed by The Amadeus Press, Cleckheaton, BD19 4TQ
Typesetting by Highlight Type Bureau Ltd, Shipley

82017 pulls away from Exeter St. Davids Station with an up pick-up goods train off the LSWR line bound for Exmouth Junction yard, date unknown.

G.W. Sharpe & Co.

CONTENTS

PREFACE

This volume covers the detailed history of the British Railways Standard Tank engines which were built between 1951 and 1957. They were designed to cover the projected requirements for intermediate and short distance haulage, mainly passenger trains, for a period of forty years. This plan was very soon curtailed, however, by the 1955 Modernisation Programme which envisaged early phasing out of steam haulage in favour of diesel and electric traction. It is the intention to cover the entire Standard locomotive history in four volumes of which this is the second to appear. Each volume will be self contained but the detailed background to the policies and design work which led up to the construction of the Standard locomotives is incorporated as the first section of Volume One which is already available. It is also the intention to include an index to the series as the last section of the fourth volume.

As pounds sterling and imperial measures together with two daily twelve hour periods of time were used during the steam era these units are used throughout the series.

The vast amount of assistance received from the railway and enthusiast community is very gratefully acknowledged by the RCTS. It has come in the form of notes, reminiscences and many photographs, some of the latter being included in this volume. I must mention a few of those who have been of exceptional assistance namely Philip Atkins, librarian of NRM York and his staff, Geoffrey Bird, Alan Clothier and Robert Urie all past senior mechanical engineers with British Railways who had first hand experience in design and operation of Standard tank engines, also Brian Sullivan who undertook the task of putting the written word for this book on computer disc.

Bibliography and Acknowledgements are shown towards the end of the book.

Accuracy is vital and care has been taken to ensure this. There are grey areas, however, from information at present available due either to missing archive documents or conflicting information available from BR records which do exist. I shall be pleased to receive any corrections or additional information from readers on behalf of the RCTS.

The shed allocations of all the locomotives described in this book have been shown in order to cover as fully as possible their complete operating history. The author has used information which appeared in The Railway Observer magazines at the time. However, subsequent perusal of other information has revealed some differences. These have been researched by RCTS members and show that information produced by British Railways was in some instances inconsistent. In fact there are variations between the allocation transfer details given to the Society at the time and internal documents produced by the Regions. There are also cases of this information differing from details written on the Engine History Cards. These differences apply mainly, but not entirely, to transfers made towards the end of the steam era. Some listed transfers also may not have materialised at this time of rapid change as events overtook plans. We are confident that the vast majority of information shown is correct.

R. K. Taylor
(Hon. Editor British Railways Standard Steam Locomotive series)
"The Meadows"
Bardon Mill
Hexham
Northumberland
NE47 7AA

SUMMARY OF BRITISH RAILWAYS
STANDARD TANK ENGINE CLASSES

WHEEL ARRANGEMENT	POWER CLASS	NUMBERS	BUILT	PERIOD OF BUILDING	NO. IN CLASS
2-6-4T	4	80000-154	BRIGHTON, DERBY, DONCASTER	1951-7	155
2-6-2T	3	82000-44	SWINDON	1952-5	45
2-6-2T	2	84000-29	CREWE, DARLINGTON	1953-7	30
				TOTAL	230

BUILDING WORKSHOPS	CLASSES			NO. OF ENGINES
	80000	82000	84000	
BRIGHTON	130			130
CREWE			20	20
DARLINGTON			10	10
DERBY	15			15
DONCASTER	10			10
SWINDON		45		45
TOTALS	155	45	30	230

ABBREVIATIONS USED IN THIS BOOK

Companies and Organisations

BR	British Railways (British Rail from 1.65)
BREL	British Rail Engineering Limited
CLC	Cheshire Lines Committee
ER	Eastern Region
G&C	Gresham and Craven Ltd.
GC	Great Central
GCR	Great Central Railway
GN	Great Northern
GNR	Great Northern Railway
GNSR	Great North of Scotland Railway
GSWR	Glasgow and South Western Railway
GW	Great Western
GWR	Great Western Railway
KWVR	Keighley and Worth Valley Railway
LBSCR	London Brighton and South Coast Railway
LCGB	Locomotive Club of Great Britain
LMR	London Midland Region
LMS	London Midland and Scottish Railway
LNER	London and North Eastern Railway
LNWR	London and North Western Railway
LSWR	London and South Western Railway
LTS	London Tilbury and Southend
LTSR	London Tilbury and Southend Railway
LYR	Lancashire and Yorkshire Railway
MR	Midland Railway
MSWJR	Midland and South Western Junction Railway
NBR	North British Railway
NER	North Eastern Railway (prior to 1923)
NER	North Eastern Region (from 1/1/1948)
NRM	National Railway Museum, York
NYMR	North Yorkshire Moors Railway
RCTS	Railway Correspondence and Travel Society
SECR	South Eastern and Chatham Railway
SLS	Stephenson Locomotive Society
SR	Southern Railway
SR	Southern Region (from 1/1/1948)
SVR	Severn Valley Railway
WD	War Department
WR	Western Region

Other Abbreviations

A/S	Area to Surface
ATC	Automatic Train Control
AWS	Automatic Warning System
CME	Chief Mechanical Engineer
CM&EE	Chief Mechanical and Electrical Engineer
Co.	Company
cyl	Cylinder
DMU	Diesel Multiple Unit
DRWG	Drawing
ECS	Empty Coaching Stock
Gal.	Gallon
IofW	Isle of Wight
Jct.	Junction
Loco.	Locomotive
MT	Mixed Traffic
Mods	Modifications
MPD	Motive Power Depot
N/A	Not Applicable
P	Four Weekly Period
PT	Pannier Tank Engine
Sigs	Signals
SWG	Standard Wire Gauge
T	Tank Engine
USSR	Union of Soviet Socialist Republics
U	Unserviceable
UK	United Kingdom
VAT	Value Added Tax
W/d	Withdrawn
W/e	Week ending

THE TANK ENGINE CLASSES

P. J. Chancellor

1. INTRODUCTION

1.1 Background to Standardisation

The following summarises the development of a series of locomotives that ran to a total of 999, starting with 70000 *Britannia*, a Class 7 Pacific design appearing in 1951 and concluding with the entry into traffic in 1960 of Standard Class 9F 2-10-0, 92220 *Evening Star*.

At the time of nationalisation there were a large number of different types of locomotives in service across the country, designed and built by the constituent railways, meeting a wide range of traffic requirements. However, following the war years there were not many modern types and even fewer that could fit a universal loading gauge.

A team drawn from all four of the constituent railway companies but led by former London Midland and Scottish men set about producing a set of designs that could be used from Penzance to Wick, which also took account of conditions in a post-war Britain requiring engines to be easily serviced and maintained. It had become increasingly difficult to find labour willing to work in the dirty environment of engine sheds and there was a need for locomotives to have low maintenance costs as well as being able to perform adequately on the often inferior fuels of the day. The theme of the designs was to be the use of standard and, as far as possible, fully interchangeable parts including items such as boilers, wheels and tenders.

The ancestry of most of the designs could be traced back to the LMS, no doubt influenced by the heavy bias of staff on the team but mainly because the designs of the other railways did not meet the defined needs. For example, Great Western

designs could not meet the L1 loading gauge, newer Southern Railway designs failed to meet the 'ease of maintenance' criteria and the London and North Eastern designs tended to have higher maintenance and fuel costs compared with similar LMS designs. However, the best of various design features were to be taken from the other railways for incorporation in the new types.

The new designs of tender engines (nine types ranging from Class 2 2-6-0 to Class 9 2-10-0) had a distinct "family" appearance with high running plates for ease of maintenance and a cab layout common to all (Fig. 1).

Three tank engine types were also developed, of Classes 2, 3 and 4, the "family" resemblance being evident in these designs too. Such features included plate frames, plain bearings on all axles (unlike some of the larger tender engines which had roller bearings on the driving axles), taper boilers, rocking grates and self-cleaning smokeboxes to reduce servicing requirements and allow relatively easy access to all moving parts. To aid this last feature the tank designs had two outside cylinders only and were fitted with Walschaert valve gear.

The first design to appear in July 1951 was the Class 4 tank, the class total reaching 155 locomotives with Classes 3 and 2 2-6-2 tank designs following totalling 45 and 30 members respectively. Despite the fact that the engines met all the key targets set for them in terms of cost and efficiency, with the run down of steam traction on British Railways all had been withdrawn within sixteen years of the first entering service with some engines being in stock with British

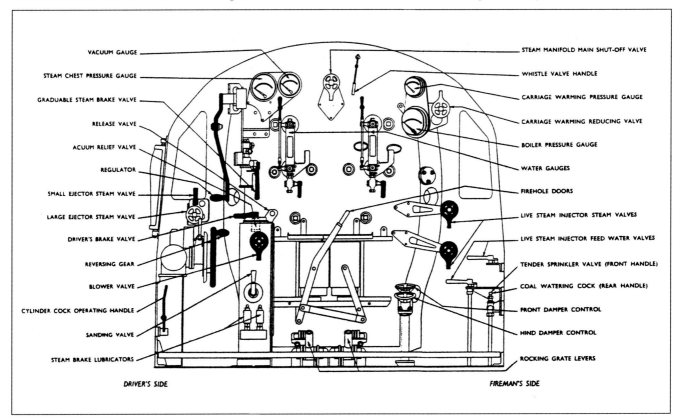

Fig. 1 Arrangement of Cab fittings – Standard Locomotive.

British Railways

Railways for as little as seven years.

Several of the Class 4 tanks however survived their journey to the scrap yard and are now preserved on various lines around the country where they look set to give many more years service than they did to their original owners.

1.2 General Design Features

Three classes of tank locomotives were included in the Standard locomotive building programme comprising a 2-6-4 design designated as a Class 4 Mixed Traffic type (4MT) and two 2-6-2 tank designs being of 3MT and 2MT power classification. All three types had similarities in design to standard tender engines with the same power classification, and they were all intended to have a life span of forty years.

All the designs featured plate frames as had the equivalent tender engines. These smaller locomotives, which included the tank engines, had narrow fireboxes with the object of being able to perform average duties with combustion rates not exceeding 45-50lb of coal per square foot of grate area per hour at 80% boiler efficiency.

Boilers used the standard 5¹/₈" diameter flue tubes and were equipped with copper inner fireboxes based on GWR/LMS Belpaire practice. All tank locomotives were fitted with rocking grates constructed in two rocking sections, front and back. (On the larger tender engines the rocking was arranged in side by side sections.)

Self Cleaning Smokeboxes were fitted as standard but the self cleaning fittings were subsequently removed from some engines during their lives. The Class 2 and 4 tanks were fitted with cast iron cylinders whilst the Class 3 engines had steel castings with cast iron liners.

Hammer blow had to conform to the recommendations of the 1928 Bridge Stress Committee such that the axle hammer-blow should not exceed 25% of the static load and that the total should not exceed 12.5 tons at five revolutions per second.

In this respect the Class 3 tanks were more damaging to the tracks than the Class 4 and 2 versions, the figures being:-

Maximum Hammerblow at 5 Revolutions per second			
	Class 4MT	Class 3MT	Class 2MT
Tons per wheel	1.91	2.17	1.53
Tons per axle	2.28	2.58	1.82
Tons per rail	5.10	5.93	4.29
Whole Locomotive	6.08	7.05	5.11

All the classes were fitted with screw reversing gear but the tanks, unlike the tender engines, had the reversing screw in the cab as opposed to being at the front end of the reversing rod. The position of the reversing handwheel was registered through gears to a rotary drum on which the percentage cut-off was shown. This drum had the 'forward gear' and 'mid gear' markings indicated by raised figures and letters and the 'backward gear' markings were indicated by recessed figures and letters on a raised portion of the drum surface and were filled in with black wax. The raised parts of the drum were polished and nickel plated to enable the figures to be more clearly seen. A notched sector plate was incorporated with the reversing handwheel which, together with the pivoted handle and catch arrangement, enabled it to be locked in almost any

position for each revolution of the wheel.

The Class 4 engines were non-standard in that the reversing hand wheel in the cab was set diagonally as opposed to 'end on' as in all the other designs. In other respects however the tanks had the standard cab layout common to all the twelve types and which had been the subject of much discussion prior to its introduction. In common with other classes, those locomotives allocated to the Western Region, plus some on the Scottish Region, had a different design of firebox door allowing more air to enter which suited the different kinds of coal used in these areas.

All axles on all engines had plain bearings. Suspension on the driving axles was by underhung leaf springs having a span of 4' 0" with sixteen leaves made from 5" x ¹/₂" plates. The bogie springs on the Class 4 engines were of 3' 6" span with plates of 5" x ⁷/₁₆" with twenty four leaves in each spring.

The pony truck bearing springs were double coils, with four sets per truck, each pair acting at each end of a yoke which rested on the crown of the axlebox. These springs consisted of separate inner and outer coils, the inner one having a length of 1' 1" and the outer 12¹/₈".

The pony truck of the 2-6-4 tanks and the leading truck of the 2-6-2 tank designs had spring side control but the trailing truck of these had swing link side control.

All locomotives were fitted with mechanical lubricators of either Silvertown or Wakefield design. The systems employed varied from that of the tender engines now described.

For the little end bearing of the connecting rod, the oil box was integral with the rod, a cork being provided in the riveted-on cover for re-filling, the cover having a spring loaded needle valve which acted as a reservoir.

The big end bearing was of a similar design except that a syphon tube with restrictor was provided instead of a needle valve.

On the 2-6-4 tanks the coupling rod crank pin and joint pin bearings were lubricated in the same way as the big end bearing but on the 2-6-2 tanks an oil hole was provided in the eye-end of the leading rod.

The expansion link die blocks contained an oil well for a pad trimming which lubricated the bearing in the die for the pin and an oil box was provided on each half of the expansion link to lubricate the slides directly for the front surface and through the die blocks to the back surface.

The radius rod was fitted with a die block in the slotted end of the rod for reversing purposes, the pin and slide surfaces being lubricated from an oil box integral with the top slide with cap-nut and cork and having a syphon tube with trimming.

The bogie slides on both sides of the bogie centre were lubricated by high capacity oil boxes with trimmings which fed the bearing surfaces via flexible pipes. Pony truck lubrication was achieved by the same method.

The trailing pony trucks of the 2-6-2 tank designs, fitted with four swing links, had the top pins lubricated by means of pipes running from flat bottomed boxes placed on the front of the bunker inside the cab, the same boxes being used for lubrication of the centre pivot pad.

In the following chapters the details of the individual classes and the variations between members of the classes are described. Readers are asked to bear in mind that engineering practices varied between Regions and that data on mileages between overhauls may not be indicative of inferior or superior performance and standards to be found at the various locations.

A major problem encountered with the compilation of data for the history of the Standard classes has been the lack of official information. In all cases accurate official records ceased to be kept when it was clear that steam motive power was on its way out and in the case of some of the Standard engines this represented up to 50% of the working life of the locomotive. For a considerable number of engines it has not proved possible to locate any official data at all. Efforts have been made to fill the gaps from actual observations although this has proved particularly difficult in the case of the tank classes which were not frequently reported and even less frequently photographed.

2. CLASS 4   2-6-4T   80000-80154

Fig. 2   80140 at Eastleigh MPD having recently been out-shopped from the Works 4 August 1961.   *E.W. Fry*

2.1 Purpose

In the years before World War 2, the Great Western and LMS vigorously pursued a policy of replacing pre-grouping secondline tender and tank engines by fewer modern and more economical 2-6-2 or 2-6-4 tanks. This policy was virtually completed by the GWR before hostilities commenced but, because of the later start, further large scale replacement remained necessary by the LMS in 1945-7. Prewar, the funds available to the LNER for locomotive renewal forbade a similar policy and consequently many of that company's secondary passenger and suburban services had to be worked by pre-grouping classes. However, to some extent this was rectified when the one hundred Thompson L1 class 2-6-4 tanks, ordered between 1944 and 1947, entered service (Fig. 3). Therefore at the time of nationalisation, the GWR, LMS and LNER were adequately provided with modern passenger tanks, and although more would become necessary, these could be supplied as annual replacements.

On the Southern Railway, however, the motive power position was less satisfactory for the postponement of the electrification programme had created an acute shortage of modern passenger tanks, particularly on the Central Division where most of the Victoria and London Bridge steam commuter services were having to be worked by the Maunsell Q class 0-6-0's (Fig. 4) and ex-LBSCR 4-4-2 tanks (Fig. 5), a most unsatisfactory state of affairs with no readily apparent solution since, with the failure of the Bulleid Leader class, no appropriate Eastleigh design existed. Consequently the problem remained at nationalisation, when with little delay assistance was sought from Derby Works where the time proven Fairburn 2-6-4 tanks were currently being constructed for the London Midland Region. The response was favourable and in April 1948 newly-built Nos. 42198/9 were despatched to the Southern Region to work a lengthy series of trials from Waterloo to Basingstoke, Victoria to Brighton, Eastbourne and Tunbridge Wells West, Charing Cross to Ashford and Victoria to Ashford via Maidstone East. With memory of the Maunsell River class 2-6-4 tanks, particular attention was given to the riding and when this proved acceptable at the highest speeds demanded by the various routes, forty-one locomotives, 42066-42106, were ordered from Brighton Works at a cost of £9,485 each (Fig. 6). Delivery was planned for the second half of 1949, but assembly difficulties with the final West Country pacifics delayed completion of the first, 42096, until July 1950 and raised the cost to £11,025 each.

Fig. 3
67755 in Darlington North Road Works yard on a date unknown. It is a Class L1 2-6-4T built by BR to a Thompson design and was completed in December 1948 but was ordered by the LNER before nationalisation.
E. Haigh Collection

Fig. 4
S R Maunsell designed Q class 0-6-0 30541 at Lymington Junction working a train from Bournemouth West to Brockenhurst via Wimborne 23 April 1962. *Rodney Lissenden*

Fig. 5
LBSCR 4-4-2T 2083 at Shoreham-by-Sea on 27 August 1936. It was classified 'I3' by the Southern Railway.
Rodney Lissenden Collection

Fig. 6
42084 working a Richmond to Darlington Bank Top train at Croft Spa in May 1952. This locomotive was built at Brighton by the SR to an LMS Fairburn design 2-6-4T and was classified 4P. It was first allocated to Stewarts Lane MPD and subsequently transferred to Darlington. *RAS Marketing*

Most of these welcome additions to Southern Region stock were sent to the Central Division, principally to Brighton and Tunbridge Wells West sheds, where they were employed on a wide range of secondary passenger duties as well as being rostered for the more exacting London commuter services. Exceptionally for a design originating on a "foreign" railway, and incorporating many unfamiliar features, they were well regarded by the men who much appreciated their free-steaming boiler, sure-footedness and comfortable cab.

Since similar acclaim was found on the Scottish and London Midland Regions, and with the Thompson L1 class plagued by hot boxes, the Fairburn 2-6-4 tank was the obvious choice for inclusion in the British Railways range of Standard classes. At first only superficial modification was thought necessary to accept the repositioning or incorporation of standard fittings but, following a detailed examination by the Brighton Drawing Office staff, it was discovered that more drastic action would be required in order to meet the L1 universal loading gauge and thereby gain virtually unrestricted running throughout the newly-created Regions.

The modifications mainly concerned the superstructure and distance across the cylinders, the former being found relatively simple to accomplish whereas the latter proved troublesome for the largest acceptable cylinder diameter, 18 inches, significantly reduced the tractive effort. Since this was considered undesirable, it became necessary to increase the working pressure to 225 lb. per sq.in. which fortunately could be accomplished by restaying the existing boiler at a closer pitch. By this means a tractive effort of 25,515 lb. at 85% working pressure was obtained as against the 24,670 lb. of the Fairburn locomotives. Officially the class was designed to work similar duties to the 51XX class 2-6-2 tanks of the WR, and the previously mentioned Fairburn and L1 class 2-6-4T's.

The redesigning was completed at Brighton in August 1950, with an initial batch of fifty-four locomotives being included in the 1951 Building Programme. Other orders followed in 1952-1956 until the class totalled 155, the details being:-

Prog-ramme	Works	Order Nos.	Engine Nos.	Total	Region
1951	Derby	O/5124	80000-9	10	Scottish
	Brighton	BR3621	80010-9	10	Southern
	Brighton	BR3621	80020-30	11	Scottish
	Brighton	BR3621	80031/2/3	3	North Eastern
	Brighton	BR3621	80034-53	20	London Midland
1952	Derby	O/6231	80054-8	5	Scottish
	Brighton	BR5271	80059-68	10	London Midland
1953	Brighton	BR5788	80069-78	10	Eastern
	Brighton	BR6166	80079/80	2	Eastern
	Brighton	BR6166	80081-8	8	London Midland
	Brighton	BR6167	80089-95	7	London Midland
	Brighton	BR6167	80096-80105	10	Eastern
	Doncaster	E0398	80106-15	10	Scottish
1954	Brighton	BR6360	80116-20	5	North Eastern
	Brighton	BR6360	80121-4	4	Scottish
	Brighton	BR6941	80125-30	6	Scottish
1956	Brighton	BR7739	80131-44	14	Eastern
	Brighton	BR7739	80145-54	10	Southern

Fifteen more, Nos. 80155-69, to be built at Brighton in 1957, were proposed for the Southern Region, but cancelled before work on order BR7739 commenced.

It was understood that the locomotives built at Doncaster had some parts fabricated at Gorton. This batch differed from the earlier engines by having the running plate cut away near the lubricator. In addition the route availability number was painted on the bunker and power classification 'Class 4' on the buffer beam.

2.2 Dimensions and Data

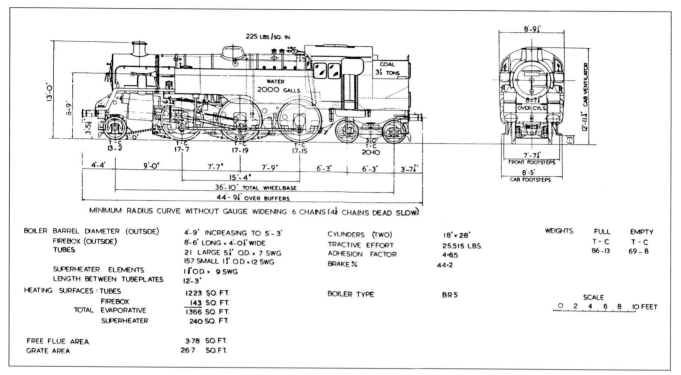

BOILER BARREL DIAMETER (OUTSIDE)	4'-9" INCREASING TO 5'-3"	
FIREBOX (OUTSIDE)	8'-6" LONG × 4'-0½" WIDE	
TUBES	21 LARGE 5¼" O.D. × 7 SWG	
	157 SMALL 1⅞" O.D. × 12 SWG	
SUPERHEATER ELEMENTS	1⅛" O.D. × 9 SWG	
LENGTH BETWEEN TUBEPLATES	12'-3"	
HEATING SURFACES : TUBES	1223 SQ. FT.	
FIREBOX	143 SQ. FT.	
TOTAL EVAPORATIVE	1366 SQ. FT.	
SUPERHEATER	240 SQ. FT.	
FREE FLUE AREA	3·78 SQ. FT.	
GRATE AREA	26·7 SQ.FT.	

CYLINDERS (TWO) 18" × 28"
TRACTIVE EFFORT 25,515 LBS.
ADHESION FACTOR 4·65
BRAKE % 44·2

BOILER TYPE BR5

WEIGHTS	FULL	EMPTY
	T - C	T - C
	86 -13	69 - 8

Fig. 7   Class 4 2-6-4T. Diagram and dimensions.   *British Railways*

Piston Swept Volume (1 cylinder)	7,125 cu in
Piston Valves (Walschaert) diameter	10" dia.
steam lap	1½"
maximum travel	6.58"
lead	¼"
exhaust clearance	nil
Maximum Cut-off	75%
Travel at 20% cut-off	3.66"
Clearance Volume as % of piston swept volume	10.8
Maximum Piston thrust	57,256 lbs
Steam Chest volume between valve heads	3,912 cu in
Steam Chest volume as % of piston swept volume	54.9
Revolving Masses-weight per cylinder	1,396 lbs
Reciprocating Masses - total weight/cylinder	757 lbs
- percentage balanced	40
- unbalanced weight/cyl	454 lbs
Ratio unbalanced weight/cylinder to total engine weight	1:427
Firebox Volume	131 cu ft
Water Surface at half glass	84 sq ft
Volume steam above half glass	80 cu ft
Total Heating Surface including firebox	1612 sq ft

Free area through tubes	Large 1.74 sq ft
	Small 2.04 sq ft
	Total 3.78 sq ft
Area through large tubes as % of Total	46.0
Total free area as % of grate area	14.2
A/S ratio - Large Tubes	1:345
- Small Tubes	1:382
Steam pipe in boiler - Bore	5 ½"
Cross sectional area	23.8 sq in
Regulator full open area	24.3 sq in
Superheater Elements Total Area	20.6 sq in
Steam pipes/Cylinders Total Area	31.8 sq in
Blast Pipe Cap diameter	4¾"
Blast Pipe area	17.7 sq in
Chimney Throat - diameter	1' 1½"
- area	1.0 sq ft
Chimney Throat area as % of grate area	3.75
Height Blast Pipe Cap to Chimney Throat	2' 7"
Taper of Chimney	1 in 14

Original power classification 4MT, May 1953 classification 4P4F. Statistical classification 4MTT. LNER route availability RA5.

Weight Full	Published Weights	Weights shown as Brighton Drawing SL/BR/95
Leading Wheels	13t 2c	13t 3c
Leading Coupled Wheels	17t 7c	18t 0c
Centre Coupled Wheels	17t 19c	18t 0c
Trailing Coupled Wheels	17t 15c	17t 16c
Bogie	20t 10c	21t 11c
Total	**86t 13c**	**88t 10c**
Adhesion factor	4.23	

2.3 Design Details

Externally there was no marked resemblance to the Fairburn 2-6-4 class since, in complying with the L1 loading gauge, Brighton had given the side tanks and bunker a pleasing curved profile which in conjunction with the deep running plate and drop ends created a distinctive appearance.

In common with other Standard classes, fittings included Eastleigh pattern boiler feed clack valves, dome regulators with external rodding, manganese steel coupled box liners, Gresham & Craven ejectors, steam sanding and combined steam and vacuum braking. The 6ft. 3in. bogie wheelbase was 3in. shorter than the Fairburn pattern and this, together with a more compact bunker, reduced the overall length by 11⅞ in. to 44ft. 9⅞ in.

Sanding was provided ahead of the leading coupled wheels and to the front and rear of the centre coupled wheels. On most engines the sanding operation was conventionally by steam, but 80000-9/34-58/81-95 employed the Downs System which in the post-war period Darlington had fitted to a number of LNER classes, including A2/1, A6, A7, B16/3, J25, J72 and T1. The system was the invention of W.Downs, a foreman at Consett, and involved a series of steam coils within the containers which kept the sand dry and free-flowing. Initially all the inventor's claims were substantiated, but after some years service the steam coils corroded and caused blockages while dismantling for repair was both difficult and costly.

Most of the secondary passenger duties envisaged for the class were of short duration with the water supply being conveniently replenished between services, but some London Midland Region duties covered longer distances and necessitated the use of track troughs. Engines employed on these duties therefore required pick-up scoops, and to ensure that Regional transfers remained possible the entire class was built with the necessary internal piping while those engines destined for the London Midland Region were additionally equipped with bi-directional water scoops and operating gear. Should Regional transfers occur, then with minimal delay and expense the external fittings could be added or removed, although in practice this never became necessary. When built the position was: full equipment - 80034-53/59-68/81-95; partial equipment - 80000-33/54-8/69-80/96-9, 80100-54.

To accommodate any water discharged from the side tanks when using track troughs all engines, whether fully or partially equipped, were provided with tall vent pipes on the tank tops. On the fireman's side these were positioned part way along the firebox, but on the left hand or driver's side of the engine they were placed adjacent to the cab lookout window, causing some loss of visibility and the possibility of glass breakage. As a result, commencing with 80059 in March 1953, the left hand vent pipe was resited further forward along the tank top to a position similar to that occupied on the right hand side of the engine. Those built earlier were not similarly modified (Figs. 8 and 9).

Speedometers were not considered necessary for secondary passenger engines when construction commenced in 1951, but opinion changed and commencing with 80059 built in March 1953 this equipment was provided (Fig. 10).

In Scotland Manson tablet exchange equipment was in regular use where there was single track with passing loops, therefore 80000-9/20-30/54-8, 80110-4/21-30 were provided with a recess low down on the left hand cab sidesheets to accept the exchange arm. However, only those engines regularly working over the single track sections were actually fitted with the equipment for all or part of their lives. These included 80004/5/20-3/6/8/9/55/7, 80111-4/21/4/6. 80114 was noted in May 1966 still so fitted.

No trouble was experienced with the fluted section connecting and coupling rods, but following the discovery of loose driving wheels on the Britannia pacifics it was decided as a precautionary measure to substitute a deeper pattern coupling rod of rectangular section. This modification first appeared on 80079 in March 1954 and was applied to all subsequent construction, except for Derby-built 80054-8 of December 1954 and January 1955.

80000 to 80120 were fitted with LNER pattern return cranks having two vertical bolts securing them to square section crank pins. In service they proved inferior to the Derby/LMS rounded type where four studs and bolts secured the return crank to the crank pin, and this pattern was employed on 80121 to 80154. Some locomotives were subsequently modified from the LNER to the LMS type, 80097 being an example, which was dealt with between May 1964 and April 1965 (Fig. 11).

The lamp bracket configuration of engines working on the London Midland, Eastern, North Eastern and Scottish Regions comprised three positions above the leading buffer beam and a fourth at the top of the smokebox door, with a similar layout on the bunker backplate. Southern Region engines, however, were provided with two additional brackets at each end, at mid-height either side of the smokebox door and two similarly spaced on the bunker backplate, to accommodate the Region's route codes. The brackets also differed by being cranked to avoid the necessity of providing base plates to support lamps carried on the smokebox doors or bunkers. No members of the class went new to the Western Region, but in later years most of those transferred there from other Regions were re-equipped with Swindon pattern brackets.

After an accident in the Erecting Shop at Eastleigh when the cab roof of 80031 was being lifted off by a crane, the cabs of most Southern Region engines were fitted with four lifting brackets.

In the late 1930's the LMS gave extended trials to the Hudd intermittent inductive system of train control on the London Tilbury and Southend Section (LTS) and when these proved successful 110 distant signals and 183 engines were

Fig. 8   80030 at Corkerhill MPD 5 November 1955. The tall vent pipe is visible adjacent to the front cab window on the driver's side as originally fitted to the early class members. This locomotive received fluted coupling rods. There appear to be signs of a corrosion problem on the lower part of the tank sides. The embellished smokebox door of Fairburn 2-6-4T 42124 can be seen on the right, this treatment was given to several Standard 2-6-4T's in the Scottish Region.   *J.L. Stevenson*

Fig. 9   80121 at Kittybrewster MPD 10 October 1955. This photograph shows the vent pipe re-positioned further forward on the driver's side. This locomotive was fitted with rectangular section coupling rods.   *T. J. Edgington*

Fig. 10   The speedometer and cable leading to the cab of 80100 at Stratford MPD 17 April 1961.   *A.G. Ellis*

Fig. 11   Another photograph at Stratford Shed showing piston, motion and return crank of 80100 17 April 1961.   This locomotive has also been fitted with rectangular section coupling rods.
A.G. Ellis

fitted with the necessary equipment. At the time of nationalisation, this section was incorporated in the London Midland Region, but in February 1949 it was transferred to the Eastern Region. Consequently, the Standard 2-6-4 tanks allotted to that Region for the LTS line services required fitting with the Hudd equipment. This work was shared by Brighton and Bow Works, with the former fitting the bogie brackets and vacuum reservoirs while Bow provided the piping, cables, hooters, visual reminders and magnetic receivers.

In May 1956, this system of train control, redesignated Automatic Warning System (AWS), was approved for use on all Regions.

Latterly engines liable to work over lines having overhead electric wires were provided with warning flashes to remind crews of the danger when changing lamps, replenishing the side tanks or climbing into the coal bunker; for example 80132 was noted so fitted on 22nd July 1963, and 80118 was another example, the detail being entered on the engine record card.

Standard equipment from new were continuous blowdown cocks. Two WR10 10mm injectors were fitted - one on each side of the locomotive. Gangway doors were fitted to the cab entrance as were access doors to the coal bunker on later construction batches.

2.3.1 Construction Costs

Bearing in mind a production time span of six years and low inflation there was no dramatic increase in the manufacturing costs. Cost data varies between sources. In the following table data from the engine history cards is given, where available, as well as that from British Railways financial accounts.

Year Built	Engine Numbers	Works	Authority		Estimated Cost £	Engine History Card Cost £	Official Cost £	Additional Fittings from new (Information from Record Cards)
1951	80010-9	Brighton	RE3337	17.11.49	11025	N/A	15277	
1951-2	80020-30	Brighton	"	"	11025	15773	15377	Recess for tablet catching
1952	80000-9	Derby	N/A		11025	15398	15453	Recess for tablet catching
1952	80031-3	Brighton	N/A		11025	N/A	15277	
1952	80034-53	Brighton	N/A		11025	15909	15472	
1953	80059-68	Brighton	RE5262	1.1.51	11600	17109	17053	Speedometer
1953-4	80069-78	Brighton	N/A		14400	17364	17324	Speedometer. Provision on bogies for ATC. Briquette tube feeders.
1954-5	80054-8	Derby	258/3	6.9.51	11600	16831	17651	Recess for tablet catching
1954	80079-95	Brighton	RE6502	29.11.51	14400	17548	17522	Speedometer. Provision on bogies for ATC.Cab lifting brackets. Briquette tube feeder.
1954	80096-8	Brighton	RE6502	29.11.51	14400	17600	N/A	Speedometer
1954	80106-15	Doncaster	RE6503	29.11.51	14400	17652	17158	Recess for tablet catching (80110-4) Speedometer. Water pickup. AWS. Balljoint Superheater. Snowplough brackets.
1955	80099-80101	Brighton	N/A		14400	18206	18195	Speedometer. Briquette tube feeder. Water scoop. Provision on bogies for ATC.
1955	80102-5	Brighton	N/A		14400	18206	18206	Speedometer. Briquette tube feeder. Water scoop. Provision on bogies for ATC.
1955	80116-20	Brighton	N/A		16200	N/A	17790	
1955	80121-30	Brighton	7477/7752	18.12.52	16200	18046	18041	Recess for tablet catching. Speedometer.
1956	80131-44	Brighton	N/A		18100	20223	20222	Water pick up. Speedometer. Briquette tube feeders. Balljoint Superheater.
1956-7	80145-54	Brighton	N/A		18100	N/A	21944	Speedometer. AWS. Cab lifting brackets.

More detailed figures are available for the fifteen locomotives constructed by Derby, these being:-

	Costs (£)			
	Erecting Shop	Other Depts.	Capital Interest	Total
80000-9	14,643	522	288	15,453
80054-8	16,761	630	260	17,651

Comparative diesel-electric locomotive costs were:-

Type 3	Bo-Bo	D6500-44	1960-1	£83,330 each
Type 3	Co-Co	D6700-29	1960-1	£86,324 each
Type 2	A1A-A1A	D5500-19	1957-8	£78,043 each

2.4 Boilers

The BR5 pattern boiler fitted to the class, apart from the closer pitched staying and standard mountings, was virtually a repeat of that carried by the Fairburn 2-6-4 tanks. Both boilers steamed well in service and were inexpensive to maintain although, possibly because of the modified spark arresting layout, the BR5 proved marginally less free steaming. On the Southern, North Eastern, Scottish and London Midland Regions, this apparently caused little concern for generally the engines were working within their capacity, but the Eastern Region in 1956 found it beneficial to strip the spark arresting equipment from the smokeboxes of 80069-80/96-9 and 80100-5/31-6, when working the LTS commuter services (see modifications 2.8). Undoubtedly these trains proved more demanding than any worked by the class elsewhere in the country and to achieve comparability with the Stanier and Fairburn 2-6-4 tanks this action was not only officially condoned, but recorded on the engine cards. Nevertheless, some misgivings must have remained for Doncaster was instructed to investigate the advantage of a double blast pipe. The necessary drawings, incorporating spark-arresting sieves, were completed in October 1957, but no action followed, so presumably the cost of modification was not considered justified in view of the pending electrification of the LTS section. On engines leaving the Eastern Region in 1962, the smokebox spark-arresting sieves were refitted on some locomotives.

Altogether 162 boilers were provided for the class, of which seven were spares to avoid delay in shops. Most were constructed at Brighton, details of the others being: Crewe 19, fitted to Derby series 80000-9/54-8 and four spares, Doncaster ten for 80106-15 and Eastleigh twelve for Brighton built 80010/2/4/5/8/9/29/32/41/4/7/51 and one spare.

To save expense, the number of different pattern boilers fitted to the Standard classes was kept to a minimum, although it was appreciated that in some instances this policy could adversely affect performance. Fortunately, this only occurred with the Class 4 75XXX 4-6-0's, where the BR4 boiler proved lacking in staying power when confronted by the longer and faster workings made possible by the increased coal and water supplies. The deficiency was overcome by fitting double blast pipes of similar design to that proposed by Doncaster for the Standard tanks, to the Southern Region series and to some of those based on the Western Region.

Boiler Numbers:-
Crewe Built   886-95, 1078-82, 1607/8 (Spare o/no BS 9/75) 967 (Spare BS 7/8440) 1368 (Spare BS 7/374)

Eastleigh   896/8. 900/2/4/6/16/18/22/4/6/8 1942 (Spare on order HO 9843)

Brighton   897/9, 901/3/5/7-15/7/9-21/3/5/7/9-39 1083-92, 1298-1334, 1562-76, 1847-70,

1598 (Spare order HO 6372) 1872 (Spare order HO 8875)

Doncaster   1335-44

Boilers were fitted as given below. As noted earlier various record cards are missing, therefore the details are incomplete. In particular it is suspected that several engines had a boiler change in the period 1962/3 and even where record cards exist the changes are not fully recorded. The numbers in brackets are the short numbers of the previous carrier of the boiler. e.g. 1303 7.60 (74) indicates that boiler 1303 was changed in 7.60 and came from locomotive 80074.

80000	886 New (No Record)
80001	887 New (No Record)
80002	888 New (No Record)
80003	889 New (No Record)
80004	890 New (No Record)
80005	891 New (No Record) Off by 5.58 to 80030
80006	892 New (No Record)
80007	893 New (No Record) Off by 12.57 to 80009
80008	894 New, 908 5.57 (22), 907 6.62 (?)
80009	895 New, 893 12.57 (07), 1322 7.63 (86)
80010	896 New, 898 8.57 (12)
80011	897 New, 901 12.56 (16), 935 2.64 (43)
80012	898 New, 904 1.57 (18), 967 3.64 (85)
80013	899 New, 896 8.57 (10), 897 4.63 (18)
80014	900 New, 1869 5.62 (153)
80015	902 New, 906 9.56 (19), 1856 5.61 (140)
80016	901 New, 919 10.56 (33), 1860 7.61 (144)
80017	903 New, 917 9.56 (31), 1312 12.60 (83)
80018	904 New, 897 1.57 (11), 930 2.63 (59)
80019	906 New, 1599 7.56 (Spare), 1859 1.64 (143)
80020	905 New (No Record) General Overhauls 12.56 and 12.62
80021	907 New, 1607 9.56 (Spare), 1344 7.62 (115)
80022	908 New (No Record) Off by 5.57 to 80008
80023	910 New, 1608 4.57 (Spare)
80024	909 New (No Record)
80025	911 New (No Record)
80026	912 New (No Record)
80027	914 New (No Record)
80028	913 New (No Record)
80029	916 New (No Record)
80030	915 New, 891 5.58 (05)
80031	917 New, 902 8.56 (15), 1854 3.61 (138)
80032	918 New, 899 2.58 (13), 929 5.63 (34)
80033	919 New, 903 10.56 (17), 1316 9.60 (87)
80034	920 New, 929 7.57 (40), 922 2.63 (39)
80035	921 New, 928 2.58 (51), 1861 1.62 (145)
80036	923 New, 926 5.58 (47)
80037	925 New, 933 9.57 (45), 1866 11.62 (150)
80038	927 New, 925 11.57 (37)
80039	930 New, 922 10.57 (41), 1857 7.62 (141)
80040	929 New, 1314 3.57 (85), 1868 9.61 (152)
80041	922 New, 934 9.57 (46), 1862 9.63 (146)
80042	931 New, 927 12.57 (38)
80043	932 New, 935 9.58 (48), 899 9.63 (32)
80044	924 New, 923 8.58 (36)
80045	933 New, 1368 8.57 (Spare) Off by 11.61 to 80127
80046	934 New, 920 8.57 (34)
80047	926 New, 921 5.58 (35)

80048   935 New removed by 3.56, 938 7.58 (52)
80049   936 New, 1083 1.58 (59)
80050   937 New, 1086 5.58 (62)
80051   928 New, 1087 12.58 (63)
80052   938 New, 937 5.58 (50)
80053   939 New, 936 2.58 (49)
80054   1080 New Off by 27.11.61 - to 80129 3.62
80055/7/8   Boilers 1078/81/2 fitted - order of fitting unknown 1082 off by 6.61 to 80106
80056   1079 New, 1574 12.60 (128)
80059   1083 New, 930 12.57 (39), 900 08.62 (14)
80060   1084 New, 1085 12.58 (61)
80061   1085 New, 924 9.58 (44)
80062   1086 New, 939 4.58 (53)
80063   1087 New, 931 1.58 (42)
80064   1088 New, 932 11.58 (43)
80065   1089 New, 1091 11.59 (67)
80066   1090 New, 1313 2.59 (84)
80067   1091 New, 1090 3.59 (66)
80068   1092 New, 1323 5.60 (94)
80069   1298 New, 1305 9.59 (76)
80070   1299 New, 1301 6.59 (72)
80071   1300 New, 1306 10.60 (77)
80072   1301 New, 1566 3.59 (120)
80073   1302 New, Off by 4.60 to 80074
80074   1303 New, 1302 6.60 (73)
80075   1304 New, 1298 1.60 (69)
80076   1305 New, 1299 8.59 (70)
80077   1306 New, 1325 8.60 (96)
80078   1307 New, 1308 12.60 (79)
80079   1308 New, 1334 12.60 (105)
80080   1309 New, 1304 1.60 (75)
80081   1310 New, 1088 1.59 (64)
80082   1311 New, 1320 12.59 (91)
80083   1312 New, 918 2.60 (?)
80084   1313 New, 1084 12.58 (60)
80085   1314 New, 967 1.57 (Spare), 934 11.63 (46)
80086   1315 New, 1322 12.59 (93) Off by 7.63 to 80009
80087   1316 New, 1092 8.60 (68)
80088   1317 New, 1310 2.59 (81)
80089   1318 New, 1089 1.60 (65)
80090   1319 New (No Record)
80091   1320 New, 1317 10.59 (88)
80092   1321 New, 1315 3.60 (86)
80093   1322 New, 1598 11.59 (Spare)
80094   1323 New, 1318 4.60 (89)
80095   1324 New, 1311 2.60 (82)
80096   1325 New, 1303 7.60 (74)
80097   1326 New, 1329 6.61 (101)
80098   1327 New, 1309 4.60 (80)
80099   1331 New, 1872 3.58 (Spare)
80100   1328 New, 1331 4.58 (99), 1326 6.61 (97)
80101   1329 New, 1307 4.61 (78)
80102   1330 New, 1333 8.58 (104), 1851 1.63 (135)
80103   1332 New, 1330 8.58 (102)
80104   1333 New, 1328 5.58 (100), 1858 9.62 (142)
80105   1334 New, 1300 11.60 (71)
80106   1335 New, 1082 6.61 (?)
80107   1336 New, 1573 12.61 (127)
80108   1337 New (No Record)
80109   1338 New (No Record)
80110   1339 New (No Record)

80111   1340 New (No Record)
80112   1341 New (No Record)
80113   1342 New, Off 11.59 80125
80114   1343 New (No Record)
80115   1344 New, 1336 1.62 (107)
80116   1562 New, Off by 11.62 to 80135
80117   1563 New (No Record)
80118   1564 New (No Record)
80119   1565 New (No Record)
80120   1566 New, Off by 3.59 to 80072
80121   1567 New (No Record)
80122   1568 New (No Record)
80123   1569 New (No Record)
80124   1570 New (No Record)
80125   1571 New, 1342 4.60 (113)
80126   1572 New (No Record)
80127   1573 New, 1368 11.61 (45)
80128   1574 New, Off by 9.60 to 80056
80129   1575 New, 1080 3.62 (54)
80130   1576 New (No Record)
80131   1847 New, 1332 10.58 (103)
80132   1848 New (No Record). Possibly changed 11.58
80133   1849 New, 1333 12.63 (102)
80134   1850 New, 1328 2.63 (104)
80135   1851 New, 1562 11.62 (116)
80136   1852 New. Carried throughout but overhauled 9.59
80137   1853 New, 1855 6.62 (139)
80138   1854 New, 903 12.60 (33)
80139   1855 New, 919 1.62 (16)
80140   1856 New, 917 2.61 (17)
80141   1857 New, 928 2.62 (35)
80142   1858 New, 1863 4.62 (147)
80143   1859 New, 933 5.63 (37)
80144   1860 New, 1324 11.60 (95)
80145   1861 New, 1864 11.61 (148)
80146   1862 New, 896 5.63 (13)
80147   1863 New, 1867 4.62 (151)
80148   1864 New, 902 6.61 (31)
80149   1865 New, 1942 1.62 (Spare)
80150   1866 New, 1853 10.62 (137)
80151   1867 New, 1865 3.62 (149)
80152   1868 New, 906 7.61 (15)
80153   1869 New, 1314 5.62 (40)
80154   1870 New. Possibly carried throughout

2.5 Livery

Variations of livery were minimal. All were painted secondary passenger black, lined in red, cream and grey. Both bunker and tank sides were lined out with the lining extending along the sides of the running plate to the front of the engine. The cylinders were lined in red only. Numbers were painted on the bunker side and smokebox numberplates were carried.

Up until 1956 the lion and wheel emblem was applied, being superseded in that year by the later totem of the lion and crown flanked by British Railways (Figs. 12 and 13).

Other variations noted were the application of larger size numbers to the bunker side on the Doncaster build, some Darlington repaints (Fig. 14) e.g. 80069, 80115/8, the customisation of various Scottish engines by their crews in the late 1950's e.g. 80127, when allocated to Corkerhill, was noted with a red backed number plate, red smokebox door hinges and handles as well as a red-backed shedplate. Some

Fig. 12   80120 at Scarborough MPD in original lined black livery with the small first crest used by BR. Power classification shown by small figure 4 above number.   *David Tyreman collection*

Fig. 13   80003 at Polmadie MPD in April 1958 again in lined black livery but displaying the second type of crest introduced by BR in 1956.
RAS Marketing

Fig. 15
80031 is the locomotive at Eastleigh 26 March 1955 with a stencilled 4P4F power classification above the number.
E.W. Fry

other Scottish engines had light blue backed smokebox number plates and shedplates and the placing of the power classification on the cab sheet below the cab window instead of the usual position above the engine number on the bunker.

2.6 Allocation and Duties

2.6.1 Distribution

Due to the widely scattered allocation of the class, and the fact that whilst allocated to a specific shed they rarely crossed regional boundaries in the course of their duties, it has been decided to break from the traditional format of the RCTS locomotive histories and give allocation and work information by region.

This chapter is therefore split into three main sections - general introduction with specimen allocations, regional duties and complete locomotive allocation summary.

Initially the class was restricted to the Southern, Scottish and London Midland Regions, but later use was extended to the Eastern Region LTS section commuter services to and from Fenchurch Street station, while in mid-1955 five commenced working from Whitby in the North Eastern Region. The Western Region did not receive an allocation until 1962 when transfers occurred from the Eastern and Southern Regions.

Specimen Allocations

January 1955	Class total 112
Corkerhill	80000/8/9/24/5/30
Polmadie	80001-3/6/7/22/3/6/7/54-8, 80111-5
Kittybrewster	80004/5/20/1/8/9, 80106-10
Tunbridge Wells West	80010-5/7/8
Brighton	80016/9/31-3
Watford	80034-8/64-8
Longsight	80039
Bletchley	80040-3/81/2/4
Bury	80044/6/60/1/86-90/3
Kentish Town	80045/7/8/59/62/3/91/2/4

Fig. 16   80002 at Polmadie MPD displaying a 4MTT power classification. The perforations under the cab ventilators and the black pipe is a spray to keep down bunker coal dust.
David Tyreman collection

Fig. 17   80032 at Eastleigh recently ex Works 17 April 1955 showing power classification 4P/4F.
L. Elsey

Fig. 18   80118 outside Scarborough shed 20 July 1955. This was a new locomotive en route to Whitby where it was first allocated.

T. J. Edgington

Newton Heath	80049-53	Corkerhill	80000/5/8/9/24/5/30/44-53,
Tilbury	80069-73/9/80		80127/8
Plaistow	80074-8/96-99, 80100/1	Polmadie	80001-3/6/7/22/3/6/7/54-8/86,
Rugby	80083/5		80106-10/29/30
St. Albans	80095	Kittybrewster	80004/20/1/8/9, 80111/2
		Three Bridges	80010-2/88/9/94
December 1957	Class total 155	Brighton	80013/31-3, 80138/43-54
Corkerhill	80000/8/9/24/5/30, 80127/8	Tunbridge Wells West	80014-9/95, 80137-42
Polmadie	80001-3/6/7/22/3/6/7/54-8,	Ashford	80034-43/59/64-6/87
	80106-10/29/30	Stirling	80060-3, 80125
Kittybrewster	80004/5/20/1/8/9, 80111-5	Stewarts Lane	80067/8/81
Brighton	80010/1/31-3, 80145-54	Tilbury	80069-80/96-99,
Tunbridge Wells West	80012-9		80100/5/31/2/4-6
Watford	80034-8/64-8	Bricklayers Arms	80082-5
Bletchley	80039/41-3/81-5	Dundee	80090, 80123/4
Chester (LMS)	80040/5/7-53/9/62/91/2	St. Rollox	80091
Newton Heath	80044/60/1	Perth	80092/3, 80126
Blackpool	80046/93	Keith	80113-5/21/2
Birkenhead	80063/86	Neville Hill	80116-20
Tilbury	80069-80	Shoeburyness	80133
Bangor	80087-90/4/5		
Plaistow	80096-9, 80100-5/31-6	December 1962	Class total 154 - 80103 withdrawn
Whitby	80116-20		in August 1962
Keith	80121/2	Ardrossan	80000
Dundee	80123/4	Beattock	80001/2
Stirling	80125	St. Margarets	80003/6/7/22/6/54/5, 80114/22
Perth	80126	Eastfield	80004/27/56/7
Neasden	80137-44	Corkerhill	80005/8/9/20/1/4/5/30/44-53,
			80127/8
December 1960	Class total 155	Three Bridges	80010-2/88/9/94

Brighton	80013/31-3, 80138/43-54
Tunbridge Wells West	80014-9, 80139-42
Hurlford	80023/8/9/91, 80111/2
Stewarts Lane	80034/68/81/4/5
Exmouth Jct	80035-43/59/64/7
Polmadie	80058/86, 80106-10/5/21/9/30
Stirling	80060-3, 80125
Eastleigh	80065/6/82/3/7/95, 80137
Swansea East Dock	80069/72/97/99, 80133/4
Shrewsbury	80070/8, 80100/2/31/2/5/6
Ardsley	80071/3-7
Croes Newydd	80079/80/96/8, 80104
Dundee	80090, 80123/4
Perth	80092/3, 80126
Machynlleth	80101/5
Hawick	80113
Neville Hill	80116-20
December 1964	Class total 123
Corkerhill	80000/4/20/4/5/45-7/51/63, 80112/28
Polmadie	80001/2/27/58/86, 80108-10/6/8/20/1/30
St. Margarets	80003/6/7/22/6/54/5,80114/22
Ayr	80005
Redhill	80011/9/32-4/68/84/5/8/9/94, 80138-42/4/5/9/51-3

Eastleigh	80012/4/5/6/8/65/6/82/3, 80150
Bournemouth	80013/81, 80134/46/7
Dumfries	80023/61, 80117/9
Perth	80028/92/3, 80126
Hurlford	80029/91, 80111
Yeovil	80035
Bath Green Park	80037/9
Exmouth Jct.	80041/2/64
Templecombe	80043/59/67
Shrewsbury	80048/70, 80100/2/13/5/6
Eastfield	80057
Greenock Ladyburn	80060
Nine Elms	80069/95, 80133/7/43/54
Leamington	80072
Croes Newydd	80078/9/80/96
Dundee	80090, 80123/4
Machynlleth	80097/8/9, 80101/4/5
Hawick	80113
Oswestry	80131/2

At 1st January 1967 only twenty-five members of the class remained as follows:-

Polmadie	80002/45/86, 80116/20
Corkerhill	80004/46, 80128
Bournemouth	80011/9/32, 80134/46
Nine Elms	80012/5/85, 80133/40/3/5/54
Eastleigh	80016, 80139/51/2

Other depots, not mentioned in the above lists, to have an allocation of the class - some only briefly, were:-

Aberdeen Ferryhill		Salisbury
Bristol Barrow Road	Kings Cross	Saltley
Crewe North		Scarborough
Dalry Road	Llanelli	Stratford
Dawsholm	March	Tonbridge
Derby	Motherwell	Weymouth
Bedford	Hamilton	
Carstairs	Holbeck	Stranraer
Dover	Lostock Hall	
Eastbourne	Neath	Willesden
Guildford	Old Oak Common	York

A few locomotives remained at the same shed throughout their service, all on the Scottish Region. They were:-
80008/9/24/5, 80127 at Corkerhill, 80058, 80130 at Polmadie and 80126 at Perth.

Some were also officially stored prior to withdrawal, dates recorded being as follows:-

	To Store	Ex-Store
1.8.62	80070/9/98, 80100/2/4/32	
9.9.62		80098, 80100
3.11.62		80104
4.11.62		80070, 80102/32

80059 appears to hold the record of the most transferred member of the class with eleven sheds.

Inter regional transfers/loans also took place. Known dates are shown below, although the list is not complete.

ER to WR	15.7.62	80069/70/2/8/9/80/96-99, 80100-2/4/5/31-6
WR to LMR	30.12.62★	80070/8/9/80/96/8, 80100-2/4/5/31/2/5/6

SR to WR | 30.12.62★ | 80035-43/59/64/7
WR to LMR | 14.7.63 | 80097/9
WR to LMR | 8.9.63 | 80072
WR to SR | 17.9.64 | 80069, 80133/4

★ These transfers were due to Regional Boundary Changes.

As one of the more numerous classes as steam declined, the Class 4 tanks featured as motive power for a number of RCTS tours.

As early as 1956 80080 worked the East London No 2 tour on 24th March. Other tours using the Class 4 tanks were:-

10 November 1956	-	80065 Hammersmith and Chiswick Branch (Fig. 64)
13 April 1958	-	80154 Sussex Coast (Fig. 65)
10 August 1958	-	80041 Northern and Eastern
19 May 1962	-	80117 The Seven Companies Railtour
14 - 23 June 1962	-	80092, 80110/29 Grand Scottish Tour
18 June 1967	-	80146 Farewell to Southern Steam

2.6.2 Eastern Region

The delivery in 1948-50 of the Thompson L1 Class 2-6-4 tanks left the Kings Cross, Liverpool Street and Marylebone suburban services adequately provided with modern motive power, but this did not apply to the newly acquired LT&S Section where Stanier and Fairburn 2-6-4 tanks were sharing the services with a number of obsolescent Whitelegg designed 4-4-2 tanks. Obviously replacement of the last mentioned was necessary, but with the provision and maintenance of motive power remaining with Derby no great urgency prevailed and consequently it was September 1953 before the first Standard

Fig. 19 LMS 4-4-2T 41945 at Plaistow MPD on date unknown. This class was originally a Whitelegg design for the LTSR but this locomotive was built by the LMS at Derby. It was classified 3P.

S.J. Rhodes

tank, 80069, was delivered to Plaistow, where it was later joined by 80070-80. After several weeks service, each in turn was despatched to Bow Works to have Hudd train control equipment fitted. In January 1954 80069-73 were transferred to Tilbury for the Fenchurch Street trains (Fig. 19).

Between November 1954 and April 1955 ten more members of the class, 80096 to 80105, were delivered to Plaistow as replacements for Fairburns 42230/1/2/48-53/6 which were transferred to Neasden to supersede a similar number of Thompson L1 class 2-6-4 tanks on the Marylebone and Metropolitan commuter services. The delivery of the final batch of fourteen locomotives, 80131-44, commenced in March 1956, with the intention of stationing all at Plaistow and transferring eight more Fairburns to the Great Central Section. However, because of an acute shortage of shed staff at Neasden it was later decided to send 80137-44 there instead. As a result of this late decision all the series left Brighton partially equipped with Hudd train control, although it was only necessary on 80131-6.

For several days before arriving at Plaistow, 80131 was borrowed by Kings Cross shed for empty coaching stock duties. The class reappeared in Kings Cross in September 1958 when they were seen to have a regular duty on the 5.39pm to Baldock, 80103/37 being amongst those noted (80103 was at the time still allocated to Plaistow, and 80137 was a Neasden engine). 80080 was exhibited at Southend Central between 1st and 3rd March 1956 in company with electric 27002, 60022 *Mallard*, 70038 *Robin Hood* as part of the Tilbury Centenary Exhibition and LTSR 4-4-2 Tank 80 *Thundersley* which was used on special trains.

Pre-war the LMS had prepared an electrification scheme for the LTS section, but with the financial stringencies of the 1930's no action was possible and the scheme remained in abeyance until incorporated in the 1955 British Railways Modernisation Plan. The civil engineering works were completed with the opening of the flyover and rebuilt Barking station on 29th September 1961 and this was followed on 6th November 1961 by electrification of the off-peak services. There was insufficient stock for the morning and evening commuter services, so these remained steam-operated as mixed steam/electric working was not possible due to the proximity of some water cranes to the overhead wiring. Full electrification was scheduled for 1st January 1962, but this had to be delayed to 18th June 1962 because of the continuing need to loan electric stock to the Great Eastern Section.

A limited number of engines were temporarily retained for goods and permanent way duties, and 80072, 80077 (noted 7.8.62) and 80131 were noted on empty coaching stock from Liverpool Street, and they were also used on North Woolwich services. However, their stay was a relatively short one as in July 1962 they were both transferred to the Western Region in company with 80069/70/8-80/96-9, 80100-2/4/5/32-6. At the end of the year 80071/3-7 left for the North Eastern Region after spending three months at March shed, some of them in store.

80103 had been laid aside with twisted frames at Plaistow in January 1962, and not being considered worthy of repair, was condemned with a mileage of 281,743 on 29th August 1962. It was cut up at Stratford in the following month, the first of the class to go. It was also the first Standard design locomotive to be condemned.

On 31st January 1958 80079 worked a Fenchurch Street – Shoeburyness train in thick fog. The driver, on approaching Upney, missed the signal and entered the next section where

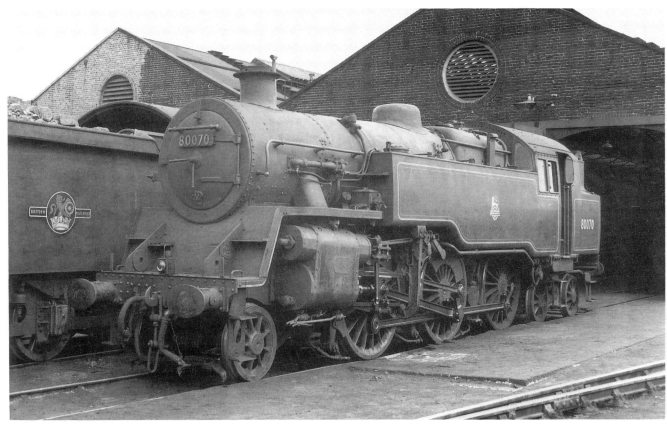

Fig. 20   80070 at Stratford MPD 10 May 1958.   *Alan Bowman*

Fig. 21   80105 entering Purfleet Station with a down stopping train 23 March 1957.   *R.C. Riley*

an 11-coach train had been stopped by signals. 80079 running bunker first, demolished two coaches completely, killed ten passengers and injured 89 others.

2.6.3 London Midland Region

At Derby the design was not considered new, merely an extension of the Fairburn series, therefore when delivery of 80034-53 commenced in April 1952, there was no attempt to group them in one Motive Power Division, a policy which lead to the following widely scattered allocation:-

Crewe North	80034	Watford	80035-8
Bletchley	80039-43	Derby	80044
Bedford	80045-7	Kentish Town	80048
Blackpool	80049	Newton Heath	80050-3

In daily service the design differences with the Fairburn and Stanier 2-6-4 tanks quickly became apparent and before the end of the year some rationalisation was found necessary with 80034 being transferred to Watford to join 80035-8, 80044 moving from Derby to join 80045-7 at Bedford, and 80049 moving from Blackpool to Newton Heath to join 80050-3. This was a much more realistic distribution, but nevertheless still did not fully exploit the economic potential of the class.

The five members of the class allocated to Watford were rostered for the Euston, Tring, Rugby, Northampton and St. Albans services, whilst the five at Bletchley worked mainly to Euston, Oxford and Cambridge. The four engines at Bedford, plus the one at Kentish Town, were similarly employed on the commuter services out of St. Pancras. Newton Heath also had five members of the class allocated to the depot, and these worked the eastern suburban services from Manchester Victoria to Oldham, Rochdale, Bury, Ashton and Stalybridge, together with a daily turn to Chester and occasional forays across the Pennines to Huddersfield.

Ten more of the class, 80059-68, were delivered between March and August 1953, and these were followed by a final batch of fifteen, 80081-95, which were delivered between March and November the following year. The allocation of these twenty-five locomotives was as follows:-

Kentish Town	80059/62/91/2/4	Bedford	80060/1/93
Saltley	80063	Watford	80064-8
Bletchley	80081-5	Bury	80086-90
St. Albans	80095		

80084 was delivered new from Brighton to Willesden for display at the International Railway Congress Exhibition during May/June 1954.

This was a scattered distribution which was partially remedied by the early transfer of 80063/93 from Saltley and Bedford to Kentish Town and Bury. 80086-90/3 practically monopolised the Bury local passenger services, including those running through to Manchester Victoria via Clifton Jct.

80064 from Watford shed performed a rescue on 1st August 1955 when it coupled ahead of LMS 10000 on the 1.35 pm Euston - Perth, following the failure of the diesel south of Harrow. Having deposited the failed diesel at Harrow, 80064 worked forward for an unknown distance.

Some sheds, in particular Bury, Newton Heath and Watford, liked the class and maintained that they were at least equal to the Stanier, Fairburn and Fowler 2-6-4 tanks, but Bedford men took the contrary view and consequently the performance of the locomotives allocated to Bedford shed, 80044-7/60/1, was often disappointing. This in turn led to

crews losing confidence in their ability to work the Bedford - St.Pancras stopping trains without taking water at Luton and thereby causing delays to other Midland Division services. Inspectors were deputed to investigate the problem but to no avail and, like the Southern Region when faced with a similar problem, the only practical solution was to replace the class at Bedford by 4-6-0's 75040-44. 80045 moved to Kentish Town, and 80044/6/60/1 were added to the Bury allocation.

In September 1956, the folly of widely scattering the class throughout the Region was at last fully appreciated and the forty-five engines were gathered together at just five sheds, these being:-

Watford	10	80034-8/64-8
Bletchley	10	80039-43/81-5
Newton Heath	5	80044/6/60/1/93
Chester	12	80045/7-53/9/62/3/86
Bangor	8	80087-92/4/5

Following its transfer to Newton Heath in February 1956, 80093 was noted on banking duties at Manchester Victoria on 11th August that year. The locomotives that were transferred to Bangor and Chester replaced a similar number of Fairburn and Stanier 2-6-4 tanks on the North Wales, Crewe and Manchester Exchange services, whilst those at Bangor also appeared regularly on Afonwen passenger trains, Penychain Summer Saturday trains and pick-up goods to Llanberis and Afonwen.

Five of the six Regions created at nationalisation (those in England and Wales) were based on the existing main line companies, a logical division, but nevertheless one which left lines penetrating deeply into adjacent Regions, often preventing the introduction of service economies or timetable improvements. To overcome this in April 1952 the administrative and commercial jurisdiction of these lines was transferred to the Region in which they were geographically sited, although at the same time leaving unchanged the existing operating arrangements. One of the lines concerned was the Great Central Railway's London Extension, much of which passed into the London Midland Region, with the Western Region gaining the section from Northolt Junction to Marylebone. This left the Eastern Region in charge of the services and motive power until February 1958 when full control was vested in the London Midland Region. About ninety engines at Neasden, Aylesbury Town, Woodford Halse and Leicester (GC) depots were involved, mainly ex-LNER classes, but including 80137-44.

The next major change occurred on 29 November 1959, when 80034-43/59/64-8/81-5/7-9/94/5, 80137-44 were transferred to the Southern Region in exchange for thirty-four Fairburns 42066-71/4-82/6-92/5-9, 42100-6. As far as the London Midland Region was concerned this was an excellent redistribution for the Fairburns were received in fine fettle whereas a high proportion of the Standard tanks despatched south were unkempt and urgently requiring works attention before re-entering traffic.

This exchange left nineteen members of the class working in the Region, 80044-53/60-3/86/90-3, until February 1960 when they were transferred to Scotland in exchange for more Fairburns, 42198, 42202/6/7/9-13/7/29/36/8/40/7/70, 42696-8. The London Midland Region was now without any member of the class for nearly three years until 1st January 1963 when the incorporation of the Western Region's Shrewsbury Division led to the return of fifteen members of the class. These were located at:-

Shrewsbury   80070/8, 80100/2
Croes Newydd   80079/80/96/8, 80104
Machynlleth   80101/5 (sub-shedded at Portmadoc)
Oswestry   80131/2/5/6 (replacing ex-GW Manor
                            class 4-6-0's)

They were mainly employed working stopping trains over the former Cambrian lines and also the Central Wales Line. Those allocated to Shrewsbury and Croes Newydd also worked over the Severn Valley line before closure on 9th September 1963. For a time the Western Region retained 80069/72/97/9 at Swansea East Dock for the Central Wales Line services, but in July 1963 80097/9 were transferred to Oswestry and Machynlleth whilst in September that year 80072 replaced Class 4 4-6-0 75000 at Leamington Spa on the Warwick Milverton shunt plus the Stratford-on-Avon and Birmingham parcel services. Occasionally, it also deputised for Ivatt 2-6-2 tanks 41231/72 on the Nuneaton parcels whilst later it worked the Solihull-Banbury Triumph/Rover car trains.

By mid-1964 a surplus of passenger tanks in Scotland led to engines being prematurely laid aside and offered for sale as scrap while the London Midland Region was temporarily short of secondary motive power. Therefore six of the condemned Scottish Region Standard tanks were reprieved, details being:-

80044/8/50, condemned June 1964, reinstated at Bangor July 1964. They were seen en route at Carlisle on 16th July 1964. 80056, 80125/9, condemned July 1964, reinstated at Lostock Hall August 1964. However, these three locomotives were reported as being damaged in transit, and appear not to have actually entered service from Lostock Hall, being condemned again in October 1964. The reprieve for 80044/50 was also brief as they had succumbed by the end of 1964, 80050 being noted in store at Bangor at the end of

September that year.

In April 1965 80070/96, 80102/32 were transferred to the Southern Region, leaving a total of fifteen engines still allocated to the Region as follows:-

80048, 80100/35/6 working from Shrewsbury, 80078-80 from Croes Newydd, 80097-9, 80101/4/5 from Machynlleth, 80131 from Bangor and 80072 from Leamington Spa. However, by mid-1965 these had also become redundant and were awaiting disposal, most being withdrawn towards the end of July.

2.6.4 North Eastern Region

80031/2/3 were allotted to the North Eastern Region, but while under construction at Brighton the Southern Region sought authority to retain them in exchange for three of its Fairburn 2-6-4 tanks, 42083/4/5. This was duly agreed and on 12th March 1952 these three engines were despatched in steam to Hornsey, from where 42085 ran light to Peterborough and on 1st March left for the north on coal empties while 42084 hauled 42083 and the unique W1 class 4-6-4 60700 to Doncaster. 42084 then continued to York, still hauling 42083.

During the following week all three commenced work on the Middlesbrough - Newcastle fast hourly services and proved so satisfactory that in December 1954 the transfer of four more Fairburns, 42072/3/93/4 was negotiated with the Southern Region. As a result when Standard tanks 80116-20, also destined for the North Eastern Region, were nearing completion at Brighton in April 1955, the Southern Region proposed retaining them and substituting the recently shopped Fairburns 42066/70/91/6/9. However, for some now forgotten reason this request was refused. Consequently, after being run-in by Brighton shed, 80116-20 were despatched to York via Neasden, which gave that shed the opportunity of overcoming, albeit temporarily, its prevailing

Fig. 22   80061 at Bedford MPD 10 October 1954.

T. J. Edgington

Fig. 23   80037 clearing Northchurch Tunnel with a down stopping train from London Euston 16 August 1952.   *E.D Bruton*

Fig. 24   80065 having just left Tring Goods yard with an up pick-up goods train 10 October 1953.   *E.D. Bruton*

Fig. 25   80069 at Shrewsbury with a Swansea via Central Wales line train 12 June 1964.   *T. J. Edgington*

Fig. 26   80135 with an Aberystwyth to Oswestry train at Talerddig on the scenic Cambrian main line 2 June 1964.   *T. J. Edgington*

motive power shortage by purloining each in turn for ten days to work the Marylebone suburban services to High Wycombe, Princes Risborough and Aylesbury.

On reaching York 80116 was used briefly on the Scarborough services before being transferred to Whitby, reaching there on 26th May 1955 with the 5.00 pm Leeds - Scarborough, normally a Class B1 4-6-0 duty. At Whitby it was later joined by 80117-20, although the last two had been intended for Malton, but because only one fitter was available at Whitby, they were sent there instead on the reasonable assumption that being new they would require little attention. Fortunately this proved correct and in partnership with the Fairburn 2-6-4 tanks 42083-5, they gave excellent service on the Malton, York, Scarborough, Stockton and Middlesbrough trains, the last mentioned working via both Battersby and Kettleness. However, on the North Eastern Region, the Standard tanks proved heavier on coal and water than did the Fairburn equivalents.

80116/9 were transferred to Scarborough in exchange for 42084/5 in February 1956 and used on passenger workings to York, Hull, Whitby and Middlesbrough until May of that year when all four returned to their previous sheds. Unlike Whitby men, crews at Scarborough preferred the Standards and considered them ideal engines for the York and Middlesbrough services. As recorded in the performance section, whilst 80116 was at Whitby, it worked the last passenger train between Loftus and Whitby West Cliff in the course of its duty with the 4.20 pm Middlesbrough - Scarborough on 3rd May 1958.

All five members of the class (80116-20) remained at Whitby, averaging 30,830 miles yearly, until replaced by diesel multiple unit sets in June 1958, when they were transferred to Leeds (Neville Hill) as replacements for classes D49 4-4-0 and B1 4-6-0 on the York, Harrogate, Thirsk, Ripon, Northallerton and Bradford (Forster Square) services. They also appeared regularly between Leeds and Harrogate on the "Yorkshire Pullman", the "Harrogate Sunday Pullman" and the through portions of Kings Cross expresses as well as assisting the heavy Newcastle - Liverpool trains between Ripon and Leeds. Various van and empty carriage stock duties were also covered as well as Leeds City to Harrogate via Wetherby local passenger trains while occasionally they substituted for B1's on the Leeds City - York - Scarborough trains, a $67\frac{1}{2}$ mile trip which necessitated taking water at York, but otherwise posed few problems (Figs. 27 and 28).

In December 1962, 80071/3-7 made redundant on the Eastern Region by the LTS electrification, were transferred from store at March to Ardsley shed to replace withdrawn Thompson L1 class 2-6-4 tanks on ECS workings, van and local goods duties around Leeds Central, Bradford Exchange and Wakefield Westgate. On these tasks they proved better engines than the L1's and when they, and 80116-20 were transferred to the Scottish Region in exchange for Fairburns 42055, 42123/42/5/65/77/96, 42204/71, 42689/99 in November 1963, most Ardsley crews were sorry to see them depart.

These eleven were the sole members of the class on the North Eastern Region, so their departure left the Region without any representatives of the Standard 4 2-6-4 tanks.

Fig. 27   80119 assisting LNER 'A3' 60036 departing the south end of Leeds City Station on a date unknown. The train is a Liverpool Lime Street to Newcastle Central express having reversed at Leeds to take up the 'Leeds Northern' route. 80119 will assist as far as Harrogate.

D.J. Montgomery

31

Fig. 28   80120 with a stopping passenger train from Leeds City to Harrogate leaving Wetherby station 9 July 1960.   *G.D. King*

Fig. 29   80116 leaves Prospect Hill Junction after propelling the train up the incline from Whitby Town and heads
for Larpool Viaduct with the 8.57am from Whitby Town to Scarborough 3 May 1958.   *S.C. Nash*

Fig. 30   80119 has just passed Eaglescliffe South Signalbox with the Eaglescliffe to Whitby pick-up goods 27 April 1957.

J.S. Phillips/Alan Bowman Collection

Fig. 31   LNER (NBR) J36 0-6-0 65259 assisting 80007 in March 1955. 80007 was working a time tabled train from Hawick to Newcastle Central which was halted at Wall where passengers were transferred to buses for Hexham. The Border Counties bridge over the River Tyne just west of Hexham had been declared unsafe due to the river flooding as a result of rapidly melting snow in the district. 80007 ran round its train in Wall Station and eased back to couple up but the reversing lever then could not be moved to the reverse position. After considerable delay 65259 arrived from Riccarton Junction to tow the whole train including 80007 back to the Scottish Region. The photograph was taken by the fireman of 65259 as the train waited for the home signal to clear outside Riccarton Junction! 80007 and Fairburn 2-6-4T 42277 had been loaned to Hawick to work these truncated services thus avoiding the need for tender first running by engines allocated to this line.

R.W. Lynn Collection

33

2.6.5 Scottish Region

By 1950 the withdrawal of many pre-Grouping engines had left the Great North of Scotland Section and the Glasgow suburban services acutely short of motive power and therefore it was necessary to allocate a high proportion of the early members of the class to the Scottish Region. Delivery of the first ten, 80000-9, was scheduled for Autumn 1951, but, with construction in arrears, Derby was forced to postpone their assembly and consequently it was Brighton-built 80020-30, completed between October 1951 and February 1952, that first saw service in Scotland.

On arrival 80020 worked briefly from Polmadie before being despatched to Kittybrewster where later it was joined by 80021/8/9, while 80024/5/30 went to Corkerhill and 80022/3/6/7 to Polmadie. At Kittybrewster the newcomers replaced withdrawn ex-GNSR Classes D40 and D41 4-4-0's and B12 4-6-0's on a variety of duties (Fig 34), including those to Ballater, both passenger and goods, and Fraserburgh as well as working some of the Aberdeen-Elgin-Keith-Inverness main line services in partnership with B1 and Stanier Class 5 4-6-0's. Apart from the need to husband the water supply on the longer duties, 80020/1/8/9 gave excellent service and proved popular with the crews. Polmadie regularly rostered 80022/3/6/7 for the Gourock, Wemyss Bay and Lanark services, and occasionally to Edinburgh (Princes Street) via Shotts, while those members of the class at Corkerhill appeared mainly on the Ardrossan, Largs, Ayr and Greenock services.

They were also often seen working Glasgow St. Enoch - Carlisle trains over the GSWR main line via Dumfries being a distance of 115½ miles. 80008 was noted with the 5.51pm Carlisle to Glasgow St. Enoch on 24th and 31st March 1953

In June 1952 Derby belatedly commenced constructing 80000-9, although only superficial progress was visible until the works reopened after the annual holiday, therefore it was not until late September 1952 when the first entered traffic, and mid-January 1953 before the last one reached Scotland. The allocation of this batch was as follows:-

Ayr 80000 (to Corkerhill in October 1952); Polmadie 80001/6/7; Motherwell 80002/3 (to Polmadie in November 1952); Kittybrewster 80004/5; Corkerhill 80008/9. Another fifteen members of the class were received between October 1954 and January 1955, 80054-8 from Derby, again a year overdue, and 80106-15 from Doncaster. All were stationed at Polmadie except 80106-10 which went to Kittybrewster. With these arrivals at Polmadie up to 50% of Glasgow Central suburban services were worked by the class. 80106-15 were the only members of the class built at Doncaster and, after some days shunting coaching stock at Doncaster they were run in on local passenger duties, including those to Cleethorpes, Sheffield, Leeds and Hull. Delivery was via the East Coast main line, with 80110/4 being borrowed en route by York for the Scarborough services. 80110 worked on the Tweedmouth-St. Boswells line during December 1954 whilst en route from Doncaster to Aberdeen Kittybrewster.

Fig. 32 80027 leaving Glasgow Central Station with a Class A passenger train and carrying a reporting number on the smokebox door on a date unknown.

David Tyreman collection

Fig. 33   80115 also leaving Glasgow Central with the 5.36pm train for Kirkhill 25 May 1962.   *W.A.C. Smith*

Fig. 34   LNER (GNSR) D41 62241 4-4-0 in Keith Shed yard 30 August 1949. These locomotives were replaced by Standard 2-6-4T's.

R.K. Taylor

Fig. 35   80027 at Polmadie shed 8 May 1954.   *W.A.C. Smith*

Fig. 36   80111 assisting a goods train from Carlisle Kingsmoor to Mossend yard at Motherwell up Beattock bank 17 June 1966.   The train has just passed Greskine signalbox.
                                                                                                   T. J. Edgington

Fig. 37   80112 near Inches with a Class B stopping train from Muirkirk to Lanark in September 1961.

T. J. Edgington

Fig. 38   80086 entering Gourock where the train will terminate on a date unknown. The River Clyde is on the right of the photograph, Gourock being a busy passenger exchange location to and from the railway owned Clyde coast steamers.

Hamish Stevenson

Fig. 39   80000 stands in Glasgow St. Enoch Station at the head of a local passenger train shortly before departure 10 April 1954.

J.L. Stevenson

Fig. 40   80025 making a spirited departure from Glasgow St. Enoch with the 9.44am train to Ardrossan South Beach 28 August 1965. There is a sharp curve leading to the bridge which carried all lines over the River Clyde. A Swindon built DMU is also in evidence

T. J. Edgington

Fig. 41   80047 stands in Greenock Princes Pier Station at the head of an ocean liner special for Glasgow St. Enoch 18 April 1964. Passengers
are from *R.M.S. Devonia*. Note that as well as carrying the 67A smokebox shed allocation plate, Corkerhill has also been painted on
the buffer beam in LNER style, Corkerhill was a former LMS shed. This probably indicates the locomotive has passed through
Cowlairs Works.   *J.L. Stevenson*

Fig. 42   80024 at Ayr station with a Girvan to Glasgow St. Enoch train in August 1958. LMS (former Caledonian Railway) 0-4-4T 55262
is also seen on station pilot duties. The Standard 2-6-4T's replaced some of these 0-4-4T's duties. The route indication can be seen
on the centre bracket on 80024's front buffer beam.   *T. J. Edgington*

Fig. 43   80023 piloting an unidentified LMS Class 5 4-6-0 with an up Express train entering Dumfries on a date unknown.

David Tyreman collection

Fig. 44   80045 with a down Special passenger train passing Crossmichael Station 15 November 1964. Crossmichael is located on the now closed portion of the Dumfries to Stranraer line, known as the 'Port Road'.

J.L. Stevenson

A final Brighton-built batch, 80121-30, was delivered between July and December 1955 and these were spread between six sheds. 80121/2 went to Kittybrewster, 80123/4 were sent to Dundee, Stirling received 80125, Perth 80126, Corkerhill received 80127/8 and Polmadie had 80129/30. The locomotive at Stirling, 80125, worked to Gleneagles, Crieff, Perth and Glasgow (Buchanan Street), whilst the Perth engine, 80126, was usually rostered for the Aberdeen or Blair Atholl services, although on 26th July 1956 it was sharing pilot/banking duties to Druimuachdar summit with Fairburn 42168. Like those delivered earlier to the Scottish Region, except 80106-9 all were provided with a recess in the left hand cab sidesheets to accommodate the Manson tablet exchange equipment.

80127 and 80000 were the first of the class to work an Ocean Liner special from Glasgow St. Enoch to Greenock Princes Pier on 13th April 1957. 80127 was kept in immaculate condition and was adorned with red and white paint at the front end.

The class was well liked by the men and in March 1954 the Scottish Region proposed exchanging its ten Fowler 2-6-4 tanks, 42400/15-23 at Greenock Ladyburn, for 80081-90 currently being delivered to the London Midland Region, but to no avail. However, to reduce the stock of boilers and spares retained at St. Rollox Works, it was agreed that they should be replaced by Fairburns 42258-66 from Stoke, Bangor, Monument Lane and Springs Branch sheds. No further transfers occurred before March 1960 when, following the Southern-London Midland Region 2-6-4 tank rationalisation, the nineteen members of the class remaining on the London Midland Region, 80044-53/60-3/86/90-3, were despatched to Scotland in exchange for Fairburn 2-6-4T's 42198, 42202/6/7/9-13/7/29/36/8/40/7/70, 42696-8. The absence of any of the 1954 Fairburn transfers was deliberate to ensure that full advantage was gained of the soft water found at most Scottish sheds. However, the benefit was far from mutual for many of the Standard tanks arrived badly run down and unkempt, and some months were to pass before all proved capable of normal Scottish availability and performance. The allocation of these transfers was as follows:-
Corkerhill 80044-53; Stirling 80060-3; Dalry Road 80086; Dundee 80090/1; and Perth 80092/3. En route to Corkerhill from Chester 80049 was borrowed by Beattock for several weeks when, in addition to banking, it was regularly rostered for the Moffat goods.

During 1960 the class attained its peak in Scotland and daily could be found working a wide range of duties, including secondary passenger, commuter, branch line, ECS, van, local goods, shunting and banking. Up until then the diesel intrusion had caused little lasting impact, for redundancy of the Standards in one area immediately led to redeployment elsewhere, frequently to the detriment of older classes working services as yet not threatened by dieselisation. As a result, their sudden appearance in a district almost inevitably foreshadowed the withdrawal of these engines or the impending closure of a line, and in time this gained them the dubbing "Vultures". This was a truly unmerited sobriquet, for the class remained in excellent fettle and was in no way responsible for the "wind of change" sweeping through Scotland. However, at one stage in mid-1962, 80026/7/54/5 were all stored at Polmadie shed.

The duty changes, and the despatch of Fairburns 42055,

42123/42/5/65/77/96, 42204/71, 42689/99 to the North Eastern Region in exchange for 80071/3-7, 80116-20 in November 1963, widened the allocation of the class in Scotland. The total of 76 locomotives was allocated as follows:-

Corkerhill	(20)	80005/8/9/20/1/4/5/30/44-53, 80127/8
Beattock	(2)	80001/2
Polmadie	(10)	80058/86, 80106-9/15/21/9/30
Eastfield	(4)	80004/27/56/7
St. Margarets	(9)	80003/6/7/22/6/54/5, 80114/22
Dumfries	(4)	80023/76, 80117/9
Perth	(4)	80028/92/3, 80126
Ardrossan	(2)	80000/77
Stirling	(5)	80060-3, 80125
Carstairs	(8)	80071/3-5, 80110/6/8/20
Dundee	(3)	80090, 80123/4
Hurlford	(4)	80029/91, 80111/2
Hawick	(1)	80113

Two engines from the Eastfield allocation 80027/57 were utilised for banking duties between Glasgow Queen Street and Cowlairs; they were fitted with uncoupling apparatus to facilitate uncoupling whilst the train concerned was kept moving.

Over the next two years further duties were lost to the diesels, although again the impact fell principally on the older classes with the Standards remaining fully active. Duties worthy of note included the Dumfries - Stranraer 'Port Road', around Carstairs, the Killin, Dalmellington, Largs and Darvel branches, from Glasgow to Gourock, Ardrossan, Wemyss Bay, Ayr and Girvan, Hawick to Carlisle and Edinburgh and between Perth and Aberdeen. Various ECS duties were also worked around the Edinburgh and Glasgow termini while 80001/2 partnered Fairburn 2-6-4 tanks at Beattock. As bankers they were found noticeably stronger, but whereas the Fairburns regularly completed two round trips before taking water, it proved advisable to top up the Standards between journeys, especially when banking goods trains.

Cowlairs now remained responsible for all repairs and, like St. Rollox earlier, not only achieved an exceptionally high standard of workmanship, but did so in 80 per cent of the time required by Eastleigh, Darlington or Derby. The average miles at this period to intermediate repair was 124,617 and to general repair 201,247. 80002/6/8/21/3/5/6/8/54/60/1, 80115/29 received repaints and general repairs in 1962, 80000/5/9/20/2/7/9/46/51/86 in 1963 and 80004/47/61/3, 80120 in March 1964. In April 1964, with dieselisation now threatening the most modern classes, all further heavy attention was forbidden while in August 1964 further instructions authorised the withdrawal of engines requiring works attention in excess of £1,000, this being reduced to £450 in June 1965. As a result 80008/9/21/30/44/48-50/2/3/6/62/71/3-7, 80106/7/15/25/7/9 were condemned prematurely in 1964, with 80071/3-5 at Carstairs and 80030/44/9/50/77, 80115 at Ardrossan being in store by June. For statistical purposes the mileages of the first five withdrawals were recorded, details being:-
80030 411,762 80044 391,450 80048 309,293
80049 316,597 80050 293,348

The London Midland Region briefly reinstated 80044/8/50/6 80125/9, but the others were sold for cutting

Fig. 45   80006 and 80114 stand outside St. Margarets MPD, Edinburgh 1 May 1965.   St. Margarets was a very cramped and dirty shed located on both sides of the East Coast mainline east of Calton Tunnel.   *N. Skinner*

Fig. 46   80063 at Dunfermline Lower Station with the 4.05pm Stirling to Edinburgh Waverley stopping train 26 March 1960.

T. J. Edgington

Fig. 47   80062 catches the evening light as it hauls a local train near Alloa 13 April 1963.   *Rodney Lissenden*

up, mostly to the Motherwell Machinery & Scrap Company, Inshaw Works, Wishaw. This company gained a handsome profit from the transaction for, after allowance for wages, administration and tax, each engine gave a return of £308.

Line and branch closures, and further dieselisation in 1964, badly affected the steam services, although the surviving members of the class remained reasonably active, including 80123/4 on the Tayport branch (a Dundee duty), 80023/61, 80116/7/9 on Dumfries to Stranraer line and 80113 on the Hawick - Carlisle service, its regular duty being 6.30am and 6.13pm return. Perth's 80028/92/3, 80126 shared the Killin branch and the Aberdeen stopping trains, with occasional spells of banking at Blair Atholl. Many local goods, van and ECS duties also remained, although the appearance of 80023 working hard at the head of the heavy Dumfries-Perth goods on 27 July 1964 was exceptional and probably the result of the booked LNER A2 Class pacific, or 73XXX Standard Class 5 4-6-0 failing just prior to taking up the duty from Glasgow onwards.

The steam presence at Glasgow Central, despite the South Clyde electrification and extensive use of diesel units and locomotives, remained reasonably strong until 4 January 1965 when the local passenger service to Carlisle via Carstairs was withdrawn. Later in the year another steam oasis also vanished with the closure of the Dumfries-Challoch Junction line on 14th June 1965, having been preceded on 3 May by the withdrawal of passenger trains between Castle Douglas and Kirkcudbright. On the latter the final services were shared by 80117 and Standard Class 4 2-6-0 76073 although goods trains continued until final closure of the branch on 14 June 1955. Local traffic during the last weeks of the 'Port Road' was worked by 80023, 80117 and Standard Class 4 2-6-0's 76073/4. Other closures affecting the class at this period,

included the Killin and Tayport branches, and the Gleneagles-Crieff line, but not all was bad for poor diesel multiple unit performance led to a welcome increase of steam on the Glasgow Central-Gourock-Wemyss Bay services.

Many ECS workings also remained, as did various van and local goods duties, and this led to the class receiving sympathetic treatment with only ten, 80003/20/2/3/9/90, 80108-10/9, being condemned and sold for cutting up in 1965, while 80057 was modified for service as a stationary boiler at Buchanan Street station, arriving there in September 1965. It had gone from this duty by 1st February 1967.

Some typical observations at Scottish Region depots were:-

9 August 1964

Corkerhill	(14)	80005/8/9/20/1/4/8/45-7/51/77, 80112/27
Eastfield	(3)	80027/57/63
Polmadie	(14)	80001/56/8/86, 80107-9/15/6/20/1/5/9/30
St. Margarets	(3)	80022/55, 80122

2 and 3 September 1965

Dundee	(1)	80124
Perth	(3)	80092/3, 80126
Polmadie	(3)	80001, 80121/30
St. Margarets	(6)	80006/22/54/5, 80113/22

1 April 1966

Ayr	(2)	80024/5

If 1965 was a year of retention, then the following year proved disastrous for by June the class was being assailed from all directions by line closures and dieselisation of a magnitude

43

hitherto not experienced in Scotland. As a result, engines which previously had been well maintained were allowed to deteriorate, leaving them unkempt, lacking smokebox numberplates and the front end shrouded by steam. Many were laid aside surplus to requirements at their home sheds; however 80024 had the honour of performing as station pilot at Glasgow St. Enoch on the last day of passenger train working, 25th June 1966. The station closed on 27th June but parcels continued to be handled until 5th June 1967. The summer did not pass without some interesting workings, which included 80004/46 of Corkerhill piloting Class 5 4-6-0's on heavy Blackpool and St. Pancras expresses as far as Kilmarnock, and Polmadie's 80045, 80120 spending July and August on the Gourock line. Other regular duties included the 7.19am Glasgow Central-Renfrew, usually headed by 80128, and banking at Beattock where in August 80091, 80111 were partnering 42058, 42125, 42693 and 76098. As might be expected withdrawals were heavy with no fewer than thirty-four members of the class being laid aside for disposal. They were 80000/1/5-7/24-8/47/51/4/5/7/8/60/1/3/91-3, 80111-4/7/8/21-4/6/30. This massacre left only 80002/45/86, 80116/20 at Polmadie and 80004/46, 80128 at Corkerhill.

In January 1967, 80086 was on loan to Beattock, where later it was joined by 80002, while 80116/20 were the regular Glasgow Central ECS pilots, and on 11th February tended the fourteen-coach special carrying the USSR Prime Minister, Mr. Kosygin, and his entourage when visiting the city, prior to travelling to Edinburgh. Both engines were well cleaned and various mechanical faults had been rectified to ensure a trouble-free performance and the avoidance of steam enshrouding the welcoming dignitaries!

80002 was laid aside in March 1967, and 80128 in the following month, but 80004/45/6/86, 80116/20 remained in stock until steam ceased in the Region on 1st May 1967. 80116 remained in regular use as Glasgow Central station pilot and 80120 was noted on a working to Gourock in mid-April. The last regular Glasgow Central workings occurred on 28th April when Class 5 44699 departed with the 6.12am Hillington West and 80004 with the 7.19am Renfrew. A few days later a visit to Polmadie found 80116/20 derelict by the coaling plant, while 80004/46, 80128 at Corkerhill were being stripped of coal and their boilers and side tanks drained. At the same time 80086 was at Beattock.

By 24th July the Polmadie engines had been joined by 80045, and all were later sold for scrap, except 80002 which was retained for carriage heating at Cowlairs. When no longer required there, it was purchased by the Keighley & Worth Valley Railway and delivered to Haworth in May 1969. Unlike most engines obtained for preservation, it was received complete and in reasonably good mechanical order, and consequently was returned to steam with the minimum of delay in April 1971.

2.6.6 Southern Region

In 1951 Derby Works was fully committed to the construction of the Standard Class 5 4-6-0's and Ivatt Class 2 2-6-2 tanks, and consequently was forced to postpone the assembly of 80000-9 for the Scottish Region until the following year. Therefore it was from Brighton Works that the first engine, 80010, entered traffic on 10th July 1951. Over the next few days it was gently run in on empty carriage duties to Hove and Preston Park, with occasional local passenger workings to and from Steyning, before replacing a Fairburn 2-6-4 tank on 18th July at the head of the 11.05am Brighton-Victoria via East Grinstead, returning on the

Fig. 48   80004 at Ballater with the 6.05pm from Aberdeen 11 August 1954.   Although a local stopping train it consists of four Gresley mainline corridor coaches.
Peter Hay

Fig. 49   80005 working the 12.25pm Aberdeen to Fraserburgh train leaving Kittybrewster 28 March 1953.   Note the Snow plough fixed below the front buffer beam.

J.L. Stevenson

Fig. 50   80004 at Fraserburgh Station with 12.28pm train for Aberdeen 21 July 1956.

T. J. Edgington

Fig. 51 80121 piloting LMS Class 5 4-6-0 45497 at Inverness Station on a train bound for Aviemore via Forres 25 April 1961. 80121 will be detached at Forres, it is no doubt piloting the train rather than running 'light engine' to conserve line occupation on the single lines involved, a common practice.
Noel A. Machell

3.52pm via Uckfield. These duties were successfully repeated for several days when, following a brief return to the Erecting Shop for inspection and minor adjustment, it was despatched on 29th July to Tunbridge Wells West for general service. At once it was rostered for duty 656, comprising the 7.47am to London Bridge via Edenbridge Town, 4.40pm London Bridge-Uckfield, and empty stock home.

Meanwhile the second engine, 80011, left Brighton Works on 20th July 1951 when, following a generally similar routine, it was set to work on the 11.05am Brighton-Victoria on 30th July and despatched to Tunbridge Wells West on 14th August. There it was charged with the shed's most onerous duty, No. 657, which comprised the 6.40am Tunbridge Wells West-Victoria via Edenbridge Town, 9.08am back to Tunbridge Wells West, 1.08pm to London Bridge via East Grinstead and the 6.30pm home, also via East Grinstead. The first engine, 80010, now allocated to Tunbridge Wells West, was noted working the 1.15pm Victoria to Tunbridge Wells and the 4.49pm return on 7th September 1951. As 80012-9 were delivered to Tunbridge Wells West in September and October 1951, so they displaced the Fairburns on most of the top-link duties, including such trains as the 11.08am Victoria-Eastbourne via Heathfield, and as a result 42095-8 were transferred to Ashford and 42099, 42102/3/5 to Exmouth Junction for sub-shedding at Bude. 80013 was displayed at Lancing Works open day, on 6th September 1951.

In regular Central Division service there was little to choose between the performance of the two classes, although 80010-9 proved more versatile because of the ability to work through the narrow tunnels to Tonbridge and Redhill, whereas the Fairburns were prohibited. This was a most useful facility, but one nevertheless of which Tunbridge Wells West could take only limited advantage for many of the shed's duties did not involve passage through the tunnels. As a result in January 1952 a more realistic appraisal was made of the Division's 2-6-4 tank allocation, with 80016 being transferred to Brighton and 80017/8, followed later by 80019, to Eastbourne. Fairburns 42099, 42102/4/6 were returned to Tunbridge Wells West in exchange.

At Brighton 80016 partnered newly-completed members of the class on duty 745, the 5.00am Brighton-Eastbourne vans, 7.52am Eastbourne-Redhill via Tonbridge, 1.05pm Redhill-Tonbridge, 4.13pm Tonbridge-Redhill, 6.09pm Redhill-Tunbridge Wells West and 7.37pm home to Eastbourne. 80017/8/9 also worked to Redhill via Tonbridge as well as assisting with the summer inter-regional services over the coast lines which took the class for the first time regularly to Hastings.

80031/2/3, completed at Brighton in February and March 1952, were destined for the North Eastern Region

Fig. 52   80016 'Running in' when new from Brighton Works working the 3.35pm Oxted to Brighton seen near Newick 24 September 1951.

S.C. Nash

but, before being despatched to Darlington for the local services, that Region agreed to accept Fairburns 42083/4/5 in lieu so these three Standards joined 80016 at Brighton. This running shed was notorious for poor maintenance, especially the Bulleid pacifics, therefore it was not long before use was being made of all four on the through services to the West, initially the 11.00am to Cardiff as far as Salisbury, returning with the Plymouth train, but later with the Bournemouth and very occasionally with the 11.30am to Plymouth. The last mentioned was seldom loaded to less than ten corridors, 350 tons, and often more which demanded much from a Class 4 2-6-4 tank, considering the adverse grades west of Fareham which, together with lengthy water stops at Chichester and Southampton, made time keeping difficult, if not impossible. However, much better running occurred on the other through services, these being considerably lighter, although again water had to be taken en route. By October 1952, 80018/9 had moved to Redhill for the stopping trains to Tonbridge and Reading, but their stay was brief with 80019 being transferred to Brighton and 80018 to Tunbridge Wells West, to which shed 80017 had returned. Early in 1953 80017/9 were noted on Reading-Redhill services. A *Railway Magazine* report at this time claimed that trials with the class on freight trains had proved less than successful.

Despite the obvious disadvantages, 1953 again saw Brighton rostering the class for the through services with 80019/32/3 and 80059-64 running in when new all being recorded in the first half of the year. Fortunately, with greater experience and more adroit use of the water cranes, time keeping was much improved.

By the Spring of that year, the Fairburn and Standard 2-6-4 tanks had taken over practically all the Oxted line London workings, with excellent results as far as Tunbridge Wells West duties were concerned, but Brighton was experiencing difficulty with some of the longer distance turns. The 3.50pm and the 6.10pm Victoria-Brighton, both having Eastbourne portions, were Standard duties and almost invariably lost four to five minutes taking water at Eridge and Oxted. Corresponding up trains similarly lost time at Eridge. Time was also lost by the 5.49pm Victoria-Groombridge via East Grinstead, another heavy train which had the added misfortune of being closely followed into Oxted by the 6.10pm Victoria-Brighton. See Appendix A for some details of typical Brighton and Tunbridge Wells West diagrams from the summer 1954 and winter 1958 working timetables.

After prolonged investigation and much reporting by the Motive Power and Traffic inspectors it was reluctantly accepted that tender engines were necessary, although it was January 1954 before Eastleigh could spare the services of Class 4 2-6-0's 76005/6. At once the delays at Eridge and Oxted ceased, but unfortunately only to be replaced by greater losses en route when the boiler proved inadequate for climbing the banks and the 5ft. 3in. coupled wheels too small on the favourable stretches of line. In April 1954 both were transferred to Dorchester and later in the year most of the offending services were taken over, with some success, by SR U1 class 2-6-0's, but it was 4th December 1958 before the ideal replacement became available, Class 4 4-6-0 75074 (Fig. 57). After initial steaming difficulties, it did exceptionally well and was regularly rostered for the 5.49pm Victoria-Groombridge

Fig. 53   80016 again, this time with 12.03 pm London Victoria to Brighton at Sheffield Park Station 16 April 1955.   *S.C. Nash*

Fig. 54   80042 on 12.45pm Eastbourne to Tunbridge Wells West descending the bank north of Heathfield Tunnel 3 June 1962.   *S.C. Nash*

Fig. 55   80083 leaving Sanderstead with the 5.37pm London Bridge to East Grinstead 1 August 1961.   *S.C. Nash*

Fig. 56   80149 passing Groombridge Junction signalbox 25 September 1959 with a stopping train from Tonbridge to Brighton.
Rodney Lissenden

Fig. 57　BR Standard Class 4 4-6-0 75074 at Eastleigh MPD 25 August 1957. This locomotive was one of three which replaced Standard Class 4 2-6-4T's to overcome delay problems taking water with London services at Eridge and Oxted.　*L. Elsey*

and the 9.20pm Tunbridge Wells West-Victoria via Edenbridge Town. In early 1959, it was joined by 75070/5 and together they eliminated most of the Oxted line problems.

From the beginning the Standards had worked regularly over the Eridge-Eastbourne line albeit with stringent speed restrictions, especially north of Horam. Many crews considered these unnecessary, therefore on 24th November 1955 brand new 80127, before dispatch to Scotland, made several test runs with a three-coach set over the line to discover whether any easement was permissible in preparation for the introduction of regular interval services over the Uckfield and Heathfield lines. Some relaxation was found possible and the revised timetable, with a dramatic increase in services, came into force in June 1956. There were many additional duties, but in the main these were fulfilled by making more extensive use of the 2-6-4 tank classes, the Standards in particular finding little difficulty in providing the increased availability.

In May 1956, with the completion in sight of the final Eastern Region series, 80131-44, the necessity for all the remaining engines of Brighton order BR 7739 was questioned and after consultation it was decided to cancel the last five, 80150-4. (It had already been agreed to cancel a further fifteen locomotives, 80155-69, in the earlier stages of building.) The decision to cancel 80150-4 was later to be rescinded when it became known that much of the material, including the boilers, was to hand and could not be purposely employed as spares. As a consequence of this indecisiveness

the assembly of these five locomotives was delayed with the last not being despatched to traffic until 26th March 1957, some three months overdue, and nearly six years after the first of the class, 80010, entered traffic in July 1951!

80154, therefore, had not only the distinction of being the final 2-6-4 tank constructed by British Railways, but also the last of a long line of engines built at Brighton Works. It also worked services on the last day of operation by the Southern Region over the 'Bluebell Line' between Sheffield Park and East Grinstead. With the delivery of 80145-54, the Southern Region allocation became:-

Brighton　　　　　　　　(15)　80010/1/31-3, 80145-54
Tunbridge Wells West　　(8)　80012-9

At Brighton the new engines took over the duties worked by the withdrawn LBSCR Atlantics (Fig. 58) as well as replacing Fairburns 42067/8/70/1/5.

In March 1958, the Southern Region made representations to have its remaining Fairburns exchanged for a like number of Standard tanks, but at the time no other Region saw the necessity of rationalising the two classes and therefore the Southern Region was left quite illogically to operate its services with a mixture of twenty-three Standards and thirty-four Fairburns. However, late the following year, the proposal went through, possibly due to problems with fitting the London Midland Region locomotives with AWS and to rationalise the holding of spare parts at depots. On 29th November 1959 the thirty-four Standard tanks, 80034-43/59/64-8/81-5/7-9,94/5, 80137-44 were exchanged for an equivalent number of Fairburns, 42066-71/4-82/6-92/5-9,

Fig. 58   SR (LBSCR) H2 4-4-2 32424 at Brighton at the head of an RCTS special composed of Pullman coaches 5 October 1952. The train ran in connection with Brighton Works Centenary and covered the main line to London Victoria in sixty minutes.

Graham S. Lloyd/Rodney Lissenden Collection

42100-6. Of these, 80137-44 from Neasden shed had originally been Eastern Region stock, but at the boundary changes of 1 February 1958 had been absorbed by the London Midland Region. For a variety of reasons the exchange was implemented slowly, thus it was March 1960 before the last Fairburn, 42101, finally departed the Southern Region, where the Standard allocation became fifty-seven locomotives, distributed as follows:-

Ashford	(15)	80034-43/59/64/5/6/87
Bricklayers Arms	(4)	80082-5
Brighton	(16)	80013/31-3,80143-54
Stewarts Lane	(3)	80067/8/81
Three Bridges	(6)	80010-2/88/9/94
Tunbridge Wells West	(13)	80014-9/95,80137-42

First recordings of the newcomers were 80081/4 working Oxted line duties on 9th December 1959, 80089 on a pick-up goods at Haywards Heath nine days later, and the following day, 19th December, 80082 heading the 3.27am London Bridge- Eastbourne. Many were received in poor mechanical order and some months elapsed before the normal high, 83 per cent, Southern Region availability was achieved.

The Kentish allocation brought the class regularly to several routes over which they had not previously worked, notably Maidstone East-Ashford, Tonbridge-Ashford, Ashford-Margate via Dover or Canterbury West, Ashford-New Romney and Ashford-Hastings. During the summer months Ashford engines 80043/59/64/5 daily penetrated as far as Eastbourne with the Wolverhampton train from Hastings, returning with the down service, while another

duty took them to Redhill.

For a week, commencing 2nd October 1960, the turntable at Weymouth was under repair and all trains from Bournemouth were worked by 80059/64-6/87/9, 80140 on loan from South Eastern and Central Divisions. Generally, the Waterloo connections were worked to time with some fast running around Wool while the slow services posed no problems, and local crews were sorry to see their departure.

In the New Year (1961) steam in Kent came under increasing pressure. Phase I of the Kent Coast electrification, Gillingham-Ramsgate and Dover via Canterbury East had been completed on 15th June 1959 and the first section of Phase II, Ramsgate-Dover, came into use on 2nd January 1961. On 12th June electric working was extended to the Sevenoaks-Dover main line and Paddock Wood-Maidstone West line. The Kent coast electrification scheme was completed on 9th October with the Maidstone East-Ashford and Ashford-Minster lines. These events, and the increasing use of diesel traction on branch services, virtually removed all of Ashford's steam duties with 80037-43/59/64-6/85 being officially transferred to Tonbridge, although most were retained to cover mechanical failures and a spate of minor derailments caused by inexperienced diesel crews. However, by mid-August 1961 80038/9/40/3/64/85 had reached Tonbridge to be employed principally on the Brighton, Redhill and Eastbourne services, together with two daily turns to Maidstone West, despite the electrification of the branch from Paddock Wood. By March 1962, no regular duties remained at Ashford and after a period in store

Fig. 59 80147 Climbing Hildenborough Bank 19 June 1960 with a Tunbridge Wells West to Sevenoaks Tubs Hill stopping train.

Rodney Lissenden

Fig. 60 80034 leaving Brookland Halt with a heavy New Romney to Ashford train in April 1962 loaded with seaside day trippers.

Brian Hilton

80035/6/67 were transferred to Exmouth Junction shed.

As the Kent electrification progressed the last steam workings at Maidstone West occurred on 16th June 1962 when 80143 headed the 5.21pm to Reading and 80065 arrived shortly afterwards with the 4.17pm from Redhill. More of the class could now be released to the South Western Division where Exmouth Junction gained 80037-43/59/64 and Eastleigh 80065/6/82/3. From Exmouth Junction the class became a familiar sight on the Exmouth and Sidmouth services and also the Bude branch while occasionally N class 2-6-0's were replaced on the Ilfracombe and Torrington stopping trains. 80040 was often sub-shedded at Launceston. Various local goods and passenger duties were also worked, including those to Honiton. At Eastleigh, 80065/6/82/3 were mainly employed on local goods and van duties, particularly around Southampton and Gosport, while occasional appearances were made on the Eastleigh-Bournemouth slows, duties on which they were joined at the end of November 1962 by 80087/95, 80137.

Further changes occurred on 30th December 1962, when yet another round of regional boundary and motive power responsibility changes transferred the lines and running sheds west of Salisbury to the Western Region. Altogether 149 engines were involved, including the twelve Standard '4' Tanks at Exmouth Junction, 80035-43/59/64/7. The Southern Region allocation of Standard 2-6-4T's then became:-

Brighton	(17)	80013/31/2/3, 80138/43-54
Eastleigh	(7)	80065/6/82/3/7/95, 80137
Stewarts Lane	(8)	80012/34/68/81/4/5/9/94
Tunbridge Wells West	(13)	80010/1/4-9/88, 80139/40/1/2

1963 proved a year of great upheaval for the class with even such stable sheds as Brighton and Tunbridge Wells West suffering from the "wind of change". The first transfers occurred in March, when Eastleigh lost 80087/95, 80137 to Guildford for empty carriage stock duties, working sets from Walton to Waterloo in the morning, thence Clapham Junction trips during the day and ECS back to Walton in the evening. 80087, probably because of its high mileage, also worked local van services to Woking or Petersfield, and piloted to Guildford. June 1963 found 80012,80148 leaving the Central Division for Feltham, whence they worked a variety of local goods, vans and ECS duties in the suburban area, on which they proved so successful that 80143/54 were similarly transferred the following month.

Other changes at this period included the transfer of 80081, 80147 to Weymouth, but with most of that shed's secondary passenger and van duties being intended for tender engines, there was little regular work and after a brief stay both were despatched to Bournemouth. There, between lengthy bouts of station pilot duties at the Bournemouth Central and West stations, useful employment was found working goods to Poole, Swanage and Ringwood, interspersed with the Southampton and Eastleigh stopping trains.

On the Central Division, the improved availability of diesel sets and Type 3 D65XX locomotives for the Oxted line services made the retention of steam unnecessary and in September 1963 Tunbridge Wells West closed as a main shed and Stewarts Lane ceased to cater for steam stock. Initially, most of the redundant Standards were transferred to Brighton,

but with that shed also in the process of closure their stay was brief and at the end of the year Redhill became the Division's principal steam MPD with an allocation of no fewer than twenty-one Standard 2-6-4T's, 80031-4/68/84/5/8/9/94, 80138-42/4/5/9/51-3. From these, the sub-sheds at Tonbridge, Tunbridge Wells West and Eastbourne were supplied, and together they operated practically all of the remaining Redhill-Tonbridge-Eastbourne steam services. Some trains were also worked to Reading, but usually these were left to the Maunsell 2-6-0's. The Standards sub-shedded at Tunbridge Wells West retained a number of workings to Three Bridges and also headed permanent way trains on Sundays, whilst those at Eastbourne covered a number of local goods duties as well as passenger services to Hailsham and Hastings. On the Uckfield line the last steam trains on 3rd January 1964 were worked by N class 2-6-0 31408, 31833 and Standard 2-6-4T's 80089,80138/49.

The Steyning line finally fell to diesels in May 1964, and in the following month Brighton shed closed to steam with Redhill gaining 80011/9 and becoming responsible for the Three Bridges sub-shed where a 2-6-4 tank was retained for working the East Grinstead line and two Ivatt Class 2 2-6-2 tanks from Guildford for the Cranleigh services. As frequently occurs with a change of motive power, the old refused to fade quietly away, for in the Spring of 1964 80011/4/7/9 deputised on numerous occasions for electric locomotives 20001/3 to and from Portsmouth with the Brighton-Plymouth through trains. Other transfers at this period took 80013 to Bournemouth, 80014/6/7 to Eastleigh and 80018 to Feltham.

Eastleigh Works ceased giving general repairs to the class in April 1964, the last being 80011/2/9, and consequently little time passed before those arriving in shops proved too run down for light attention and had to be condemned. 80010/87,80148 were the first Southern Region members of the class to go in June 1964 with 80017/31 following before the end of the year. Final mileages were ridiculously low, those for 80010, the first of the class to enter service in July 1951, being as follows:-

June	1955	Light Intermediate	130,076
August	1957	General Repair	206,088
August	1959	Light Intermediate	291,946
February	1962	Light Intermediate	373,348
At Withdrawal	14 June 1964		458,035

On the South Western Division the class was normally restricted to secondary duties, therefore the appearance of 80064 on 25th May 1964 heading the 5.30pm Waterloo-Bournemouth West express from Eastleigh was worthy of comment. That evening, it was booked for the 7.22pm Eastleigh-Bournemouth Central slow and consequently was standing on its train when Bulleid Merchant Navy pacific 35028 *Clan Line* came to a halt with failed injectors. The changeover was quickly completed and with a delay of only seven minutes 80064 was away and gave such a spirited performance that no further time was lost to Bournemouth Central.

A regular Bournemouth duty was introduced over the full length of the Somerset & Dorset line, the roster covering the 1.10pm Bournemouth-Bath Green Park and the 7.05pm return. In August 1964, 80069,80133/4 were received from the Western Region, the first two going to Nine Elms for ECS, goods and van duties while 80134 was sent to Bournemouth to join 80013/81,80146/7 on the Eastleigh,

Fig. 61
80015 passing Vauxhall 30 April 1966 with ECS from London Waterloo to Clapham Junction.
Peter Groom

Fig. 62
80146 with a local passenger train from Eastleigh to Bournemouth passing through the New Forest in May 1967. *T.J. Edgington*

Lymington and Swanage services. Incidentally, on arrival 80134 was found to be in such poor condition, that the clinkered firebox could only be cleared by the use of crowbars. In November that year 80095,80137/43/54 were also transferred to Nine Elms from Feltham.

The Tonbridge-Reading line succumbed to diesel sets on 4th January 1965, the Maunsell 2-6-0's being the principal victims, although the Standards lost their Tonbridge-Redhill work and the sub-shed at Tonbridge closed with 80138 going to Bournemouth and 80139 to Eastleigh. Most of the Tonbridge-Eastbourne services remained, with four engines being stabled at Tunbridge Wells West and six at Eastbourne. A number of turns to Three Bridges were also worked by the Tunbridge Wells West engines while Eastbourne retained responsibility for several local goods duties as well as the Hailsham services. Two parcels trains between Redhill and Tonbridge were intentionally left steam-operated to provide change over turns for the two sub-sheds.

On 1st March 1965, the diesel services were extended to Tunbridge Wells West and the steam workings shortened to operate from there to Eastbourne, with a dwindling number to Three Bridges. This, however, was the swan song for on 13th June 1965 the Cuckoo Line closed north of Hailsham and, except for a few penetrating workings from outside, steam came to an end on the Central Division. On the last day of regular steam, Saturday 12th June 1965, 80011/84, 80141/4 were in charge of the services, with 80144 heading the six-coach British Railways' "Cuckoo Line Farewell" excursion from Eastbourne to Tunbridge Wells West and return.

The last of the Eastbourne and Tunbridge Wells West engines reached the main shed on Sunday evening 13th June 1965, and during the following week, after minor repairs and boiler washouts, they were despatched by Redhill to Eastleigh 80011, Bournemouth 80019/32, Feltham 80033/4/68/85/9 80094, 80140/1 and Salisbury 80142/4/5/51/2 (mostly to store), 80084/8 failed to pass inspection, the former having badly worn tyres and the latter fractured steam piping, and

Fig. 63 80146 again, working a Weymouth to Bournemouth Central train near Upwey 3 July 1967. On the SR Parcels trains were usually known as 'Van trains'.

S.C. Nash

both were laid aside until sold to Birds Commercial Motors, Morriston for scrapping. All of those members of the class sent to Feltham, except 80085/94, were still in store at Feltham on 24th October 1965.

In April 1965, 80070/96, 80102/32 were received from the London Midland Region, 80096 being sent to Bournemouth and the others to store at Feltham. All proved badly run down and were quickly condemned, 80132 being the last in early January 1966. By April 1966, withdrawal had reduced the class to twenty-eight members on the Southern Region, shared between four running sheds:-

Bournemouth   (7)   80011/3/9/32, 80134/8/46
Eastleigh   (7)   80016/65/82/83, 80139/51/2
Feltham   (5)   80033/68/85/94, 80140
Nine Elms   (9)   80012/5/89/95, 80133/43-5/54

Those at Nine Elms were mainly employed on ECS and van workings between Waterloo, Clapham Junction and Walton, and the Kensington Olympia passenger services, but at Feltham little work remained with most being laid aside and suffering cannibalisation to retain those at Nine Elms in traffic. As a result, all of the Feltham members of the class had been condemned by the Autumn, except 80085 and 80140 which were transferred to Nine Elms. At Eastleigh, 80011 frequently acted as works pilot while other duties for the class included the Bournemouth and Salisbury slows, vans and goods to Southampton, Portsmouth and Havant, and a duty

based on Basingstoke which included carriage piloting and the daily freight to Andover and Ludgershall. At Bournemouth, 80011/3/9/32, 80134/8/46 worked the Swanage and Lymington branches, the Weymouth slows, and various local goods and van duties with periods of carriage shunting and banking at Poole.

Typical observations made during depot visits towards the end of steam recorded the following:-

28th February 1965
Bournemouth   (6)   80013/81, 80134/46/7/50
Eastleigh Works   (1)   80014
Eastleigh Depot   (11)   80015-8/65/6/83/7, 80139/49/53

21st March 1965
Feltham   (1)   80143
Nine Elms   (3)   80095, 80133/7

20th February 1966
Bournemouth   (6)   80013/9/37/85, 80134/46
Eastleigh Depot   (7)   80065/82/3/96, 80102/32/9
Salisbury   (2)   80151/2

6th March 1966
Bournemouth   (8)   80011/3/9/83/5/94, 80134/46

55

19th February 1967

Bournemouth	(4)	80011/9/32,80134
Eastleigh Depot	(2)	80138/9
Salisbury	(1)	80152

The dieselisation of the Swanage services on 5th September 1966 gave the Lymington line the distinction of being the only regular steam-operated branch in Southern England. An Ivatt Class 2 2-6-2 tank, often 41316, stabled overnight at Lymington Town for the evening and early morning services, but a Standard worked those during the day. Further withdrawals during the year left only 80012/5/85, 80133/40/3/5/54 at Nine Elms, 80016, 80139/51/2 at Eastleigh and 80011/9/32, 80134/46 at Bournemouth. The Lymington branch remained steam-operated until the week ending 1st April 1967 with 41230 and 80134 sharing the services on Easter Monday and 80152 working those of the final day.

In April 1967 the booked duties at Nine Elms fell to four, three covering ECS and van workings and the fourth the Clapham Junction-Kensington Olympia passenger services, 80015, 80133/40/3 being the most regular performers. Eastleigh had two "home" duties, one a van and goods working to Southampton and the other going further afield to Portsmouth and Havant, working a variety of local passenger, van and goods jobs. There was also the Basingstoke-based duty, which now included a van train to Reading. At Bournemouth the sole regular surviving duty comprised the 7.51am to Weymouth, returning with the 11.18am. On Saturdays one of the Nine Elms duties was extended to include the 11.05am Waterloo-Basingstoke while an Eastleigh engine worked the 12.48pm to Bournemouth and the 4.28pm return. However, in emergencies more demanding work was undertaken, for example on 10th June 1967 80145 worked the 7.18am Waterloo-Salisbury.

More withdrawals occurred during the early months of 1967 which left only eleven members of the class in stock on 9th July 1967, the day that steam ceased on the Southern Region. They were 80011/5/6/85,80133/4/9/40/3/6/52. Among the last in service were 80011 and 80146, the former working ECS at Waterloo on 7th July and the latter as station pilot at Bournemouth Central during the following day. Throughout the previous week there was a gradual movement of engines to Weymouth and Salisbury for storage, this being accelerated later until by 29th July those at Salisbury included 80015/6/9, 80133/9/43/6/51/2/4 while 80011, 80134 resided at Weymouth. Four members of the class, 80012/85, 80140/5, remained at Nine Elms while 80151 was at Basingstoke on 22nd July awaiting despatch to Woodham Brothers at Barry Dock via Salisbury. This was a most fortuitous disposal for, like most other sales to this scrap metal merchant, scrapping was long delayed and therefore it remained virtually intact until purchased in March 1975 by the Anglian Locomotive Group for preservation on the Stour Valley Railway at Chappel & Wakes Colne.

80154 became a celebrity engine being utilised to work the last trains over the Bluebell Line, the "Sussex Coast Ltd" on 13th April 1958, the "Surrey Rambler" on 5th June 1966 and the "Four Counties" Tour on 9th June 1966 (Fig. 65).

Fig. 64 80065 hauling RCTS Hammersmith and Chiswick branch Railtour seen at Hammersmith Grove Road 10 November 1956.

Philip J. Kelley

Fig. 65   80154 with RCTS Newhaven to Brighton special train 'Sussex Coast Ltd' on 13 April 1958.   *L. Elsey*

2.6.7 Western Region

The Western Region's dislike of the Britannia pacifics and the Class 4 75XXX 4-6-0's also extended to the Standard 2-6-4 tanks, although in mitigation it has to be recorded that with several GWR-designed 2-6-2 tank classes in stock, there was no demand for their services during the first decade of nationalisation. However, withdrawal took its toll of these classes and, following the LTS electrification, twenty one Standard 2-6-4T's were transferred from the Eastern Region in July 1962 and allocated to Western Region depots as follows:-

Croes Newydd	(2)	80079/80
Machynlleth	(1)	80105
Old Oak Common	(6)	80070/98,80102/4/31/2
Shrewsbury	(6)	80078/96,80100/1/35/6
Swansea East Dock	(6)	80069/72/97/9,80133/4

Those sent to Old Oak Common were immediately laid aside in store, although later limited use was made of 80070/98, 80131 on Paddington ECS duties before all six were transferred to Shrewsbury and Croes Newydd by November 1962. At Swansea East Dock and Shrewsbury they replaced the Fowler 2-6-4 tanks on the Central Wales line and proved very popular, with many crews considering them ideal engines for this difficult route. Many of the Cambrian services were also worked while those at Shrewsbury and Croes Newydd regularly worked over the Severn Valley line to Kidderminster and Hartlebury until closure. 80101/5 were sub-shedded at Portmadoc for both passenger and freight duties, including the Pwllheli-Machynlleth goods. The class had occasional duties on the Carmarthen-Aberystwyth route where they deputised for Manor class 4-6-0's.

Most of these engines, however, only came briefly under Western Region control for on 1st January 1963 a further rationalisation of motive power found the Shrewsbury District transferred to the London Midland Region. By now fifteen members of the class, 80070/8/9/80/96/8, 80100/1/2/4/5/31/2/5/6, were allocated to Shrewsbury and Croes Newydd, and these now came under London Midland control. The six at Swansea East Dock, 80069/72/97/8, 80133/4, were retained by the Western Region for working over the Central Wales line in partnership with the London Midland series at Shrewsbury, but by mid-year most were redundant with 80072/97/9 being transferred away to Leamington Spa, Oswestry and Machynlleth respectively, while 80069,80133/4 became Southern Region stock in August 1964, following their transfer to Nine Elms and Feltham. Prior to this, in March 1963, 80133 had moved to Neath (Court Sart) shed, and appeared on duties to Pontypool Road (7.40am out and 10.55am return) as well as the 5.05pm Swansea-Porthcawl and the 8.05pm Porthcawl-Neath.

At the same time that Shrewsbury was transferred away from Western Region control, former Southern Region sheds in Devon and Cornwall came under Western Region control. The sheds involved were Barnstaple, Exmouth Junction, Wadebridge and Yeovil Town, and involved twelve members of the Standard Class 4 2-6-4 tanks, 80035-43/59/64/7, which were allocated to Exmouth Junction. Although nominally stationed at Exmouth Junction shed, two were sub-shedded at Exmouth and one each at Bude, Launceston and Okehampton. On 10th August 1963 80039 was working the Yeovil Town-Junction shuttle services with a two coach GWR auto set and 80035/41/2 the Sidmouth Junction-Sidmouth-Exmouth branch, while later in the year regular appearances were being made on the North Cornwall line working to Padstow and occasionally on the Exeter-Plymouth trains via the former Southern Railway route.

By April 1964, the North Cornwall lines services were being monopolised by the Standard Class 4 tanks, while during the summer months a shortage of light pacifics at Exmouth Junction led to frequent appearances on the Ilfracombe line, including the through coaches of the "Atlantic Coast Express". Time keeping was excellent with 80037 on 6th June performing particularly well with the nine coach 11.05am ex-Waterloo from Exeter Central to Ilfracombe.

On 9th July 80043 worked the 7.40pm Okehampton-Bude, 80064 the 8.20pm Halwill-Launceston and 80037 the 7.20pm Bude-Halwill, whilst on 31st July 80037/8/41 were sharing the Bude branch and 80042/59 respectively working the 3.10pm Padstow-Exeter Central and the 6.20pm Bude-Okehampton. On the same day 80035/9/43 were in charge of the Exmouth branch and Sidmouth Junction-Exmouth services, with 80067 assisting pannier tanks banking trains between the St.Davids and Central stations at Exeter.

From 6th September 1964, services over all the ex-Southern Region West Country lines were severely curtailed while additionally the workings to Plymouth and North Devon were dieselised. However, the North Cornwall service between Okehampton and Padstow remained steam operated by 75XXX class 4-6-0's, N class 2-6-0's and 80037/9/42/3/64 until January 1965. 80064 became a regular performer on an N class duty based at Wadebridge for the Delabole slate traffic. With such a limited use for the class those stopped for repairs were condemned, with 80040 being despatched to Crewe for cutting up in May 1964 and 80036/8 laid aside at Exmouth Junction awaiting sale. Others

more fortunate were transferred away from the district for further service, with 80035 going to Yeovil Town and 80043/59/67 going to Templecombe on the Somerset & Dorset line. However, 80041 remained active at Exmouth Junction, often shunting at Exeter Central or replacing failed diesels, until mid-1965 when it too gravitated to Templecombe, to where 80037 had also been transferred as a replacement for the withdrawn 80067. 80043/59/67 were noted on Templecombe shed on 28th February 1965, but twelve months later on 12th February 1966 80019/39 had replaced 80059/67. Generally employment was found on the stopping trains to Bath or Bournemouth, but occasionally piloting, local goods and shunting duties were performed. On the withdrawal of 80035 in April 1965, 80039 replaced it at Yeovil Town, this locomotive being noted on the 3.20pm Bath Green Park-Templecombe on 10th April before official transfer.

On 12th September 1965, a special excursion ran from Waterloo to North Devon, being Bulleid pacific hauled to Exeter Central where 80039 + 43 took charge to Barnstaple, at which point the train divided with 80039 heading the front portion to Ilfracombe and 80043 the rear portion to Torrington. The special proved so successful that it was repeated on 30th October 1965 with the same motive power, although on this occasion 80043 worked to Ilfracombe and 80039 to Torrington. These were the final North Devon steam workings and since Exmouth Junction no longer possessed any members of the class, both engines had to be borrowed from Templecombe. 80037 remained allocated to Templecombe until withdrawal in March 1966, but in October and November 1965 it had gravitated to Gloucester shed and was working from there.

On 5th March 1966, the last day of normal traffic on the

Fig. 66   80037 leaving Evercreech Junction 31 July 1965 with the 4.18pm Templecombe to Bath Green Park.   *Hugh Ballantyne*

Fig. 67   80043 taking water at Evercreech Junction at the head of the 4.18pm train to Bath Green Park, 7th August 1965. Driver Bill Gunning is on the platform turning off the tap whilst his fireman tries to avoid getting wet! Ivatt Class 2 2-6-2T 41223 stands in the 'middle road' and will occupy the same platform as 80043 after its departure, with the 5pm departure to Highbridge. Bill Gunning was one of three brothers who were all senior drivers at Bath Shed.   *Hugh Ballantyne*

Fig. 68   80138 leaving Bath Green Park station with the 1.10pm local train to Templecombe, 20 October 1965. The locomotive outside the shed is 82044, LMS '8F' 2-8-0 48525 and 82004 are behind the train and Diesel Electric D88 can be seen in the station. The wooden coach body was used by the Bath Shed Mutual Improvement Class.   *Hugh Ballantyne*

Somerset & Dorset line, 80043 worked the 7.35am Templecombe-Bath, the 4.12pm Bath-Templecombe and then piloted 80041 from Templecombe with the 6.46pm Bournemouth Central-Bath while 80037 headed the 5.37pm Bournemouth Central-Templecombe and 80138 from Bournemouth shed worked the 6.10pm Bath-Templecombe. The following day, Sunday 6th March, 80043 and Class 8F 48706 worked a special from Bath to Bournemouth Central whilst 80037/9/41 had returned to Green Park shed. The same month also saw 80037/41/3, the last three Western Region members of the class, condemned and sold to J.Cashmore, Newport for cutting up, although not before 80043 had been used as an exhibit at the Bristol Bath Road Diesel Depot open day on 30th April 1966.

2.6.8 Allocation Summary

80000 9.52 Ayr, 10.52 Corkerhill, 9.61 Hurlford, 1.62 Corkerhill, 10.62 Ardrossan, 6.64 Corkerhill,

80001 10.52 Polmadie, 5.62 Beattock, 5.64 Polmadie,

80002 10.52 Motherwell, P11.52 Polmadie, 5.62 Beattock, 5.64 Polmadie,

80003 10.52 Motherwell, P11.52 Polmadie, 6.62 St. Margarets,

80004 11.52 Kittybrewster 6.61 Beattock, 12.62 Eastfield, 8.64 Dawsholm, 10.64 Corkerhill,

80005 11.52 Kittybrewster, 7.59 Corkerhill, 10.64 Ayr, 3.65 Beattock, 11.65 Polmadie,

80006 P11.52 Polmadie, 6.61 Beattock, 8.61 Polmadie, 6.62 St. Margarets,

80007 P12.52 Polmadie, 3.55 Hawick, 4.55 Polmadie, 6.62 St. Margarets, 11.65 Polmadie,

80008 P12.52 Corkerhill,

80009 1.53 Corkerhill,,

80010 7.51 Tunbridge Wells West, 10.56 Brighton, 3.59 Three Bridges, 1.63 Tunbridge Wells West, 9.63 Brighton,

80011 7.51 Tunbridge Wells West, 10.56 Brighton, 3.59 Three Bridges, 1.63 Tunbridge Wells West, 9.63 Brighton, 6.64 Redhill, 6.65 Eastleigh, 10.65 Bournemouth,1.66 Guildford, 2.66 Bournemouth,

80012 8.51 Tunbridge Wells West, 4.58 Brighton, 3.59 Three Bridges, 1.63 Stewarts Lane, 6.63 Feltham, 11.64 Eastleigh, 10.65 Nine Elms,

80013 9.51 Tunbridge Wells West, 1.59 Brighton, 6.64 Bournemouth,

80014 9.51 Tunbridge Wells West, 9.63 Brighton, 6.64 Eastleigh,

80015 9.51 Tunbridge Wells West, 6.56 Brighton, 10.56 Tunbridge Wells West, 9.63 Eastleigh, 10.65 Nine Elms,

80016 9.51 Tunbridge Wells West, 3.52 Brighton, 10.56 Tunbridge Wells West, 9.63 Brighton, 6.64 Eastleigh,

80017 9.51 Tunbridge Wells West, 1.52 Brighton, 3.52 Eastbourne, 10.52 Tunbridge Wells West, 6.56 Brighton, 10.56 Tunbridge Wells West, 9.63 Brighton, 6.64 Eastleigh,

80018 10.51 Tunbridge Wells West, 1.52 Brighton, 3.52 Eastbourne, 10.52 Redhill, 3.53 Tunbridge Wells West, 6.56 Brighton, 10.56 Tunbridge Wells West, 9.63 Brighton, 6.64 Feltham, 11.64 Eastleigh,

80019 10.51 Tunbridge Wells West, 1.52 Brighton, 6.52 Eastbourne, 10.52 Redhill, 3.53 Brighton, 10.56 Tunbridge Wells West, 9.63 Brighton, 6.64 Redhill, 6.65 Bournemouth,

80020 10.51 Kittybrewster, 6.61 Ardrossan, 7.61 Corkerhill,

80021 11.51 Kittybrewster, 6.61 Ardrossan, 7.61 Corkerhill,

80022 11.51 Polmadie, 6.62 St. Margarets,

80023 11.51 Polmadie, 6.62 Stranraer, 10.62 Hurlford, 3.63 Dumfries,

80024 P12.51 Corkerhill,

80025 P12.51 Corkerhill,

80026 P12.51 Corkerhill, 1.52 Polmadie, 8.62 St. Margarets,

80027 1.52 Polmadie, 12.62 Eastfield, P12.64 Polmadie,

80028 1.52 Kittybrewster, 6.61 Ardrossan, 6.62 Hurlford, 6.63 Stranraer, 11.63 Perth,

80029 1.52 Kittybrewster, 6.61 Ardrossan, 6.62 Hurlford,

80030 2.52 Ayr, 3.52 Corkerhill, 10.58 Ardrossan, 2.59 Corkerhill,

80031 (Originally intended for NER) 2.52 Brighton, 1.64 Redhill,

80032 (Originally intended for NER) 2.52 Brighton, 1.64 Redhill, 6.65 Bournemouth,

80033 (Originally intended for NER) 3.52 Brighton, 1.64 Redhill, 6.65 Feltham (stored),

80034 (Originally intended for SR) 5.52 Crewe North, 5.52 Watford, 12.59 Ashford, 5.62 Stewarts Lane, 7.63 Brighton, 1.64 Redhill, 6.65 Feltham (stored),

80035 (Originally intended for SR) 5.52 Watford, 12.59 Ashford, 5.62 Exmouth Jct., 9.64 Yeovil, 1.65 Exmouth Jct., 2.65 Yeovil,

80036 (Originally intended for SR) 5.52 Watford, 12.59 Ashford, 5.62 Exmouth Jct.,

80037 (Originally intended for SR) 5.52 Watford, 12.59 Ashford, 6.61 Tonbridge, 6.62 Exmouth Jct., 1.65 Bath (Green Park), 2.65 Exmouth Jct., 6.65 Templecombe,

80038 (Originally intended for SR) P6.52 Watford, 12.59 Ashford, 6.61 Tonbridge, 6.62 Exmouth Jct., 7.63 Yeovil 9.63 Exmouth Jct.,

80039 (Originally intended for SR) P6.52 Bletchley, P12.53 Longsight, P2.55 Bletchley, 12.59 Ashford 6.61 Tonbridge, 6.62 Exmouth Jct., 1.65 Bath (Green Park), 2.65 Exmouth Jct., 5.65 Yeovil, 7.65 Templecombe,

80040 P6.52 Bletchley, P6.57 Chester (LMS), 12.59 Ashford, 6.61 Tonbridge, 6.62 Exmouth Jct.,

80041 P7.52 Bletchley, 12.59 Ashford, 6.61 Tonbridge, 6.62 Exmouth Jct., 6.65 Templecombe,

80042 P7.52 Bletchley, 12.59 Ashford, 6.61 Tonbridge Jct., 6.62 Exmouth Jct.

80043 P7.52 Bletchley, 12.59 Dover, 2.60 Ashford, 6.61 Tonbridge, 6.62 Exmouth Jct., 9.64 Templecombe,

80044 P8.52 Derby, 12.52 Bedford, 1.55 Bury, 2.56 Newton Heath, 3.60 Corkerhill, Withdrawn P6.64 Re-instated 7.64 Bangor,

80045 P9.52 Bedford, P1.55 Kentish Town, 9.56 Chester (LMS), 5.60 Corkerhill, 3.65 Beattock, 11.65 Polmadie.

80046 P9.52 Bedford, P1.55 Bury, P2.56 Newton

Heath, 10.57 Blackpool, 2.60 Corkerhill,

80047 P10.52 Bedford, P1.53 Kentish Town, 9.56 Chester (LMS), 3.60 Corkerhill,

80048 P10.52 Kentish Town, 9.56 Chester (LMS), 4.60 Corkerhill, Withdrawn 6/64 Re-instated P7.64 Bangor, P9.64 Shrewsbury,

80049 P10.52 Blackpool, P11.52 Newton Heath, P9.56 Chester (LMS), 5.60 Corkerhill,

80050 P11.52 Newton Heath, P9.56 Chester (LMS), 4.60 Corkerhill, Withdrawn 6.64 Re-instated 7.64 Bangor,

80051 P11.52 Newton Heath, P9.56 Chester (LMS), 5.60 Corkerhill,

80052 P12.52 Newton Heath, 4.54 Blackpool, 5.54 Newton Heath, P9.56 Chester (LMS), 3.60 Corkerhill,

80053 P12.52 Newton Heath, P9.56 Chester (LMS), 5.60 Corkerhill,

80054 P12.54 Polmadie, 8.62 St. Margarets, 11.65 Greenock (Ladyburn),

80055 P12.54 Polmadie, 8.62 St. Margarets

80056 P12.54 Polmadie, 12.62 Eastfield, Withdrawn 6.64 Re-instated P8.64 Lostock Hall,

80057 P12.54 Polmadie, 12.62 Eastfield, 2.65 Polmadie

80058 P1.55 Polmadie,

80059 P3.53 Kentish Town, P9.56 Chester (LMS), P5.58 Bangor, P10.58 Neasden, 12.59 Dover, 2.60 Ashford, 6.61 Tonbridge, 6.62 Exmouth Jct., 9.64 Templecombe, 6.65 Bristol (Barrow Road), 7.65 Bath (Green Park),

80060 P3.53 Bedford, P1.55 Bury, P2.56 Newton Heath, 2.60 Stirling, 7.64 St. Margarets, 8.64 Greenock (Ladyburn), P12.65 Polmadie,

80061 P4.53 Bedford, P1.55 Bury, P2.56 Newton Heath, 3.60 Stirling, 8.64 Dumfries, 7.65 Polmadie,

80062 P4.53 Kentish Town, 9.56 Chester (LMS), P2.58 Birkenhead, 3.60 Stirling, 7.64 Greenock (Ladyburn), 8.64 Stirling,

80063 P5.53 Saltley, P10.54 Kentish Town, P9.56 Chester (LMS), P2.57 Birkenhead, 3.60 Stirling, 7.64 Corkerhill,

80064 P6.53 Watford, 12.59 Dover, 2.60 Ashford, 6.61 Tonbridge, 6.62 Exmouth Jct., 6.65 Bristol (Barrow Road),

80065 P6.53 Watford, 12.59 Dover, 2.60 Ashford, 6.61 Tonbridge, 6.62 Eastleigh,

80066 P7.53 Watford, 12.59 Stewarts Lane, 2.60 Ashford, 6.61 Tonbridge, 6.62 Eastleigh,

80067 P8.53 Watford, 12.59 Stewarts Lane, 5.62 Exmouth Jct., 9.64 Templecombe, 6.65 Bristol (Barrow Road),

80068 P8.53 Watford, 12.59 Stewarts Lane, 9.63 Brighton, 1.64 Redhill, 6.65 Feltham, (stored),

80069 9.53 Plaistow, 1.54 Tilbury, 7.62 Swansea (East Dock), 3.64 Llanelly, 8.64 Nine Elms,

80070 10.53 Plaistow, 1.54 Tilbury, 7.62 Old Oak Common, 11.62 Shrewsbury, 2.63 Croes Newydd, 3.63 Shrewsbury, 4.65 Eastleigh,

80071 10.53 Plaistow, 1.54 Tilbury, 7.62 Stratford, 9.62 March, 12.62 Ardsley, 10.63 Carstairs,

80072 11.53 Plaistow, 1.54 Tilbury, 7.62 Swansea (East Dock), 9.63 Leamington, P6.65 Shrewsbury,

80073 11.53 Plaistow, 1.54 Tilbury, 7.62 Stratford, 9.62 March, 12.62 Ardsley, 10.63 Carstairs,

80074 11.53 Plaistow, 11.56 Tilbury, 7.62 Stratford, 9.62 March, 12.62 Ardsley, 10.63 Carstairs,

80075 12.53 Plaistow, 11.56 Tilbury, 7.62 Stratford, 9.62 March, 12.62 Ardsley, 11.63 Carstairs,

80076 12.53 Plaistow, 11.56 Tilbury, 7.62 Stratford, 9.62 March, 12.62 Ardsley, 10.63 Dumfries,

80077 1.54 Plaistow, 11.56 Tilbury, 7.62 Stratford, 9.62 March, 12.62 Ardsley, 10.63 Ardrossan, 7.64 Corkerhill,

80078 2.54 Plaistow, 11.56 Tilbury, 6.62 Stratford, 7.62 Shrewsbury, 2.63 Croes Newydd,

80079 3.54 Plaistow, 3.54 Tilbury, 6.62 Stratford, 7.62 Croes Newydd,

80080 3.54 Plaistow, 5.54 Tilbury, 7.62 Croes Newydd,

80081 P3.54 Bletchley, P11.59 Willesden, 12.59 Stewarts Lane, 7.63 Weymouth, 7.63 Bournemouth,

80082 P4.54 Bletchley, 12.59 Bricklayers Arms, 6.62 Eastleigh,

80083 P5.54 Bletchley, P1.55 Rugby, P2.55 Bletchley, P10.58 Neasden, 12.59 Bricklayers Arms, 6.62 Eastleigh,

80084 P5.54 Bletchley, P11.59 Willesden, 12.59 Bricklayers Arms, 6.62 Stewarts Lane, 9.63 Brighton, 1.64 Redhill,

80085 P5.54 Bletchley, 1.55 Rugby, P2.55 Bletchley, 12.59 Bricklayers Arms, 2.61 Ashford, 6.61 Tonbridge, 6.62 Stewarts Lane, 9.63 Brighton, 1.64 Redhill, 1.65 Redhill (stored), 6.65 Feltham, 10.66 Nine Elms,

80086 P6.54 Bury, P6.56 Newton Heath, P9.56 Chester, (LMS), P2.57 Birkenhead, P2.58 Chester (LMS), 5.60 Dalry Road, 10.60 Carstairs, 11.60 Polmadie,

80087 P6.54 Bury, P9.56 Bangor, 12.59 Three Bridges, 2.60 Ashford, 5.61 Three Bridges, 12.62 Eastleigh, 3.63 Guildford, 9.63 Eastleigh,

80088 P7.54 Bury, P9.56 Bangor, 12.59 Three Bridges, 1.63 Tunbridge Wells West, 9.63 Brighton, 1.64 Redhill,

80089 P8.54 Bury, P8.56 Bangor, 12.59 Three Bridges, 1.63 Stewarts Lane, 9.63 Brighton, 1.64 Redhill, 6.65 Feltham (stored), 11.65 Nine Elms,

80090 P8.54 Bury, P9.56 Bangor, P12.58 Birkenhead, 2.60 Dundee,

80091 P9.54 Kentish Town, P9.56 Bangor, P10.57 Chester (LMS), 5.60 Dundee, 9.60 St. Rollox, 5.62 Hurlford, 4.66 Beattock,

80092 P9.54 Kentish Town, P9.56 Bangor, P12.56 Willesden, P1.57 Bangor, P10.57 Chester (LMS), 3.60 Perth,

80093 P10.54 Bedford, P1.55 Bury, P2.56 Newton Heath, P10.57 Blackpool, 3.60 Perth,

80094 P10.54 Kentish Town, P9.56 Bangor, P10.59 Birkenhead, 12.59 Three Bridges, 1.63 Stewarts Lane, 9.63 Brighton, 1.64 Redhill, 1.65 Redhill (stored), 6.65 Feltham,

80095 P11.54 St. Albans, P9.56 Bangor, P10.59 Birkenhead, 12.59 Tunbridge Wells West, 12.62 Eastleigh, 3.63 Guildford, 9.63 Feltham, 11.64 Nine Elms

80096 P11.54 Plaistow, P10.59 Tilbury, 7.62 Shrewsbury, 11.62 Croes Newydd, 3.63 Machynlleth, 9.63 Croes Newydd, 4.65 Bournemouth,

80097 12.54 Plaistow, P10.59 Tilbury, 6.62 Stratford, 7.62 Swansea (East Dock), 7.63 Oswestry, 6.64 Machynlleth,

80098 12.54 Plaistow, 10.59 Tilbury, 07.62 Old Oak Common, P9.62 Shrewsbury, 11.62 Croes Newydd, 3.63 Machynlleth,

80099 1.55 Plaistow, 10.59 Tilbury, 6.62 Stratford, 7.62 Swansea (East Dock), 7.63 Machynlleth,

80100 1.55 Plaistow, 10.59 Tilbury, 6.62 Stratford, 7.62 Shrewsbury,

80101 2.55 Plaistow, 10.59 Tilbury, 6.62 Stratford, 7.62 Shrewsbury, P9.62 Machynlleth, 2.63 Croes Newydd, 3.63 Machynlleth,

80102 3.55 Plaistow, 10.59 Tilbury, 7.62 Old Oak Common, 11.62 Shrewsbury, P6.64 Bangor, 9.64 Shrewsbury, 4.65 Eastleigh,

80103 3.55 Plaistow, 10.59 Tilbury,

80104 3.55 Plaistow, 10.59 Tilbury, 7.62 Old Oak Common, 11.62 Croes Newydd, 3.63 Machynlleth,

80105 4.55 Plaistow, 11.59 Tilbury, 7.62 Machynlleth, P9.62 Shrewsbury, P10.62 Machynlleth, 2.63 Croes Newydd, 3.63 Machynlleth,

80106 10.54 Kittybrewster, 5.57 Polmadie,

80107 10.54 Kittybrewster, 5.57 Polmadie,

80108 11.54 Kittybrewster, 5.57 Polmadie,

80109 11.54 Kittybrewster, 5.57 Polmadie, 3.59 Hamilton, 9.59 Polmadie,

80110 11.54 Kittybrewster, 6.57 Polmadie, 9.63 Carstairs, 5.64 Polmadie,

80111 11.54 Polmadie, 5.57 Kittybrewster, 6.61 Corkerhill, 6.61 Hurlford, 4.66 Beattock,

80112 12.54 Polmadie, 5.57 Kittybrewster, 6.61 Corkerhill, 6.61 Hurlford, 6.64 Corkerhill,

80113 P12.54 Polmadie, 6.57 Kittybrewster, 5.60 Keith, 6.61 Hawick, 1.66 St. Margarets,

80114 P12.54 Polmadie, 5.57 Kittybrewster, 9.60 Keith, 6.61 Hawick, 3.62 St. Margarets,

80115 P12.54 Polmadie, 5.57 Kittybrewster, 9.60 Keith, 6.61 Ferryhill, 8.61 Polmadie, 12.63 Ardrossan, 7.64 Polmadie,

80116 5.55 York, 5.55 Whitby, 2.56 Scarborough, 5.56 Whitby, 6.58 Neville Hill, 6.63 Holbeck, 10.63 Dumfries, 11.63 Carstairs, 4.64 Polmadie.

80117 5.55 Whitby, 6.58 Neville Hill, 10.63 Dumfries, 11.65 Beattock, 11.65 Polmadie,

80118 6.55 Whitby, 6.58 Neville Hill, 10.63 Carstairs, 4.64 Polmadie,

80119 6.55 Whitby, 2.56 Scarborough, 5.56 Whitby, 6.58 Neville Hill, 10.63 Carstairs, 11.63 Dumfries,

80120 7.55 Whitby, 6.58 Neville Hill, 10.63 Carstairs, 5.64 Polmadie,

80121 7.55 Kittybrewster, 11.55 Keith, 6.61 Ferryhill, 7.61 Polmadie,

80122 8.55 Kittybrewster, 11.55 Keith, 6.61 Dalry Road, 5.62 St. Margarets, 11.65 Greenock (Ladyburn),

80123 9.55 Dundee (Tay Bridge), 4.65 Polmadie,

80124 9.55 Dundee (Tay Bridge), P12.65 St. Margarets,

80125 10.55 Stirling, Withdrawn 6.64 Re-instated 8.64 Lostock Hall,

80126 10.55 Perth,

80127 11.55 Corkerhill,

80128 11.55 Corkerhill, 9.61 Hurlford, 1.62 Corkerhill,

80129 12.55 Polmadie, Withdrawn 6.64 Re-instated, 8.64 Lostock Hall,

80130 12.55 Polmadie,

80131 2.56 Kings Cross, 3.56 Plaistow, 10.59 Tilbury, 7.62 Old Oak Common, 8.62 Shrewsbury, 1.63 Oswestry, P1.65 Bangor,

80132 3.56 Plaistow, 10.59 Tilbury, 7.62 Old Oak Common, 11.62 Shrewsbury, 1.63 Oswestry, P1.65 Bangor, 4.65 Eastleigh,

80133 3.56 Plaistow, 10.59 Shoeburyness, 7.62 Swansea (East Dock), 3.63 Neath (Court Sart), 6.64 Llanelly, 8.64 Feltham, 11.64 Nine Elms,

80134 4.56 Plaistow, 10.59 Tilbury, 7.62 Swansea (East Dock), 3.64 Llanelly, 8.64 Feltham, 9.64 Bournemouth,

80135 4.56 Plaistow, 10.59 Tilbury, 7.62 Shrewsbury, 1.63 Oswestry, 9.64 Shrewsbury,

80136 5.56 Plaistow, 10.59 Tilbury, 7.62 Shrewsbury, 1.63 Oswestry, 6.64 Machynlleth, 9.64 Shrewsbury,

80137 5.56 Neasden, 12.59 Tunbridge Wells West, 12.62 Eastleigh, 3.63 Guildford, 9.63 Feltham, 11.64 Nine Elms,

80138 6.56 Neasden, 12.59 Tunbridge Wells West, 3.61 Brighton, 1.64 Redhill, 2.65 Bournemouth,

80139 6.56 Neasden, 12.59 Tunbridge Wells West, 9.63 Brighton, 1.64 Redhill, 2.65 Eastleigh

80140 7.56 Neasden, 12.59 Tunbridge Wells West, 9.63 Brighton, 1.64 Redhill, 6.65 Feltham (stored), 10.66 Nine Elms,

80141 7.56 Neasden, 12.59 Tunbridge Wells West, 9.63 Brighton, 1.64 Redhill, 6.65 Feltham (stored), 11.65 Nine Elms,

80142 8.56 Neasden, 12.59 Tunbridge Wells West, 9.63 Brighton, 1.64 Redhill, 6.65 Salisbury (stored), 2.66 Eastleigh,

80143 9.56 Neasden, 12.59 Brighton, 6.63 Feltham, 11.64 Nine Elms,

80144 9.56 Neasden, 12.59 Brighton, 1.64 Redhill, 6.65 Salisbury (stored), 11.65 Eastleigh, 2.66 Nine Elms,

80145 10.56 Brighton, 1.64 Redhill, 6.65 Salisbury (stored), 2.66 Nine Elms,

80146 10.56 Brighton, 9.63 Eastleigh, 1.64 Bournemouth,

80147 11.56 Brighton, 7.63 Weymouth, 7.63 Bournemouth,

80148 11.56 Brighton, 6.63 Feltham,

80149 12.56 Brighton, 1.64 Redhill,

80150 12.56 Brighton, 9.63 Eastleigh,

80151 1.57 Brighton, 1.64 Redhill, 6.65 Salisbury (stored), 10.66 Eastleigh,

80152 2.57 Brighton, 1.64 Redhill, 6.65 Salisbury (stored), 10.66 Eastleigh,

80153 2.57 Brighton, 1.64 Redhill,

80154 3.57 Brighton, 6.63 Feltham, 11.64 Nine Elms,

Fig. 69   80154 and one other member of the Class at Feltham Shed 20 August 1964.

Peter Groom

2.7 Service Performance

As discussed in other chapters, the Class 4 tanks were seen as capable performers but due to the nature of their work they rarely featured when it came to logs of the work undertaken.

One area where they performed regularly on high speed work alongside their LMS companions was on the Chester to Birkenhead service. A recorder was active towards the end of their service in 1965/66 noting the best times per class over the stretch of line from Hooton to Upton-by-Chester Halt (6.7 miles), the load being 5 or 6 coaches.

A Stanier Class 4 was timed at 7.52 minutes start to stop with a maximum speed of 75 mph. Remarkably, 82005, a Standard Class 3 tank put in a time of only 8.04 minutes, with a maximum of 74 mph, while 80094 came in third – 8.29 minutes and 67 mph, but still a creditable performance.

One log of a performance with 80030 did appear in the *Railway Magazine* in August 1952, when the locomotive was only six months old, and details are as follows.

"The venue (of these runs) was the Glasgow and South Western Ayr main line, and the day a Saturday, when a clear road down this route is not very easy to obtain; the down run was made on the 1.5pm from St. Enoch, stopping first at Troon, 35.1 miles, in 44 min. (all but equal to the Glasgow-Ayr 50 min. non-stop booking), and the return was on the 3.45pm from Girvan to Glasgow. The same non-corridor eight-coach set of 226 tons was used in both directions; gross load was 245 tons down and 240 tons back. The driver and fireman were A.Mann and J.MacLachlan respectively, of Corkerhill shed.

With these engines, the first valve of the regulator, fully open, gives a steam-chest pressure seldom less than 30 to 40 lb. below the boiler pressure; the boiler proved to be free steaming, as with all the Standard engines, and pressure was kept at 220 to 225 lb. without difficulty. In starting, Driver Mann used 55 per cent. cut-off, dropped to 35 by Cumberland Street and to 25 at the end of the first two miles, increased to 35 in recovering from Paisley slack, and then dropped back to 25 by Elderslie. Soon after Milliken Park, however, adverse signals resulted finally in a dead stand between Lochside and Beith.

It was from this stop that the speed capacity of the engine was demonstrated in remarkable fashion. Less than two miles after restarting, the driver had linked up to 25 per cent; for five miles the first valve was open far enough to give 180 lb. of steam in the valve-chest, then was eased to give 165 lb. only for $2\frac{1}{2}$ miles, and then further to give only 145 lb. for $3\frac{1}{2}$ miles. For $6\frac{1}{2}$ miles from the stop the line is virtually level; then comes a downgrade averaging 1 in 450. Yet, with such easy working as this, No. 80030 was doing 50 m.p.h. in less than two miles from the start (Beith), $59\frac{1}{2}$ at Brownhill Junction, $65\frac{1}{2}$ at Dalry, 74 at Kilwinning, and 76 at Byrehill Junction (a little less than 11 miles from the start), while the full first valve from here onwards produced no less than 81 m.p.h. at the foot of the 1 in 450, through Irvine.

Nemesis then followed, in two signal stops and a check which made the train $6\frac{3}{4}$ min. late into Troon. On the unobstructed lengths the engine had gained all but two min. from Glasgow out to Elderslie, and $1\frac{3}{4}$ min. more between Beith and Irvine; without checks it may be assumed that the tank could have reached Troon, 35.1 miles from Glasgow, in $38\frac{1}{4}$ min. net, nearly 6 min. inside booked time. Signal checks and numerous station stops robbed the rest of the run of much of its interest, though time was gained on every unchecked section, concluding with a start to stop time of 6 min. 54 sec. over the 5.2 miles, largely downhill, from Dailly to Girvan, with a maximum of $69\frac{1}{2}$ m.p.h. The total net gain to the engine was about 11 min. between Glasgow and Girvan.

The first step of the return journey from Girvan up to Dailly was the only one on which the engine showed any slight weakness and it was in climbing. The immediate start is $\frac{1}{2}$ mile downhill, including a short strip at 1 in 50 but this produced nothing better than $34\frac{1}{2}$ m.p.h., after which the 1 in 72 up past Killochan brought the rate down to a steady

24½, making the first 3.1 miles, to post 58¾, take 7 min. 46 sec. A top speed of 55 m.p.h. was reached in the subsequent dip, but even so, the 5.2 miles to Dailly took 11 min 4 sec., instead of the 9½min. allowed. However, allowance must be made for the fact that the engine was starting "cold".

Nevertheless, this was of little consequence, for 80030 all but picked up the lost time on the next sharply undulating stage, running the 7.1 miles to Maybole in 10 min. 36 sec. start to stop, against a schedule of 12 min. With 56 m.p.h. at Kilkerran, the 1½ miles mainly at 1 in 70 to post 51¾ were carried at a minimum of 44 m.p.h. The sharp drop out of Maybole produced a maximum of 74 m.p.h., and despite a slight signal check, the 9.0 miles to Ayr were run in 11 min. 12 sec. start to stop. As to the working of 80030 over this stretch, Driver Mann was using the main valve up Killochan bank, with steam chest pressure up to 195lb., and cut-off increasing from 35 to 40 per cent; from Dailly to Maybole, also, up to full regulator was employed on the uphill lengths, with maximum steam chest pressures of 200 and 205 lb., and cut-offs of 30 to 40 per cent., reduced to 20 with the first valve downhill.

From Ayr there are numerous stops with this train, and time was kept on all stages as far as Bogside, from which there is a non-stop run to Paisley. But the interest of the run was greatly enhanced by the train being diverted from Brownhill Junction on to the Lochwinnoch loop, which is a totally different proposition from the main line in its grading. Here the tank did some really magnificent work. A mile and a half after leaving Bogside, the driver linked up to 30 per cent., and a mile later to 25 per cent., with the first valve of the regulator giving 190lb. in the steam chest; this resulted in an acceleration to 56 m.p.h. up 4½ miles of the 1 in 450. The cross-over from fast to slow at Dalry No. 3 box is beautifully laid out, and can be taken at 50 m.p.h., which Mann did, then opening out to full regulator (200 to 210 lb. steam-chest pressure) with 25 per cent cut-off. An acceleration from 50 to 64 m.p.h. followed, in 2½ miles of level track, and the 1½ miles up at 1 in 100 past Kilbirnie was "rushed" at a minimum of 52½ m.p.h. 80030 then swept up to 77 m.p.h. on the descent to Lochwinnoch, but was brought down to 50 by signals at Kilbarchan; 61½ was reached at Cart Junction, after which came the usual Elderslie slack. Nevertheless, Paisley was reached on time despite the diversion; the 21.4 miles of the direct line from Bogside to Paisley are allowed 26 min., but the 22.3 miles of the loop had been run in 25 min. 53 sec., start to stop. Mr. Nelson comments on the perfect riding qualities of the 2-6-4 tank, and describes these as two of the smoothest footplate trips that he has ever enjoyed. Water consumption was moderate, 1,800 gal. on the outward journey and no more than 1,750 gal. on the return or 28.6 and 27.4 gal. per mile respectively".

SCOTTISH REGION: BOGSIDE- PAISLEY

Engine: Standard class "4" 2-6-4 tank 80030
Load: 8 coaches, 226 tons tare, 240 tons gross

Dist Miles		Sched min	Actual min. sec.	Speeds m.p.h.
0.0	BOGSIDE	0	0 00	—-
2.3	KILWINNING	4	4 15	45/56
5.2	Dalry No. 3	7	7 47	*50
5.8	Dalry	—	8 28	52½
7.6	Brownhill Jct.	—	10 17	64½
9.6	Kilbirnie	—	12 18	52½
13.1	Lochwinnoch	—	15 40	77
			sigs	51
17.3	Kilbarchan	—	19 27	54½
18.5	Johnstone North	—	20 46	59
19.3	Cart Jct.	—	21 34	61½
20.3	Elderslie	$22	22 24	*45
22.3	PAISLEY (Gill St.)	$26	25 53	—

* Speed restriction
$ Schedule is via Beith, 0.9 mile shorter

An article published in *Trains Illustrated* for August 1958 written by the well known NER expert and historian Ken Hoole perhaps typifies the everyday work of the class in the 1950's and early 1960's. It is reproduced here in full.

Footplate farewell to the Whitby-Loftus line
by K.Hoole

By the courtesy of the Motive Power Superintendent of the North Eastern Region I was able recently to travel on the footplate over one of the most difficult lines in the country, from Scarborough to Middlesbrough and back. Unfortunately a section of 15 miles in the middle of the route has now been closed and my journey actually took place on the last day that the whole line was open; in fact, ours was the last train over part of the now closed section. Never have I been photographed so many times as I was that fine Saturday evening!

My journey began at Scarborough, where in platform 1A I joined the 11.40am to Middlesbrough, consisting of Standard Class "4" 2-6-4 tank 80116 and five bogies. The normal load for this time of year is two bogies; the extra three were for the expected number wanting to make a last journey over the line, and they were certainly needed. Because the load was five coaches the engine was not allowed to propel the train out of any of the main platforms, as is usual, but only from platform 1A, whence propelling movements are permitted with five coaches. This involves quite a walk from the other platforms and it is usual to allow three minutes' grace to passengers, so that our departure was put back to 11.43am. Actually we left at 11.44, and after we had propelled our train over the points leading to the Whitby line they were changed and the signal pulled off so rapidly that we were at rest for only 15 seconds. A transient track circuit now controls the single line through Falsgrave Tunnel and as far as Gallows Close signalbox, where our first tablet was picked up; then speed increased rapidly until we were doing 40 m.p.h. past Northstead sidings and a maximum of 43 m.p.h. was reached before the brakes were applied for the 30 m.p.h. restriction round the curves through closed Scalby station.

From Scalby to Cloughton the line is a switchback with gradients (among others) of 1 in 60 up, 1 in 74 down and 1 in 55 up. Cloughton station stands on what appears to be the longest level stretch of line on the whole route (¾ mile), but after that climbing starts in earnest, commencing at 1 in 90 and gradually stiffening through 1 in 78, 71 and 54 to a final 1 in 41, which starts at the north end of Stainton Dale station. With the regulator approximately three-quarters open and a cut-off of 40 per cent we climbed steadily at 17-18 m.p.h., accelerating slightly to 20 m.p.h. just before the summit. After a 45 second halt at Ravenscar the regulator was opened just long enough to start us off from the platform and on to the long 1 in 39 descent to Fyling Hall; we were then allowed to coast down with the speed frequently checked by the brakes. Although the gradient is alleged to be constant at 1 in 39 it varies and the section below the disused brick-works is steeper than the upper part of the bank; this was particularly noticeable on the return journey. At Fyling Hall the porter dealt with a couple of passengers and then locked up and joined the train himself, for this was the last day on which the small station was to be manned; it is now an unstaffed halt.

After the Robin Hoods Bay stop came the second stiff climb, this time for 1½ miles at 1 in 43 up to the cliffs, from where we could look across the bay to Ravenscar and trace the course of the line we had descended some 15 minutes ago. We climbed at 19-20 m.p.h. on three-quarter regulator and 30-35 per cent cut-off, and here the boiler pressure dropped to 180 lb; normally it was kept nicely under blowing off point at 215 lb. Once over the top the line descends at gradients varying between 1 in 50 and 1 in 39 over the Esk Viaduct until Prospect Hill Junction is reached, whereupon it starts to climb again at 1 in 60 to Whitby West Cliff. At West Cliff Driver Pearson and Fireman Ingram were relieved by two more Whitby men, Driver T.A.Sutherland and Fireman P. Appleton; Driver Pearson and his mate had previously worked 80116 from Whitby to Scarborough on the 8.57am train. The relieving crew had a long day in front of them as they were due to work a Whitby West Cliff-Middlesbrough-Whitby West Cliff-Whitby Town-Whitby West Cliff-Scarborough-Whitby West Cliff-Whitby Town itinerary before returning to shed.

We took water at West Cliff and on leaving kept steam on long enough to get us up the short 1 in 60 stretch immediately off the platform end; it was then shut off for the long 1 in 60 descent almost to the seashore south of Sandsend, whence there is a 1 in 62 climb into Sandsend station, for the last few hundred yards of which steam was put on again. From Sandsend the line again runs on the cliff edge before it reaches the 1,657 yds.-long Sandsend Tunnel, climbing all the time at 1 in 57. This tunnel can prove most difficult, particularly in bad weather, but on this fine sunny day 80116 had no difficulty at all and we charged through at 24 m.p.h. to emerge on the cliffs for about ¼ mile until we went underground again in the 308 yds.-long Kettleness Tunnel, through which the line rises at 1 in 62.

Immediately north of Kettleness Tunnel I noticed a shallow cutting leading to the original site of the line round the cliffs. Before the line was completed the company building it – the Whitby, Redcar and Middlesbrough Union Railway – ran into financial difficulties and work was suspended for some years before they reached agreement with the North Eastern Railway for the latter to complete the line. When the NER took over they found that a large part of the original line had fallen into the sea and decided to construct two tunnels so that the line could be diverted to a more suitable and safer route.

After Kettleness, with its fine example of NER Central Division semaphore signal, we had a little more climbing to do but steam was soon shut off for the 1 in 73 descent to Hinderwell, on which we reached our highest speed so far - 48 m.p.h. From Hinderwell the line dropped again, this time at 1 in 63, to Staithes but here speed was not allowed to mount so high and so we came to a halt at the platform.

Numerous enthusiasts jumped out of the train and hurried down the station approach road to take a photograph of us crossing the well-known Staithes Viaduct, with its unique wind gauge. Now that the line is closed perhaps it can be revealed that the gauge was most unreliable and that the bell, alleged to sound only when it was unsafe for a train to cross, could be heard ringing on the calmest days. The story is told of a driver bringing a train southwards in one of the worst winter gales who rang up from Loftus to ask if the bell was ringing. When told it wasn't, he commented "It.... well should be. Keep everything clear as I'm not going to waste any time on that bridge". Sure enough, he crossed the bridge at such a rate that he was unable to stop in the station and had to set back.

Once over the viaduct we were climbing again, this time for 2½ miles at 1 in 61, with the 993 yds.-long Grinkle Tunnel on an easier 1 in 326 section at the summit. Immediately beyond the tunnel we passed the remains of the closed Grinkle station (originally Easington), and set off down a 1 in 49 stretch extending to Loftus and the end of the now closed section. Here we crossed Class L1 2-6-4 tank No. 67754 on the 12.27pm Middlesbrough-Scarborough, and I noticed that the engine had been specially cleaned for the occasion.

On the other side of Loftus is the Kilton Embankment, formerly the Kilton Viaduct, which was buried in 1911 to safeguard against iron-stone mining subsidences; part of the viaduct can still be seen at the north end of the embankment. At the south end of it is the single platform of the now derelict Skinningrove station, at which some trains made unadvertised stops to pick up workmen from the nearby steel works. Below Skinningrove station one can descry two levels of the zig-zag by means of which trains reached the bottom of the valley to serve ironstone mines and the gasworks. For some time the ironstone has been carried up the hillside by an aerial ropeway and the only traffic has been to and from the gasworks; the driver told me that even this had ceased a few days previously and that the coal was to be taken by road from Loftus station, so presumably the zig-zag track will now be taken up.

Beyond Skinningrove the line enters an area known as Carlin How, with the site of the old NER locomotive shed on the left-hand side and the steelworks' sidings on the right: the signal box at Crag Hall controls the entrance to the sidings and it also marks the end of the single line sections which extends from Scarborough, so that here we gave up the tablet for the last time. After a very slow run over the points splitting the single line into double track we set off up the 1 in 64 leading to Hunt Cliff, where once again the line runs high above the sea. Between Crag Hall and Brotton it takes a very roundabout route, chosen purposely to enable it to serve ironstone mines on Warsett Hill, now all closed and derelict; on this section we passed Class 3 2-6-0 77012 returning to Whitby shed after overhaul. After Brotton signs of derelict ironstone mines and the sidings and signalboxes that once served them become more prevalent, and approaching Guisborough it is possible to discern traces of the old Cleveland Railway that was built 100 years ago to foster the ironstone mining.

Guisborough station is, of course, a terminus at the end of a spur and consequently we had to reverse into the station from Guisborough signalbox. From here to Middlesbrough there was nothing of note and we should have arrived a few

Fig. 70   80116 on the coast near Kettleness on a day unknown with a local train from Whitby to Middlesbrough.   *K. Hoole*

Fig. 71   80116 with the 11.40 Scarborough to Middlesbrough train leaving Hinderwell 3 May 1958.   *S.C. Nash*

minutes early had we not been held by signals for four minutes at North Ormesby box, so that we eventually pulled into Middlesbrough station at 2.27pm. two minutes late.

When the passengers had all disembarked 80116 pushed back the set, uncoupled, drew ahead, ran round the coaches and proceeded to the shed, where it was found that the hopper ashpan doors were jammed and the concerted efforts of the driver, fireman and myself failed to free them. The ashpan appeared to be full and it had to be emptied somehow before we set off again, so the fireman prepared to throw out the ashes and clinker using the long shovel. However, the driver went under the engine and discovered that a piece of metal was jamming the front door of the ashpan: whilst he held the metal clear with a bar I operated the lever and we managed to bypass the obstruction and get the doors open. This had taken the best part of twenty minutes, but then the rocking grate decided to jam, necessitating another ten minutes work on the part of the driver and fireman to clear it. After this the engine had to be turned and refuelled, and it was a bare ten minutes before departure time that we finally backed down on to the train.

From the first stop at Ormesby we tackled the $1^{1}/_{2}$ miles of 1 in 44 to Nunthorpe at 19 m.p.h. with fully open regulator and approximately 35 per cent cut-off. In this direction we stopped at Skinningrove station to pick up four workmen, before the excitement of the day began at Loftus, where we were welcomed by a large crowd who had come to see the last train to Whitby. A headboard was affixed to the front of the engine and we became "The Economist" as far as Whitby Town.

From Loftus we went up the 1 in 49 to the summit near Grinkle with regulator fully open again, approximately 35 per cent cut-off, 215lb. "on the clock" and speed steady at 17 m.p.h. On the 1 in 61 down to Staithes, speed was restrained because of the permanent 15 m.p.h. restriction round the curves at Grinkle Park.

At Staithes we were met by another crowd and at Kettleness we passed the last northbound train, the 4.27pm from Scarborough with L1 67754. Many of the passengers from 67754's train were on the platforms to see the last two trains pass and a number of them joined our train for the run to Whitby. Many photographs were taken, including some by a press photographer who held us up for a few minutes; in the end the driver tired of waiting and after warning the photographer he set off, leaving the man to get aboard whilst we were moving slowly away. The same thing happened at Sandsend. This time our press friend refused to get into the first coach, where a door was held open by the station-master, but insisted on trying to board the rear of the train, with the result that he was left behind.

Detonators heralded our arrival at West Cliff, where we arrived 4 min. late and left $3^{1}/_{2}$ min. in arrears, after taking water. In this direction we were booked to run down to Whitby Town and if we had had on only the usual two coaches we should have been allowed afterwards to propel them back up to Prospect Hill, there to reverse and set course once more for Scarborough; as we had five on, we had to be assisted up to West Cliff by Class A8 4-6-2 tank 69861, which led the way back to West Cliff and there uncoupled.

The climb to Hawsker at 1 in 58,43, 39, 50, 45 and finally 1 in 46 necessitated full regulator again and about 40 per cent cut-off (boiler pressure was 210 lb.) and No. 80116 slogged

away with the speed falling to a minimum of 14 m.p.h. Soon from the cliff-top we could see our last hurdle across the bay - the long and gruelling 1 in 39 to Ravenscar. After Robin Hoods Bay and Fyling Hall the regulator was fully opened for the last time, with 35 per cent cut-off, and No. 80116 pegged away with speed gradually falling to a mere 13 m.p.h. half-way up. Each beat of the exhaust sounded like a shot from a gun as it echoed around the hills and quarries and it was easy to tell where the gradient eased off near the brickworks; with the controls untouched No. 80116 accelerated here to 22 m.p.h. and the change in the exhaust rhythm was most noticeable.

From Ravenscar to Scarborough there are ten miles of almost continual downhill and for once the fireman was able to take things a little more easily. We stopped at Stainton Dale, Hayburn Wyke and Cloughton, and handed over the last tablet at Gallows Close before running through Falsgrave Tunnel and coming to a stand opposite Londesborough Road excursion station just after 7.28pm. After a 15 second stop, the train was propelled gently back into Platform 1A.

In readiness for working back to Whitby at 8.15pm, the centre three coaches had to be taken out of the five-coach train which, incidentally, weighed 143 tons tare, and as there was no pilot available No. 80116 had to do this. Then she had to be turned, coaled and watered at the shed, but this was accomplished smartly and she left for home promptly at 8.15.

2.8 Modifications as a result of Service Experience

By 1951, the Fairburn tanks had become well established on the London Midland, Scottish and Southern Regions, therefore it was inevitable that crews should compare these well-liked engines with the British Railways derivative. The Standards were considered equally reliable and capable in addition to being found easier for daily preparation, service and disposal. In many ways they proved to be more akin to the Fowler 2-6-4 tanks than the Fairburns, their acceleration and work on the banks being excellent whereas at speed there was less evidence of the Fairburn's free-running. As a result the Standards were usually preferred where duties involved frequent stops or awkwardly sited gradients while the Fairburns gained precedence when stops were limited and periods of fast running were demanded.

At speed, the riding of large passenger tanks is usually inferior to that of equivalent tender engines, although in this respect the Fairburn design proved superior to the Fowler, Stanier and Thompson 2-6-4 tanks. This also remained true for the Standard locomotives, but there were complaints of "fore and aft" vibration when the class was accelerating away from stops and when working hard climbing banks at relatively low speeds. This vibration was most apparent to passengers travelling in the leading coach, but it was also noticeable in the second and third coaches, particularly of trains composed entirely of ex-LMS stock. This vibration also applied to other BR classes, including the Britannia pacifics, and when investigated was found to result from the drawbar spring magnifying the shaking motion left when balancing two-cylinder engines for hammer blow. This vibration can be effectively smothered by establishing the correct relationship between the unbalanced reciprocating weight and that of the engine, with one important proviso, this is that no artificial amplifier present along the couplings of the train which can collect the smothered impulses, and by generating a resonant effect, magnify them and reintroduce the vibration. Just such an amplifier was present in the drawbar spring of all BR classes and when this was modified the phenomenon disappeared.

On the Southern Region there were complaints of the water consumption being considerably heavier than that of the Fairburn 2-6-4 tanks. The crews at Brighton and Tunbridge Wells West sheds proved so adamant that inspectors were instructed to ride the footplate of 80010-9/31/2/3 and investigate the complaints, but to no avail, for the dipping of tanks at stops en route suggested that the water consumption for similar duties was approximately equal to that of the Fairburns. A variation in the tank capacities of the two 2-6-4 tank classes was then suspected, but after draining the water from the tanks of 80019 and 42103, 80019 was found to carry 1,994 gallons and the Fairburn 2,028 gallons, a difference of only thirty-four gallons and insufficient to be noticeable in normal service. With no practical solution being discovered, the problem was passed to the Brighton Drawing Office where by calculation it was found that the actual water available in the tanks to feed the Standard boiler was only 1,803 gallons, a loss of 191 gallons, whereas the Fairburn boiler had the use of 1,998 gallons (a difference of 10 per cent), so the crews were correct, although not for the right reason. In later years this wasted gallonage led to the Standards being replaced on the Bedford-St. Pancras and the Victoria-Uckfield-Brighton services by similarly powered Class 4 75XXX 4-6-0 tender engines, which had a greater water capacity.

Many modifications were made to engines during their lifetime, mostly of a minor nature. Some were well documented, others being very vague in their description. Similar modifications were given different reference numbers depending on the Works involved.

It should be noted that because a locomotive does not appear in the list it cannot be assumed that it was not modified; several cases were found of modifications being listed on a history card but not on a record card for instance. Very few locomotives have both cards still in existence and for some engines no documents have been traced.

The modification affecting most engines was the fitting of Hudd ATC, later called AWS. Modification numbers quoted were WSC 850, CSO 584, CSO 792 and RWE 6960.

Modification Dates:-

11.53	80069/70	8.57	80010
12.53	80072-5	9.59	80125
1.54	80076/7	4.60	80059
2.54	80078	5.60	80129
3.54	80079	6.60	80012/52, 80139
4.54	80080	7.60	80021/37
12.54	80096/7	10.60	80030/49
1.55	80098	12.60	80056
2.55	80099, 80100	2.61	80032
3.55	80101/2	4.61	80053
4.55	80103	10.61	80044
5.55	80104/5	11.61	80127
3.56	80131/2	12.61	80048, 80107
4.56	80133	1.62	80050, 80115/8
5.56	80134	2.62	80017/62
6.56	80136	3.62	80116/9

The original Hudd type did not require a battery to operate it but the later BR version did and to accommodate this a modification to the water space below the coal bunker was required. It is probable that many of the earlier conversions were not modified for the BR system, for example 80104.

Undated modifications were made to the following engines:-
80002/3/7/11/3-6/8/9/24/8/31/3-6/8-43/5/6/54/5/7/8/60/1/3-8/81-5/7 88-91/5, 80102/9/13/22/3/6/8/30/7/40-54

It was recorded that AWS was removed from 80079 1.57, and it was removed from 80133/4 by 3.65 and 10.66 respectively.

Speedometers were fitted as follows:-
From new	80059-80154
8.57	80010
7.60	80037
4.64	80012
Undated	80011/3-6/8/9/31-4/9/41/7/54/7/8

Speedometer removed
Undated	80107

Modification of Piston for Continuous Blowdown Valve
Modification Reference E3329. Cost of modification £1-00
5.57	80039
6.57	80044/8/9/50/2/3/62
7.57	80034
8.57	80089
9.57	80037/91
10.57	80041
11.57	80038/92/4

Removal of Downs Sanding Gear
Modification References E4341 E4343 E5777. Job Reference 5777 (see memorandum in Appendix B).
Costs £30.13s.4d (£30.66) to £38.4s.9d (£38.24)
3.57	80040	2.58	80051
5.57	80039	3.58	80053
9.57	80034	5.58	80047/50
10.57	80037/41	6.58	80036/52
11.57	80038	7.58	80048
12.57	80042	9.58	80044
1.58	80049	11.58	80043
		6.62	80008

Provision and Fitting of Non Return Valves on water pick-up pipes. Job reference R3701. Cost £20.13s.4d (£20.66)
10.54	80046/63	7.56	80065
12.54	80048	11.57	80038
1.55	80034/45	12.57	80042
4.55	80047	1.58	80049
5.55	80039/41	2.58	80051
7.55	80040	4.58	80035
10.55	80037	5.58	80050
2.56	80062	6.58	80052
3.56	80053	9.58	80044
5.56	80064	10.58	80061
6.56	80054/60	11.58	80043

Job References R4361, CSO 568, MEE 193 Cost £3.13s.0d
(£3.65)

1.55	80034	12.55	80055
4.55	80047	1.56	80030
5.55	80003/39/41	2.56	80062
6.55	80035	5.56	80064
8.55	80038/61	6.56	80060
9.55	80042	7.56	80065
10.55	80037	12.56	80067
11.55	80053		

Provision and Fitting of Atomiser Control.
Job References R7192 CSO 569 Cost £150.0s.0d (£150.00)

5.57	80039	3.58	80053
8.57	80045/6	5.58	80047
9.57	80034/7	6.58	80036/52
10.57	80041	9.58	80044
11.57	80038	11.58	80043
1.58	80049	2.62	80062
2.58	80051	6.62	80008

Steam operated Cylinder Cocks
Undated 80133/5/6

Provision of Cab Side Screens
Job Reference 5/4175
Cost £6.19.6d (£6.97) to £10.12s.6d (£10.62)

12.54	80048	8.55	80036
1.55	80034/45	9.55	80042
3.55	80037	12.55	80050/3
5.55	80038/47	Undated	80043
6.55	80035/40		

Fitting of Antiglare Screens.
Job Reference W11504, costs not known

10.56	80032	2.57	80012
11.56	80033	8.57	80010
1.57	80011	Undated	80016

Safety chain fitted in Self Cleaning Smokebox
Job Reference CME 329 Cost £1.10s.6d (£1.52)

9.58	80125	10.59	80129
10.58	80115	10.60	80030
11.58	80121/32	6.61	80106
1.59	80127	10.61	80044
4.59	80008	Undated	80131

Fitting of Cab Lifting Hooks - to SR engines following an accident whilst lifting the roof of 80031.
No costs or references known.

6.60	80012	7.60	80037

Undated 80011/7/33-6/68/81/7, 80138/42-7/9/51/3

Briquette tube feeder. No reference number or costs.

4.54	80073	4.60	80094
5.54	80069/70/2/5/8/9/80	2.61	80140
1.60	80089		

Undated80036/40/1/3/65/7/71/6/7/81/2/4/7/8/96-9
80100-5/31-4/6/9/43/7/8

It is possible that this was original equipment on some of these engines.

Removal of Water Pick-up Shute. No reference number or costs known.
By 6.56 80071★

6.56	80075-9/96/7/9, 80100-3/5 All ★		
9.56	80069/70/2, 80104	All ★	
10.58	80131★	5.60	80038/41/73★,80150★
1.60	80089	6.60	80074★
2.60	80080★	7.60	80037
3.60	80039/42/83	Undated	80043/59/64/6/8/82/7
4.60	80094		

All locomotives marked ★ were not listed as being fitted with scoops. It is possible that confusion exists between the removal of the scoop and the rest of the pick-up equipment with which all engines were fitted.

Removal of Smokebox Self Cleaning Apparatus. No reference numbers or costs known.

9.56	80072, 80104	8.58	80102/3
10.56	80078	10.58	80131
11.56	80073	6.59	80070, 80134
12.56	80069/71/5-7/9/80/96/7/8, 80101/5/36		
4.58	80100	7.59	80133
5.58	80099	Undated	80138

It is suggested that at least 80070/2, 80100/2/4/31/3 were refitted subsequently, possibly in 1962 or 1963.

Removal of Continuous Blowdown Valves. No reference numbers or costs known.

4.56	80076	10.57	80105
9.56	80077	11.57	80097
10.56	80078	3.58	80099
12.56	80074	4.58	80100
2.57	80071	Undated	80101/4

Costs not known for any of the following modifications.

Fitting of Internal Gauge Frame pipes. No reference numbers.
Undated 80035/8/41/3/7/9/50/1/3/60/1/3/81/4/92/4/5,
80137-41/3/4

G&C Graduable brake valve for engine and train also
G&C Ejector valve for train both fitted
Undated 80080 80133/5/6

Fitting of Storm Sheets. No reference numbers.

2.61	80032

Undated 80012/6/8/31/58/60/1,80110/6★/8★/20/33/5
★ Later removed.

Steam Brake Valve and Pipes modified
Undated 80011/6 80148/51

Piston Packing Modification. Reference HO8895

2.57	80018	1.59	80146
3.58	80032	Undated	80014/6

Fitting of Manual Blowdown Valve and Silencer.

3.60	80137	Undated	80043/65/82/4
5.61	80064		

Fitting of Snowplough
(and consequential turning of buffer beam vacuum pipes upwards).   Undated   80020,80109

Fitted and removed 80021/8, 80107/11/6 Undated

Provision for fitting was also made on 80097 but subsequently removed.

Modification to steam ejector Valve Handle –
Drawing SL/BR/1209

	80016	Undated
Steps welded to pony truck frame	80016	Undated
Injector outflow pipes modified	80016	Undated
Tool box drilled for drawhole TL/65/60	80017	Undated
New type ALFLOC Proportional Briquette Dispenser fitted Drawing W11403	80018	Undated
Manganese liners to bogie truck bearing	80020	Undated
Lamp bulb on reversing screw indicator	80030	1.56
Expansion link die block modification	80031	Undated
Fitting of tank steadying brackets	80043/81	Undated
Fitting of coal bunker access doors	80069	6.56
	80071/5	2.57
	80073	11.56
	80076	Undated
	80078	10.56
Modification to bottom bunker door fastening	80048	12.61
	80053	4.61
Fitting of cab gangway doors	80069	6.56
	80071/5	2.57
	80077	Undated
Two Southern Region fusible plugs	80082	Undated
Balljoint superheater 80097/8,80109/31/3/4/6		Undated
	80105	10.57
Cab weatherboard modification	80094	Undated

Injector modifications - all involved the removal of the left hand injector and addition of a second injector on the right hand side under the steps:-

8mm	80096	7 .57
	80105	10.57
	80097/8/9,80101/3/4/31/5/6	Undated
10mm	80100/2/9/17/9/32/3/4★	Undated
	★ see below	

Replacement of right hand injector as well with 8mm type (i.e. engines fitted with a pair of 8mm injectors on the right hand side)   80080, 80116/33/6 Undated

★80133 had 2 8mm injectors superseded by 2 10mm injectors.
★80136 had 2 8mm injectors superseded by 1 10mm and 1 8mm injector.

Also reported that under job 5674/14 the draw hook rubbers were changed on 80034-50 (no further details are known).

On transfer to the Western Region in 1962 the following locomotives were recorded as receiving Alfloc water treatment equipment 80069/70/2/8-80/96-8, 80100-2/4/5/31-6.

2.8.1 Experiments
In addition to the permanent modifications listed above a number of experiments were carried out, particularly on the earlier engines. The method of showing experiments is unclear. Experiment numbers were shown on the engine record cards, however several of these were subsequently crossed through. This could mean that it was intended to carry out an experiment but it was not actually done, or alternatively (and this is the preferred theory), those crossed through were subsequently terminated. Very few details can be attributed to any of these experiment numbers. Those marked ★ had the number crossed through.

Experiment Number	Date	Engines
1323	Undated	80095
M/D/L 1332	Undated	80060 (Concluded 7.57)
	10.5.56	80064
1384	Undated	80068
M/D/L 1389	Undated	80039
E1871	8.57	80045
2081	Undated	80010★/7 80147★
2216	Undated	80010-5/7/8
2243	Undated	80014★/5★
2244	Undated	80014★
2249	Undated	80014★
2253	Undated	80016★
2254	Undated	80010/9
2263	Undated	80012★/3★/4/5★/7★
2273	Undated	80012★/5/9
2276	Undated	80010★/5★
2286	Undated	80014/5★
2289	Undated	80154
2335	Undated	80031
2338	12.51	80016
	Undated	80031

Two further numbers were detailed as follows:-
ST/L/19 Valve and Valve Set in Stainless Steel
80097/8   11.57 - 4.59
80104   Undated
ST/L/20 Regulator Valve Modification
80097/8   11.57 - 9.59
80099   3.58 - 9.59
80100   4.58 - 9.59
80105   10.57 - 9.59
80014 appears to have had a series of modifications made, although details of most are not to hand.

Listed on the record card are:-
HO 8770 (Part done)
HO 7116 Mods 3 and 6
HO 6327 Mods 2, 4 and 6
HO 6192
HO 6306 Mods 2 and 3
Also noted are 'Aligning ball bearings for return cranks' and 'Metcalfe wheel flange lubricators fitted experiment HO 71' Finally the Regions had their own requirements for lamp brackets based on types used by the four pre-nationalisation main line companies.

80079 modified again in preservation with LMR pattern at the front end and SR on rear of coal bunker. 80059 is recorded as modified with additional lamp irons.

2.9 Running Costs and Maintenance

The original intention was to concentrate all intermediate and general repairs at Derby and Darlington, with the former accepting responsibility for engines working on the London Midland and Southern Regions while Darlington catered for those of the Scottish, Eastern and North Eastern Regions. As might be anticipated the Southern and Scottish Regions raised strong objections to this arbitrary decision for not only did they foresee the lengthy disappearance of engines despatched to works, but also difficulties occurring if major faults developed after their return to traffic. Consequently, following further consideration in March 1952, it was agreed that each Region should provide its own maintenance for the class. High mileages were worked between successive heavy repairs, therefore only 80000-2/4-6/8/9/11-29/31-4/7/9-41/5-7/51/9-61/3/85/6/8,80100/2/4 received a second general overhaul prior to withdrawal, according to history cards which are available.

Repainting did not automatically indicate a general repair for Eastleigh and Darlington frequently renewed the livery of high mileage engines at the intermediate stage. Officially 80154, the last built, survived on a series of intermediate repairs, although at an earlier period it is probable that the attention given by Eastleigh in April-June 1964 would have warranted a higher classification.

Its record card reads:-
New engine 26 March 1957

To Eastleigh Works	To Traffic	Mileage	Repair
16.6.59	4.7.59	122,841	Light Intermediate
12.8.60	20.8.60	174,314	Not-classified
16.11.61	16.12.61	238,053	Light Intermediate
10.4.63	19.4.63	283,025	Not-classified
10.6.63	14.6.63	286,664	Not-classified
20.4.64	13.6.64	309,674	Heavy Intermediate
2.4.67	Withdrawn	413,536	

In contrast No. 80019 received two general repairs:-

To Works	To Traffic	Mileage	Repair	Remarks
16.9.53	15.11.53	72,070	Casual	Brighton
9.3.54	26.3.54	88,120	Casual	Brighton
29.6.54	7.7.54	96,896	Casual	Brighton
19.1.55	10.2.55	124,905	Light Intermediate	Derby
3.10.55	14.10.55	153,240	Casual	Brighton
26.4.56	11.3.56	171,773	Casual	Brighton
5.7.56	18.8.56	176,998	General	Eastleigh
28.8.58	20.9.58	272,277	Light Intermediate	Eastleigh
27.11.59	12.12.59	293,048	Casual	Ashford
4.12.61	6.1.62	364,104	Light Intermediate	Eastleigh
23.1.64	7.3.64	420,977	General	Eastleigh
19.3.67	Withdrawn	514,045		

The Southern Region ceased entering mileages on their engine cards in April 1964 but most running sheds still recorded the weekly mileages of their engines and it is from these figures, and the works proposal sheets, that the 1964-7 totals have been compiled.

The average cost of repairs varied considerably between the various works, details for 1958-9 being:-

Works	Intermediate Repair	General Repair	Days in Works for General Repair
Cowlairs	£1,504	£2,894	18.3
Darlington	£2,017	£2,643	28.1
Derby	£1,786	£3,377	33.9
Eastleigh	£1,584	£2,963	23.3

At Cowlairs, Derby and Eastleigh boilers were left in the frames at intermediate repair whereas Darlington followed Eastern/North Eastern Region practice by lifting boilers at all classified repairs on the principle that "little and often" was better practice than seeking very high mileages between general repairs. This increased the cost of intermediate repair, but, since much of this was recouped at the next visit to works, the overall cost per engine mile was similar for either system. Obviously, the soft Scottish water influenced Cowlairs' excellent performance, although this alone could not account for the rapid return of engines to traffic, suggesting that as far as works practice was concerned, little was to be learnt from the English establishments.

2.9.1 Eastern Region
Casual attention and adjustment to the Hudd ATC equipment was received at Bow, but all heavy repairs were the responsibility of Stratford where intermediate repairs were received by 80069-80/96-8, 80101/2/4/5 between February 1956 and October 1957; the average mileage being 147,854. However, after the New Works ceased maintaining steam stock in mid-1957, difficulties arose with the turntable in the Old Works and as a result the class was transferred to Darlington in November 1957, with the additional work there being compensated by the despatch of North Eastern Region 76xxx Class 4 2-6-0's to Stratford.

2.9.2 London Midland Region
All heavy repairs were undertaken by Derby until the last of the original allocation was transferred to the Scottish Region in exchange for Fairburn 2-6-4 tanks in February 1960. General repairs commenced with 80085 in January 1957 and ceased with 80092 in March 1960, the average mileage being 157,491.

When the class returned to the Region in January 1963, following the transfer of 80070/8-80/96/8,80100-2/4/5/31/2/5/6 from the Western Region, all were maintained by Crewe where 80102/35/6 received general repairs in February 1963, November 1962 and January 1963 respectively. At this period Crewe was also responsible for 80069/72/97/9, 80133/4 of the Western Region, although only two, 80133/4 in February and May 1963, required general repairs.

2.9.3 North Eastern Region
80116-20 were delivered to the North Eastern Region in mid-1955 and therefore were not scheduled for major works attention before maintenance responsibility was transferred from Stratford to Darlington in November 1957. The average mileage worked since new was 168,494. 80120, however, following a heavy intermediate overhaul at Darlington in April 1959, did not require further major attention until February 1964 after being transferred to the Scottish Region

Fig. 72   80033 temporarily seen as an 0-6-4T at Brighton 3 February 1958. SR (former LBSCR) 'E4' 0-6-2T 32565 is cautiously moving the crippled locomotive.   *Rodney Lissenden*

Fig. 73   80089 in Ex-Works condition at Eastleigh MPD 11 July 1962.   *Noel A. Machell*

and to the care of Cowlairs. 80119 was the last of the class dealt with at Darlington.

Of the Eastern Region series, Darlington gave general repairs to 80099, 80100/2-4/31/2 in 1958, 80069/70/2/5/6 in 1959, 80071/3/4/7-80/96/8, 80105 in 1960 and 80097, 80100/1 in 1961. Of the remainder 80137-44, as a result of boundary changes, were transferred to the London Midland Region in February 1958 and to the Southern Region in November 1959, with intermediate repairs being received at Derby between August 1958 and January 1959, and general repairs at Eastleigh in 1960-3. 80133-6 received intermediate overhauls at Darlington in 1959 and general repairs at Crewe in 1962-3 following their transfer to the Western and London Midland Regions.

2.9.4 Scottish Region
At first all major repairs were concentrated at St. Rollox, where 80000-2/4-9/20-9 received general repairs between September 1956 and December 1957, the average mileage being 190,432. Thereafter, commencing with 80003 in April 1958, the responsibility for intermediate and general repair was transferred to Cowlairs until major steam overhaul ceased with 80047/63 in April 1964. Occasionally, to avoid the lengthy return journey across the Region to Glasgow, engines working on the Great North of Scotland section were given light attention at Inverurie, 80115 was noted 20.5.61. 80020/8/9 were known to have received attention at all three Scottish Region works.

2.9.5 Southern Region
Most heavy attention was provided by Eastleigh, with 80019 in August 1956 being the first to receive a general repair and 80012 in May 1964 the last. In 1960-4 the average mileages to intermediate and general repairs were 109,138 and 201,461 respectively, with the 282,356 miles worked by 80146 from new in October 1956 to June 1963 being the highest general repair mileage recorded. In May 1957 80014 received a general repair at Brighton while intermediate attention was given by Derby to 80019/33 in January/February 1955 and by Ashford to 80148/52 in January 1959.

Casual repairs were shared by Eastleigh and Brighton Works until the latter closed in March 1958 while occasional visits were made to Ashford Works for casual repair, tank welding and weighing until the cessation of locomotive repairs in June 1962.

2.9.6 Western Region
There is no record of any member of the class being repaired at Swindon, Wolverhampton or Caerphilly, those working in the Region being maintained by Crewe if transferred from the North Eastern Region and by Eastleigh if received from the Southern Region.

2.9.7 Statistics
During the period 1953-9 the London Midland, Eastern, Scottish and Southern Regions collated the costs of operating and maintaining the class, the repair and yearly mileages and the percentage availability. This information was tabulated centrally for comparison between the Regions and with details of similar pre-nationalisation classes, the Fairburn and Thompson 2-6-4 tanks.

Table 1 Yearly Mileages

Region	London Midland	Eastern & N. Eastern	Scottish	Southern
80XXX Class				
1953	34,143	—	43,035	35,506
1954	29,937	43,857	38,151	37,571
1955	29,403	40,067	34,472	40,433
1956	28,573	35,302	37,239	39,947
1957	28,172	36,141	35,641	45,139
1958	28,977	33,742	32,329	44,443
1959	28,629	33,187	26,948	35,429
Average per engine 1953-9	29,691	37,049	35,402	39,781
Fairburn				
1953	32,404	40,109	34,324	33,124
1954	32,260	35,471	34,825	34,580
1955	31,219	32,920	33,465	32,758
1956	32,047	35,029	34,954	35,955
1957	29,468	33,611	35,030	35,215
1958	28,540	31,802	33,963	32,307
1959	27,983	29,860	31,218	-
Average per engine 1953-9	30,560	34,115	33,968	33,990

Table 2 Yearly Mileages and Percentage Availability 1953-9

Class	Mileage	Availability
80XXX	35,513	79%
Fairburn	33,159	77%
Stanier	31,218	72%
Fowler	32,244	76%
Thompson L1	29,541	68%
GWR 61XX	27,561	72%★
		(★Data for 1956 only)

Table 3 Repair Mileages 1956-9				
80XXX Class				
	To Intermediate Repair		To General Repair	
Region	Miles	Months	Miles	Months
London Midland	91,797	30	153,269	61
Eastern	85,506	33	159,274	50
Scottish	87,134	27	89,584	60
Southern	98,644	23	214,798	62
Average per engine	90,770	28	179,231	58
Fairburn Class				
	To Intermediate Repair		To General Repair	
Region	Miles	Months	Miles	Months
London Midland	79,599	26	154,497	56
Southern	69,783	24	188,505	62
Average per engine	74,691	25	161,501	59
Thompson L1 Class				
	To Intermediate Repair		To General Repair	
Region	Miles	Months	Miles	Months
Eastern	71,623	20	114,634	42
North Eastern	73,548	22	117,360	44
Average per engine	72,585	21	115,997	43

Table 4 Repair Costs 1955-7				
80XXX Class Region	Works	No of Engines	Pence per mile	New Pence per mile
London Midland	Derby	45	8.66	3.61
Scottish	St. Rollox	46	6.43	2.68
Southern	Eastleigh	23	6.14	2.56
Average per engine			7.25	3.02
Fairburn Class Region	Works	No of Engines	Pence per mile	New Pence per mile
London Midland	Derby	102	8.98	3.74
Scottish	St. Rollox	106	5.90	2.46
Southern	Eastleigh	34	7.51	3.13
Average per engine			7.42	3.09
Thompson L1 Class Region	Works	No of Engines	Pence per mile	New Pence per mile
Eastern & North Eastern	Darlington	100	9.65	4.02

All these tables reflect the wisdom of modifying and updating an excellent LMS design as the Standard Class 4 2-6-4 tanks proved superior on all counts to other contemporary large passenger tank classes. The L1's in particular were found greatly inferior, except in boiler maintenance where again the simple Doncaster construction and round top firebox gave exceptionally low running costs.

All steam classes have their failings, that of the Standard 2-6-4 tanks being the main steam pipes which demanded more frequent attention than desirable, although not affecting the availability and performance so severely as the hot boxes of the L1's or the Fairburn's small superheater tubes. In service the Standard engines proved a thoroughly good investment, the tragedy being that their conception came towards the end of British steam locomotion.

Due to the incomplete records it cannot be said with certainty which engines took the class mileage records. As noted previously in the early years average yearly mileages were around 30,000 but by 1964 a more common figure was in the 20,000 miles range. However, 80008, a Corkerhill engine for all of its twelve year life span was credited with running 66,157 miles in 1953. Several engines accumulated over half a million miles with 80011/32, both Southern Region engines for their entire life span of fifteen years, running at least 530,000 miles whilst 80115/29 appear to have amassed only about 230,000 miles in total.

2.10 Construction, Withdrawal and Disposal Information

The first of the class to be withdrawn (and also the first of the Standard classes to go) was 80103 from Tilbury on the LTS section, on 29th August 1962. No further inroads were made until 80040 succumbed on 6th May 1964. Other 1964 withdrawals were 80008-10/7/21/30/1/6/8/44/9/50/2/3/6/62/71/3-7/87, 80106/7/15/25/7/9/48, a total of 31 engines.

1965 and 1966 saw 44 and 54 withdrawals respectively, leaving only 25 out of 155 remaining on the books for 1967 of which 11 locomotives, 80011/5/6/85, 80133/4/9/40/3/6/52, were the last survivors all being taken out of service on 9th July with the end of Southern Region steam. It could be argued that 80002 was the last of the class to work for British Railways as following withdrawal in March 1967 from Polmadie, it was relegated to carriage heating duties at

Fig. 74   80143 bereft of smokebox numberplate and in a very rundown condition at Nine Elms MPD 11 March 1967. Seven months later it was sold for scrap.

Peter Groom

Eastfield and was still present on 11th September 1967. It is believed that it did not cease work until 1969.

In BR service the longest lived was 80011 being just short of its 16th birthday when withdrawn. 80103 had the shortest life at 7 years 5 months.

Under the 'Sold From' column where the location of sale has not been confirmed the final depot of allocation is shown, this being denoted by the use of brackets.

Year End Totals for the Class

1951	17	1957-61	155	1962	154
1952	54			1963	154
1953	72			1964	123
1954	108			1965	79
1955	131			1966	25
1956	151			1967	nil

SUMMARY

Engine	New	Withdrawn	Sold From	Disposal
80000	26.9.52	31.12.66	Corkerhill	Sold 2.67. Shipbreaking Industries, Faslane. On site 4.4.67.
80001	14.10.52	17.7.66	Eastfield	Sold to Shipbreaking Industries, Faslane. Cut up 10.66.
80002	17.10.52	1.3.67	Eastfield	Sold 3.69 Keighley & Worth Valley Railway for preservation.
80003	24.10.52	6.3.65	St. Margarets	Sold 6.65 to Shipbreaking Industries, Faslane.
80004	4.11.52	1.5.67	Corkerhill	Sold 8.67 to G.H.Campbell, Airdrie.
80005	13.11.52	9.8.66	(Polmadie)	Sold 10.66 to Motherwell Machinery and Scrap, Inshaw Works - on site 21.10.66.
80006	24.11.52	2.9.66	St. Margarets	Sold 12.66 to Shipbreaking Industries, Faslane.
80007	8.12.52	17.7.66	Eastfield	Sold 10.66 to Shipbreaking Industries, Faslane.
80008	15.12.52	13.7.64	Corkerhill	Sold 3.65 to Motherwell Machinery and Scrap, Inshaw Works.
80009	30.12.52	24.9.64	Corkerhill	Sold 3.65 to Motherwell Machinery and Scrap, Inshaw Works.
80010	10.7.51	14.6.64	(Brighton)	Sold 2.65 to J.Cashmore Newport - Moved Fratton to Westbury 17.3.65.
80011	21.7.51	9.7.67	(Bournemouth)	Sold 11.67 to Birds Commercial Motors, Risca.
80012	17.8.51	19.3.67	Salisbury	Sold 8.67 to J. Buttigieg, Newport.
80013	28.8.51	19.9.66	Bournemouth	Sold 10.66 to R.A.King, Norwich (At Ipswich Top Yard 20.11.66).
80014	5.9.51	2.5.65	Eastleigh	Birds Commercial Motors, Bynea 9.65.
80015	14.9.51	9.7.67	Salisbury	Sold 11.67. Birds Commercial Motors, Risca 12.67-at Gloucester 11.67.
80016	20.9.51	9.7.67	Salisbury	Sold 10.67. Birds Commercial Motors, Risca 11.67-at Gloucester 6.11.67.

80017	8.10.51	13.9.64	(Eastleigh)	J.Cashmore, Newport 2-3 1965.
80018	13.10.51	11.4.65	Eastleigh	Sold 8.65. G.Cohen, Morriston.
80019	20.10.51	19.3.67	Bournemouth	J. Buttigieg, Newport 8.67.
80020	27.10.51	26.6.65	(Corkerhill)	Motherwell Machinery and Scrap, Inshaw Works 9.65.
80021	10.11.51	13.7.64	Corkerhill	Motherwell Machinery and Scrap, Inshaw Works 3.65.
80022	20.11.51	26.6.65	(St. Margarets)	Motherwell Machinery and Scrap, Inshaw Works 9.65.
80023	27.11.51	2.10.65	Carstairs	Shipbreaking Industries, Faslane 11.65.
80024	7.12.51	24.8.66	Corkerhill	Shipbreaking Industries, Faslane 10.66.
80025	13.12.51	24.8.66	Corkerhill	Shipbreaking Industries, Faslane 10.66.
80026	20.12.51	2.9.66	St. Margarets	Shipbreaking Industries, Faslane 12.66.
80027	4.1.52	29.11.66	Polmadie	Sold 2.67. Motherwell Machinery and Scrap, Inshaw Works. On site 4.4.67. Still present 27.5.67.
80028	11.1.52	26.9.66	Perth	G.H.Campbell, Airdrie 12.66.
80029	22.1.52	16.12.65	(Hurlford)	Shipbreaking Industries, Faslane 2.66.
80030	5.2.52	8.6.64	Ardrossan	Arnott Young, West of Scotland Shipbreakers, Troon 2.65.
80031	2.2.52	20.9.64	Redhill	Steel Supply Co., West Drayton 3.65.
80032	4.3.52	29.1.67	(Bournemouth)	J.Cashmore, Newport 5.67.
80033	18.3.52	2.10.66	Eastleigh	J.Cashmore, Newport 3.67.
80034	5.4.52	2.1.66	Feltham	Cox and Danks, Park Royal 4.66.
80035	17.5.52	21.4.65	Yeovil	Sold 2.6.65 tender No.16/230/522T/96. Birds Commercial Motors, Bynea 7.65.
80036	24.5.52	9.11.64	Exmouth Jct.	Sold 2.2.65 tender No. 17/230/522T/60. J.Cashmore, Newport 3.65.
80037	24.5.52	7.3.66	Templecombe	Sold 6.4.66 tender No. 17/230/522T/210. J.Cashmore, Newport 6.66.
80038	7.6.52	7.9.64	Exmouth Jct	Sold 2.2.65 tender No. 17/230/522T/60. J.Cashmore, Newport 4.65.
80039	18.6.52	21.1.66	Bath Green Park	Sold 4.3.66 tender No. 17/230/522T/203. J.Cashmore, Newport 3.66.
80040	27.6.52	6.5.64	Exmouth Jct.	Crewe Works 7.64.
80041	5.7.52	7.3.66	Templecombe	Sold 6.4.66 tender No. 17/230/522T/210. J.Cashmore, Newport 6.66.
80042	15.7.52	6.2.65	(Exmouth Jct.)	Sold 5.3.65 tender No. 17/230/522T/71. R.S.Hayes, Bridgend 5.65.
80043	24.7.52	7.3.66	Templecombe	Sold 6.4.66 tender No. 17/230/522T/210. J.Cashmore, Newport 7.66.
80044	21.8.52	14.11.64	Bangor	Crewe Works 1.65. (Withdrawn 12.6.64, reinstated 8.64).
80045	4.9.52	1.5.67	Polmadie	G.H.Campbell, Airdrie 8.67.
80046	17.9.52	1.5.67	Corkerhill	G.H.Campbell, Airdrie 8.67.
80047	30.9.52	24.8.66	Corkerhill	Shipbreaking Industries, Faslane 10.66.
80048	13.10.52	17.7.65	Shrewsbury	Birds Commercial Motors, Morriston 9-10.65. (Withdrawn 12.6.64, reinstated 7.64)
80049	24.10.52	8.6.64	Ardrossan	Arnott Young, West of Scotland Shipbreakers, Troon 1-2.65.
80050	6.11.52	21.11.64	Bangor	Central Wagon Co., Ince 7.65. (Withdrawn 8.6.64, reinstated 8.64).
80051	21.11.52	17.8.66	Corkerhill	Shipbreaking Industries, Faslane 10.66.
80052	5.12.52	7.7.64	Dumfries	Motherwell Machinery and Scrap, Inshaw Works 3.65.
80053	22.12.52	7.7.64	Corkerhill	Motherwell Machinery and Scrap, Inshaw Works 3.65.
80054	4.12.54	29.6.66	(Greenock)	Motherwell Machinery and Scrap, Inshaw Works 8.65.
80055	23.12.54	2.9.66	St. Margarets	Shipbreaking Industries, Faslane 10.66.
80056	30.12.54	10.10.64	(Lostock Hall)	Crewe Works 11.64. (Withdrawn 29.6.64, reinstated 8.64).
80057	31.12.54	31.12.66	Polmadie	Shipbreaking Industries, Faslane 4.67.
80058	8.1.55	17.7.66	Eastfield	Shipbreaking Industries, Faslane 10.66.
80059	3.3.53	18.11.65	Bath Green Park	Sold 30.12.65 tender No. 16/230/522T/179. J. Buttigieg, Newport 1.66.
80060	19.3.53	7.2.66	(Polmadie)	Motherwell Machinery and Scrap, Inshaw Works 5.66.
80061	8.4.53	31.12.66	Polmadie	Shipbreaking Industries, Faslane 4.67. On site 15.4.67.
80062	29.4.53	12.10.64	Stirling	Motherwell Machinery and Scrap, Inshaw Works 2.65.
80063	19.5.53	24.8.66	Corkerhill	Shipbreaking Industries, Faslane 11.66.
80064	9.6.53	8.65	(Barrow Road)	Sold 24.9.65 tender No. 16/230/522T/142. Woodham Brothers, Barry 1.66.
80065	25.6.53	4.9.66	Eastleigh	J.Cashmore, Newport 1.67.
80066	15.7.53	13.6.65	(Eastleigh)	Birds Commercial Motors, Morriston 10.65.
80067	4.8.53	3.6.65	Barrow Road	Sold 28.7.65 tender No. 16/230/522T/116. Woodham Brothers, Barry 8-9.65.
80068	21.8.53	2.10.66	Eastleigh	J.Cashmore, Newport 2-3.67.
80069	30.9.53	23.1.66	(Nine Elms)	Cox and Danks, Park Royal 4.66.
80070	9.10.53	20.6.65	Eastleigh	Cox and Danks, Park Royal 10.65.
80071	21.10.53	30.7.64	Carstairs	Motherwell Machinery and Scrap, Inshaw Works 2.65.
80072	3.11.53	24.7.65	Shrewsbury	Woodham Brothers, Barry 1.66.
80073	13.11.53	30.7.64	Carstairs	Motherwell Machinery and Scrap, Inshaw Works 2.65.

80074	27.11.53	30.7.64	Carstairs	Motherwell Machinery and Scrap, Inshaw Works 2.65.
80075	10.12.53	30.7.64	Carstairs	Motherwell Machinery and Scrap, Inshaw Works 2.65.
80076	23.12.53	30.7.64	Dumfries	Motherwell Machinery and Scrap, Inshaw Works 2.65.
80077	12.1.54	12.10.64	Corkerhill	Motherwell Machinery and Scrap, Inshaw Works 3.65.
80078	2.2.54	24.7.65	Shrewsbury	Woodham Brothers, Barry 6.66.
80079	5.3.54	24.7.65	Croes Newydd	Woodham Brothers, Barry 1.66.
80080	18.3.54	24.7.65	Croes Newydd	Woodham Brothers, Barry 1.66.
80081	31.3.54	8.6.65	(Bournemouth)	Birds Commercial Motors, Morriston 10.65.
80082	15.4.54	4.9.66	Eastleigh	J.Cashmore, Newport 1.67.
80083	3.5.54	7.8.66	(Eastleigh)	G.Cohen, Morriston 1.67.
80084	14.5.54	13.6.65	(Redhill)	Birds Commercial Motors, Morriston 10.65.
80085	28.5.54	9.7.67	Salisbury	Birds Commercial Motors, Morriston 10.67.Observed at Gloucester 11.11.67 and at Risca 11.67.
80086	14.6.54	1.5.67	(Polmadie)	J.McWilliam and Sons, Shettleston 2.68.
80087	29.6.54	14.6.64	Eastleigh	J.Cashmore, Newport 2.65.
80088	14.7.54	13.6.65	(Redhill)	Birds Commercial Motors, Swansea 10.65.
80089	3.8.54	2.10.66	(Nine Elms)	J.Cashmore, Newport 3.67.
80090	12.8.54	27.3.65	(Dundee)	Shipbreaking Industries, Faslane 5.65.
80091	10.9.54	29.11.66	Beattock	Motherwell Machinery and Scrap, Inshaw Works 2.67.
80092	24.9.54	26.9.66	Perth	G.H.Campbell, Airdrie 12.66.
80093	11.10.54	26.9.66	Perth	G.H.Campbell, Airdrie 12.66.
80094	25.10.54	31.7.66	(Feltham)	G.Cohen, Morriston 2.67.
80095	9.11.54	2.10.66	(Nine Elms)	J.Cashmore, Newport 3.67.
80096	23.11.54	26.12.65	(Eastleigh)	T.W.Ward, Ringwood Goods Yard 3.66.
80097	9.12.54	24.7.65	Machynlleth	Woodham Brothers, Barry 1.66.
80098	22.12.54	24.7.65	Machynlleth	Woodham Brothers, Barry 1.66.
80099	17.1.55	8.5.65	(Machynlleth)	G.Cohen, Morriston 7.65.
80100	31.1.55	24.7.65	Shrewsbury	Woodham Brothers, Barry 1.66.
80101	7.2.55	17.7.65	Machynlleth	Birds Commercial Motors, Morriston 10.65.
80102	1.3.55	5.12.65	(Eastleigh)	T.W. Ward, Ringwood Goods Yard 3.66.
80103	16.3.55	29.8.62	(Shoeburyness)	Stratford Works 9.62.
80104	31.3.55	24.7.65	Machynlleth	Woodham Brothers, Barry 1.66.
80105	19.4.55	24.7.65	Machynlleth	Woodham Brothers, Barry 1.66.
80106	22.10.54	12.10.64	Polmadie	Motherwell Machinery and Scrap, Inshaw Works 2.65.
80107	29.10.54	14.9.64	Polmadie	Motherwell Machinery and Scrap, Inshaw Works 2.65.
80108	5.11.54	8.5.65	Polmadie	Sold 6.65 to Motherwell Machinery and Scrap, Inshaw Works 7.65.
80109	18.11.54	13.11.65	(Polmadie)	J.McWilliam & Sons, Shettleston 2.66.
80110	18.11.54	8.5.65	Polmadie	Sold 6.65 to Motherwell Machinery and Scrap, Inshaw Works 7.65.
80111	26.11,54	29.11.66	Beattock	Motherwell Machinery and Scrap, Inshaw Works 2.67.
80112	3.12.54	24.8.66	Corkerhill	Shipbreaking Industries, Faslane 10.66.
80113	14.12.54	2.9.66	St. Margarets	Shipbreaking Industries, Faslane 12.66.
80114	29.12.54	31.12.66	St. Margarets	Sold 3.67 to Shipbreaking Industries, Faslane. On site 15.4.67.
80115	31.12.54	12.10.64	Polmadie	Motherwell Machinery and Scrap, Inshaw Works 2.65.
80116	4.5.55	1.5.67	Polmadie	G.H.Campbell, Airdrie 8.67.
80117	19.5.55	3.3.66	(Polmadie)	Motherwell Machinery and Scrap, Inshaw Works 5.66.
80118	15.6.55	29.11.66	Polmadie	Motherwell Machinery and Scrap, Inshaw Works 2.67.
80119	21.6.55	29.5.65	Dumfries	Motherwell Machinery and Scrap, Inshaw Works 8.65.
80120	6.7.55	1.5.67	Polmadie	G.H.Campbell, Airdrie 5.67.
80121	22.7.55	2.6.66	(Polmadie)	Shipbreaking Industries, Faslane 8.66.
80122	8.8.55	31.12.66	Polmadie	Shipbreaking Industries, Faslane on site 15.4.67.
80123	9.9.55	17.8.66	Polmadie	Shipbreaking Industries, Faslane 11.66.
80124	22.9.55	9.12.66	St. Margarets	Shipbreaking Industries, Faslane 3.67.
80125	6.10.55	10.10.64	Crewe	Sold 2.65. Maden and McKee, Stanley, Liverpool 5.65. (Withdrawn 7.7.64, reinstated 9.64).
80126	20.10.55	19.11.66	Perth	Sold 12.66. G.H.Campbell, Airdrie 1.67.
80127	7.11.55	30.7.64	(Corkerhill)	Motherwell Machinery and Scrap, Inshaw Works 10.64.
80128	23.11.55	4.4.67	Corkerhill	P. & W. McLellan, Langloan 8.67.
80129	9.12.55	10.10.64	(Lostock Hall)	Crewe Works 11.64. (Withdrawn 7.7.64, reinstated 8.64).
80130	22.12.55	17.8.66	Polmadie	Shipbreaking Industries, Faslane 11.66.
80131	2.3.56	8.5.65	(Bangor)	G.Cohen, Morriston 7.65.
80132	15.3.56	9.1.66	Eastleigh	Sold 2.66. G.Cohen – cut up at Eastleigh by 4.66.
80133	28.3.56	9.7.67	(Nine Elms)	Sold 10.67. Birds Commercial Motors, Risca. At Gloucester 11.67.

80134	20.4.56	9.7.67	Salisbury	Birds Commercial Motors, Risca 10.67.
80135	30.4.56	24.7.65	(Shrewsbury)	Woodham Brothers, Barry 1.66.
80136	11.5.56	24.7.65	Shrewsbury	Woodham Brothers, Barry 6.66
80137	28.5.56	31.10.65	Eastleigh	Sold 1.66. Cox & Danks, Park Royal 1.66.
80138	12.6.56	2.10.66	(Bournemouth)	J.Cashmore, Newport 2.67.
80139	26.6.56	9.7.67	(Eastleigh)	Sold 10.67. Birds Commercial Motors, Risca. At Gloucester 11.67.
80140	10.7.56	9.7.67	Salisbury	Birds Commercial Motors, Risca 11.67.
80141	25.7.56	9.1.66	Nine Elms	Cox & Danks, Park Royal 3.66.
80142	9.8.56	3.3.66	Eastleigh	Birds Commercial Motors, Bridgend 6.66.
80143	10.9.56	9.7.67	(Nine Elms)	Sold 10.67. Birds Commercial Motors, Risca. At Gloucester 11.67.
80144	25.9.56	15.5.66	(Nine Elms)	Birds Commercial Motors, Bridgend 9.66.
80145	16.10.56	25.6.67	Salisbury	J.Cashmore, Newport 11.67.
80146	30.10.56	9.7.67	(Bournemouth)	Sold 10.67. Birds Commercial Motors, Risca 12.67. At Gloucester 11.67.
80147	15.11.56	13.6.65	Bournemouth	Birds Commercial Motors, Morriston 1.66.
80148	29.11.56	14.6.64	Redhill	Steel Supply Co., West Drayton 3.65.
80149	13.12.56	7.3.65	Eastleigh	Cox & Danks, Park Royal 6.65.
80150	28.12.56	17.10.65	Eastleigh	Woodham Brothers, Barry 1.66.
80151	18.1.57	7.5.67	Eastleigh	Woodham Brothers, Barry 8.67.
80152	6.2.57	9.7.67	Salisbury	Sold 10.67. Birds Commercial Motors, Risca 11.67. At Gloucester 11.67.
80153	25.2.57	7.3.65	Eastleigh	Cox & Danks, Park Royal 6.65.
80154	26.3.57	2.4.67	Salisbury	J. Buttigieg, Newport 8.67.

As noted above 80044/8/50 were withdrawn in June 1964, and 80056, 80125/9 were withdrawn in July 1964 by the Scottish Region but were reinstated by the London Midland Region in August or September 1964.

80064/72/8/9/80/97/8, 80100/4/5/35/6/50/1 were later resold for preservation, 80002 was sold direct by BR for preservation.

2.11 Preservation

Approximately ten percent of the class remains, most of the survivors being consigned to Woodham Brothers at Barry. Some of the preserved examples have already completed one spell of service and have been returned to service following a second full overhaul, whilst others are still in 'ex-scrap yard' condition.

Some of the preservation societies have provided considerable assistance in compiling this chapter, and their valuable help is gratefully acknowledged.

80002 - purchased for £2,700 by the Keighley and Worth Valley Railway in March 1969 from British Railways (see letter of acceptance of bid - appendix C). The locomotive was moved from Eastfield on 20th May 1969 being towed south by Brush Type 4 D1810 (advice of despatch appendix C). Following an appeal for funds to retube the boiler this task was completed in the spring of 1971 prior to a mid-year return to service in BR lined black livery. It ran 770 miles in the season before the front pony truck was removed and sent to BREL Horwich for overhaul. It was on display at an exhibition held at Newcastle Central station from 7th-14th October 1972 along with other preserved steam locomotives and items of passenger rolling stock. By 1975 it was out of service with boiler problems and what at first seemed like small repairs being required to various parts of the boiler developed into a major rebuilding project to the extent that for instance the copper firebox has been replaced by one of steel construction. Following all this work the engine was returned to work in 1995 and continues to be based on the Keighley and Worth Valley Railway.

80064 - A scheme to purchase this locomotive (the 80064 Loco Fund) was started in 1970. Additional members joined in 1972 which enabled the £4,000 purchase price to be raised and also the additional £810 needed to move the locomotive from Woodham Brothers at Barry to Buckfastleigh in South Devon where the engine arrived in February 1973.

The engine was stripped down during 1974; by February 1976 the chassis had been re-wheeled but the locomotive did not steam again until February 1981. Nearly all the restoration tasks were carried out by group members and the job was completed in 1982 at a cost of £18,000. This included the fitting of air brakes and a Westinghouse pump and the application of BR black livery. Examples of the fund raising literature are to be found in appendix C.

When restoration was complete the locomotive was transferred to the Torbay line on 17th June 1982. Unfortunately a long term agreement to operate the engine on this route could not be reached and a move to the Bluebell Railway took place, departure from Torbay being on 15th March 1983. Sheffield Park was reached on 21st March and following remedial work the engine entered service on 16th June.

Following expiry of its boiler certificate 80064 returned in 1992 to the South Devon Railway (as the Dart Valley Railway is now called) but was moved again to the Bluebell Railway in 1997.

80072 - Moved from Woodham Brothers, Barry via Swindon Works to the Llangollen Railway, this engine had donated parts to many of its fellows before departure (for example cab roof to 80079). It has not yet returned to service.

80078 - Purchased from Woodham Brothers, Barry in March 1975 by the Southern Steam Trust the engine left the scrapyard on 23rd September 1976 going direct to Swanage, being the 84th engine to move from Barry. Little progress had been made however when the Swanage Railway ran into financial problems, the locomotive being sold to the 'Project 78' group in May 1991, to help raise funds for the railway but also to speed up restoration work. Subsequently the engine has been incorporated into the restoration programme of Southern Locomotives Ltd (see 80104) and it is hoped to return the engine to traffic at Swanage by early 1998.

Fig. 75   80080 is seen leaving Nottingham for Derby on a Steam Shuttle Service 4 June 1989.

Hugh Ballantyne

80079 – Moved from the Barry yard of Woodham Brothers in May 1971 to the Severn Valley Railway having been purchased in March of that year. It returned to service on 16th April 1977 in BR plain black livery although it was later lined out. The engine was restored to mainline condition and appeared on BR on several occasions including the Liverpool and Manchester Railway '150' celebrations at Rainhill in 1980. It also hauled the first train over Bridgnorth road by-pass new bridge on the SVR on 5th March 1983.

After completion of ten years service the locomotive underwent a further overhaul returning to traffic in April 1993 in unlined black. Once again it has been on mainline activities and one of its first duties being to work over the Central Wales line to Carmarthen and the West Wales branches to Milford Haven, Tenby and Fishguard Harbour. Several of the outings have been in company with 80080. During the 1993/4 winter break the locomotive was again lined out, and it has worked since on SVR services and the main line.

80080 (Fig. 75) – This engine was selected in preference to 80150 by the Peak Railway Society due to the condition of its boiler. It was purchased from Woodham Brothers at Barry for £9,000 + VAT in October 1980, and it left the yard on 4th November 1980, arriving at Matlock on 6th November.

In 1983 the engine was moved, in pieces, to the Midland Railway Centre at Butterley and ownership passed to '80080 Locomotive Holdings Ltd.' By 1985 the bunker and tanks had been refitted, and during 1986 work was undertaken on the boiler. The engine was restored, in BR lined black, to mainline condition and has made several appearances including workings on the Cambrian line, Nottingham to Skegness, Carlisle to Kirkby Stephen, the Folkestone Harbour branch and areas of South West England. The engine remains based at the Midland Railway Centre.

80097 – Owned by the Bury Standard 4 Group, this engine was moved to the East Lancashire Railway from Barry in 1985. The official purchase date was 14th May and the asking price £9,000. Ownership is officially vested in the Barry Steam Locomotive Co. Ltd. Little progress was made prior to 1991, the previous three years having been spent in building covered accommodation to carry out the restoration work.

Work completed by the end of 1994 was the stripping of the engine, re-profiling the tyres and refitting of the wheel sets plus the preparation of many of the component parts. The costs of restoration to mid-1994 exceeded £40,000.

80098 – Originally purchased for spares on 1st March 1983 for £9,000 + VAT by 80080 Loco Holdings, it is now intended that the locomotive will be restored to working order, stripping started in 1993 at the Midland Railway

Centre, Butterley (see invoice appendix C). By coincidence this engine finished its service carrying the boiler originally fitted to 80080. 80098 is based at the Midland Railway Centre.

80100 - The Brighton Standard 4 Fund selected this locomotive from Barry scrap yard in February 1976. Purchase was concluded on 12th September 1978, the price being £8,500 but the total payment on the day was much higher as Southern Railway Class S15 30847 and Standard Class 9F 92240 were also bought on this date. 80100 was the first Barry locomotive to be purchased for the Bluebell Railway to which it was moved in October 1978.

Unlike many of the other subsequent purchases from the yard, the new owners were allowed to collect missing pieces from other residents so that a relatively complete engine was obtained. 80100 has been put aside for restoration at Sheffield Park whilst efforts are concentrated on the Fund's other locomotive, 78059 which is to be rebuilt as a 2-6-2 tank, to be given the number 84030.

80104 - This was intended to be a companion to 80078, being purchased in December 1980 from Woodhams as a long term project. It stayed at Barry until September 1984 before moving to Swanage. It had received a cosmetic repaint by April 1986 but no further work had been carried out when purchase was agreed with the Port Line Locomotive Project, ownership passing in January 1988. Subsequently a new grouping was formed specifically to work on the locomotive and this was formalised as the 80104 Locomotive Project Limited in 1990. The people involved were also heavily committed to work on Bulleid Pacific 34072 and little visible progress was made on 80104, by now moved to the group's Swindon Works site.

At the end of February 1991 80104 'as a kit of parts' was moved again, this time to the Avon Valley Railway at Bitton where slow progress had been made. In November 1994 ownership changed to Southern Locomotives Ltd. and the engine moved back to Swanage in October 1995 where it has now been returned to traffic using the boiler from 80078 (No.1308).

80105 - Woodham Brothers sold this locomotive in 1973 and it is now owned by 'Locomotive Owners Group (Scotland) Ltd.' Originally at Falkirk, the engine is now at Bo'ness undergoing restoration.

80135 - Originally purchased by the North Yorkshire Moors Railway in 1973 (again from Woodham Brothers) the locomotive was sold to Jos de Crau in 1976 and first entered service on the NYMR in 1980. It received boiler repairs in 1982 (the boiler going to the Severn Valley Railway for the work to be carried out) and it re-entered traffic in 1985. This engine has been in service on the NYMR in lined green livery which was never carried by the class in BR service although the shade of green has not always been the authentic shade used by British Railways. Having completed ten years running the locomotive was withdrawn again in 1995. Restoration is now under way with a planned return to service during 1997.

80136 - Owned by 'The 80136 Locomotive Fund' the engine is under restoration at Cheddleton. Woodham Brothers sold this locomotive for £8,500 + VAT at 8% in March 1979. Removal from Barry was undertaken by Sunters Ltd. of Northallerton for £2,850 in August 1979. The engine was completely dismantled by 1982. In order to restore the engine many parts have had to be made from scratch and this group have, in addition to making these for their own locomotive, provided parts for others of the class, for example top feed clack boxes for 80080.

A set of connecting rods was required but the type of steel originally specified (EN 1005) ceased being manufactured in the late 1950s. To be able to get an order large enough to justify a new production lot the group arranged with the other owners to have a bulk order made. 25 forgings were produced by J.Hesketh (Bury) and other Standard locomotives to benefit from this scheme included 80072, 78059 (to become 84030) and class 9F 92214. Further work on 80136 has been contracted out with the aim of a return to service in 1997.

80150 - Possibly the last of the class to leave Barry, 80150 was purchased by the Wales Railway Centre, Cardiff in 1988 for £9,500 + VAT. Only cosmetic restoration had been undertaken by 1993 and it was subsequently moved back to Barry for storage in the former bus depot.

80151 - The Stour Valley Railway Preservation Society selected this engine from Barry, purchase taking place on 8th June 1974, the asking price being £6,600. Transportation to Chappel & Wakes Colne cost a further £2,000.

When BR requested a high price for the Chappel site 80151 had to be sold to raise the funds and ownership passed to the '80151 Locomotive Company Ltd.'.

Restoration started in 1988 with the wheelsets going to Swindon. Since that time the work carried out (to mid-1993) had cost £40,000 with an estimate of a similar sum still to be spent before the engine is fit for service.

Fig. 76   80032 with the 1.59pm Brockenhurst to Lymington Pier at a location about 2¹/₂ miles north of Lymington, 10th September 1966.   *M. Mensing*

Fig. 77   80041 departing from Bailey Gate on the Southern section of the Somerset and Dorset line with a stopping train from Templecombe to Bournemouth West, 30th December 1965.   *G.W. Morrison*

Fig. 78   80072 leaving Lapworth with the 7.30am Leamington Spa to Birmingham Snow Hill, 2nd July 1964.
M. Mensing

Fig. 79   80079 working a 'Santa Special' approaching Bewdley at Northwood Farm on the Severn Valley Railway,
11th December 1982.
Hugh Ballantyne

Fig. 80   80080 & 80079 with a special train passing Sutton Bridge Junction at Shrewsbury en route from Shrewsbury to Carmarthen via the Central Wales line and Llanelly 9 October 1993.   *Hugh Ballantyne*

Fig. 81   80094 working 12.5pm Reading South to Redhill train about one mile east of Betchworth Station 22 October 1964.   *Hugh Ballantyne*

Fig. 82   80101 stands in Stratford Shed yard ER minus piston and coupling rods 7 May 1962   *R.C. Riley*

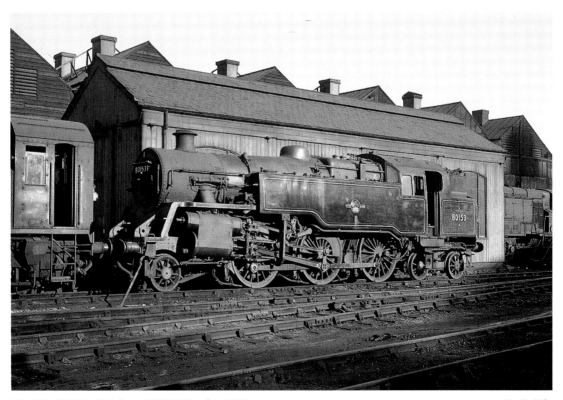

Fig. 83   80153 at Brighton MPD 7 October 1962   *R.C. Riley*

Fig. 84   82004 with the 1.45pm Shrewsbury to Hartlebury approaching Bewdley, 20th June 1959. The line on the right leads to Tenbury Wells.   *M. Mensing*

Fig. 85   82008 working the 4.28pm Worcester Foregate Street to Malvern Wells local train approaching Malvern Wells, 3rd May 1958.   *M. Mensing*

Fig. 86   82016 at Eastleigh MPD, 17th August 1961.   *G.W. Morrison*

Fig. 87   82037 with 3.35 Bristol Temple Meads to Bath Green Park passing under the A4 road bridge west of Bath, 13th May 1964.
                                                                                                                              M. Mensing

Fig. 88   82038 at Worcester MPD 23 September 1955.   *R.C. Riley*

Fig. 89   82041 at Bath Green Park 12 July 1960. Note WR colour of station nameboard.   *R.C. Riley*

Fig. 90   82041 leaving Bath Green Park with 2pm train to Bristol Temple Meads 6 March 1965   *Hugh Ballantyne*

Fig. 91   84008 standing in Northampton Castle station at the head of a push-pull set which was likely to form the 10.13am service to Wellingborough on Whit Monday, 6th June 1960.   *M. Mensing*

3. CLASS 3   2-6-2T   82000-44

Fig. 92   82007 at Swindon MPD 15 June 1952 awaiting despatch to its first allocation at Tyseley.   *R.C. Riley*

3.1 Purpose

The main reason for the introduction of this class of engine, as with the Standard Class 3 2-6-0 77xxx, was the existence of a number of bridges having a 16 Ton axle load restriction, which the Class 4 2-6-4T design could not meet, whilst a more powerful engine than a Class 2 category was desirable.

3.2 Construction

Unlike other classes it was not possible in this case to modify an Ivatt LMS design, as there was no existing LMS boiler to suit engines in the Class 3 category, the Ivatt Class 4 mogul boiler being too heavy. It was therefore decided to adapt the Swindon No. 4 boiler, which had been constructed for use on the GWR 2-6-2T's of the 5100 and 8100 classes, and also on the 5600 0-6-2T's. This course of action allowed the existing flange blocks to be made use of, but the barrel was shortened by $5^{13}/_{16}$ inches, and a dome was added to what had been a domeless boiler.

In other respects, including construction detail, the boiler and fittings were brought into line with the new standard specification, with an 18-element superheater in place of the Swindon 7-element design, and as such was designated BR6. The design life of the class was 40 years.

The engines were built as follows:-

1952 Swindon Nos. 82000-9 Lot No. 392   Authority
RE 3337
17.11.49

1952 Swindon Nos. 82010-19 Lot No. 393   Authority
RE 3337
17.11.49

1954 Swindon Nos. 82020-29 Lot No. 398
Authority
RE 5267
1954/5 Swindon Nos. 82030-34 Lot No. 399   4.1.51
under 1952
renewal programme

1955 Swindon Nos. 82035-44 Lot No.410   Authority
RE 6403
29.11.51
under 1953
renewal programme

In the Western Region Building Programme for 1954, Swindon Lot Nos. were shown as follows:- Lot 415, 82045-54 for the Western Region and Lot 416, 82055-62 for the North Eastern Region, but in the event these were never built. The costs for each engine were:-

Nos.	Estimated Cost	Final Cost
82000-9	£9,450	£12,995
82010-19	£9,450	£12,859
82020-29	£10,290	£14,504
82030-34	£10,290	£14,632
82035-44	£11,320	£14,627

All except 82010-29 were built with GWR type ATC

Fig. 93   GWR 51XX 2-6-2T 4165 stands in Tyseley shed yard 22 May 1949.   *J.F. Ward Collection*

Fig. 94   Preserved GWR 56XX 0-6-2T 6697 stands at the head of a demonstration goods train at Great Western Society's Didcot premises 30 August 1981.
                                                             J.F. Ward

Fig. 95   82017/8 Under construction in Swindon Works 'A' Shop nearing completion 24 August 1952.

T. E. Williams collection/NRM, York

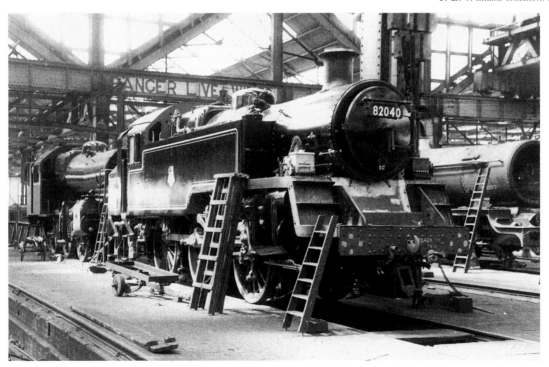

Fig. 96   82040/1 Under construction at Swindon 8 May 1955.

David Tyreman collection

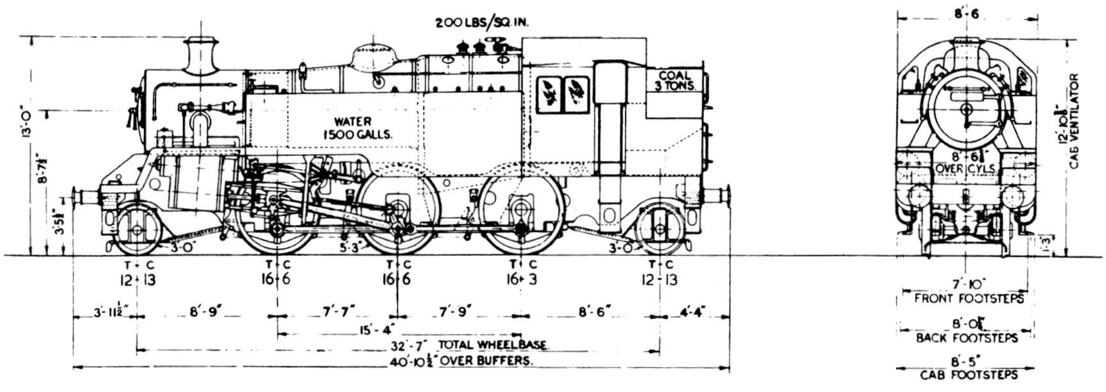

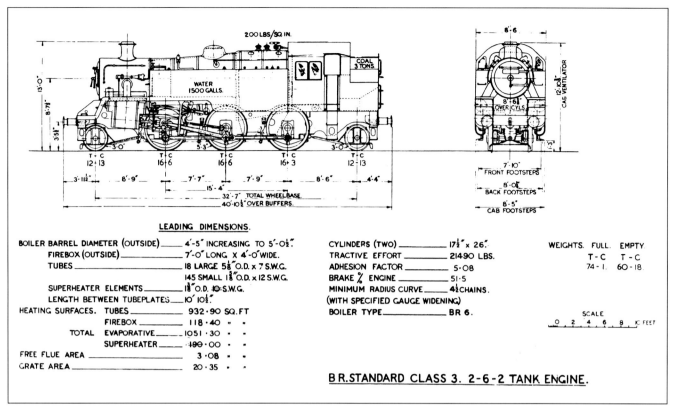

LEADING DIMENSIONS.

BOILER BARREL DIAMETER (OUTSIDE) ______ 4'-5" INCREASING TO 5'-0½"
FIREBOX (OUTSIDE) ______ 7'-0" LONG X 4'-0" WIDE.
TUBES ______ 18 LARGE 5⅛" O.D. x 7 S.W.G.
145 SMALL 1⅝" O.D. x 12 S.W.G.
SUPERHEATER ELEMENTS ______ 1⅜" O.D. ~~10~~ S.W.G.
LENGTH BETWEEN TUBEPLATES ______ 10' 10½"
HEATING SURFACES. TUBES ______ 932·90 SQ. FT
FIREBOX ______ 118·40 " "
TOTAL EVAPORATIVE ______ 1051·30 " "
SUPERHEATER ______ ~~190~~·00 " "
FREE FLUE AREA ______ 3·08 " "
GRATE AREA ______ 20·35 " "

CYLINDERS (TWO) ______ 17½" x 26"
TRACTIVE EFFORT ______ 21490 LBS.
ADHESION FACTOR ______ 5·08
BRAKE % ENGINE ______ 51·5
MINIMUM RADIUS CURVE ______ 4½ CHAINS.
(WITH SPECIFIED GAUGE WIDENING)
BOILER TYPE ______ BR 6.

WEIGHTS.	FULL.	EMPTY
	T-C	T-C
	74-1.	60-18

SCALE
0 2 4 6 8 10 FEET

B R. STANDARD CLASS 3. 2-6-2 TANK ENGINE.

Fig. 97 BR '3' 2-6-2T Diagram and Dimensions, 3 tons coal capacity 82000-29/31-5 *British Railways*

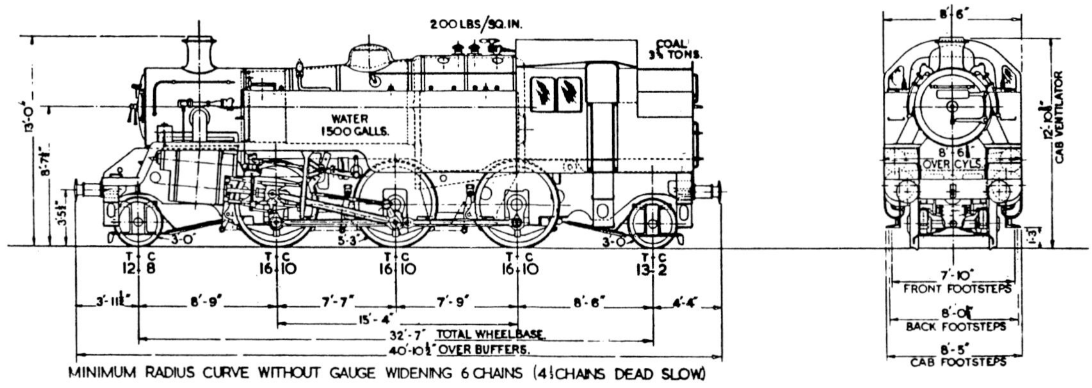

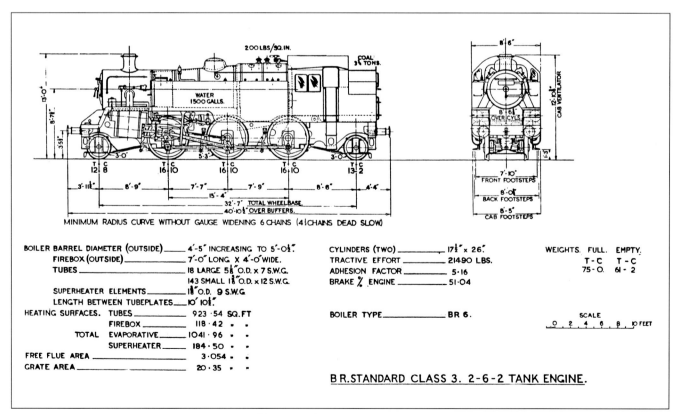

MINIMUM RADIUS CURVE WITHOUT GAUGE WIDENING 6 CHAINS (4½ CHAINS DEAD SLOW)

BOILER BARREL DIAMETER (OUTSIDE) ______ 4'-5" INCREASING TO 5'-0½"
FIREBOX (OUTSIDE) ______ 7'-0" LONG X 4'-0" WIDE.
TUBES ______ 18 LARGE 5⅛" O.D. x 7 S.W.G.
143 SMALL 1⅝" O.D. x 12 S.W.G.
SUPERHEATER ELEMENTS ______ 1⅜" O.D. 9 S.W.G.
LENGTH BETWEEN TUBEPLATES ______ 10' 10½"
HEATING SURFACES. TUBES ______ 923·54 SQ. FT
FIREBOX ______ 118·42 " "
TOTAL EVAPORATIVE ______ 1041·96 " "
SUPERHEATER ______ 184·50 " "
FREE FLUE AREA ______ 3·054 " "
GRATE AREA ______ 20·35 " "

CYLINDERS (TWO) ______ 17½" x 26"
TRACTIVE EFFORT ______ 21490 LBS.
ADHESION FACTOR ______ 5·16
BRAKE % ENGINE ______ 51·04

BOILER TYPE ______ BR 6.

WEIGHTS.	FULL.	EMPTY.
	T-C	T-C
	75-0.	61-2

SCALE
0 2 4 6 8 10 FEET

B R. STANDARD CLASS 3. 2-6-2 TANK ENGINE.

Fig. 98 BR '3' 2-6-2T Diagram and Dimensions, 3¾ tons coal capacity 82030/6-44 *British Railways*

which explains why 82000-9 were more expensive to build than 82010-19.

As seen with other classes the costs given on the engine record cards do not tally with other sources, 82000-6 being quoted at £13,999, 82020 at £14,523 and 82031 at £14,651. 82036 and 82043 are quoted at the price given above.

3.3 Dimensions and Data

Those additions to information supporting the official diagrams (Figs. 97 & 98) are as follows:-

Piston Swept Volume (1 cylinder)			6,254 cu in
Piston Valves (Walschaert)	diameter		10"
	steam lap		$1^1/_2$"
	maximum travel		6.25"
	lead		$^1/_4$"
	exhaust clearance		nil
Maximum Cut-off			75%
Travel at 20% cut-off			3.62"
Clearance Volume as % of piston swept volume			11.6
Maximum Piston thrust			48,106 lbs
Steam Chest volume between valve heads			3,037 cu in
Steam Chest volume as % of piston swept volume			48.5
Revolving Masses-weight per cylinder			1,189lbs
Reciprocating Masses	- total weight/cylinder		737lbs
	- percentage balanced		50
	- unbalanced weight/cyl		368lbs
Ratio unbalanced weight/cylinder to total engine weight			1:451
Firebox Volume			107 cu ft
	Heating Surface		118.4 sq ft
	Water Surface at half glass		72 sq ft
	Volume steam above half glass		76 cu ft
	Heating surface tubes		932.9 sq ft
Total heating surface including firebox			1051.3 sq ft
Superheater surface area: 82000-29/31-5			184.5 sq ft
	82030/6-44		190 sq. ft
Free area through tubes	Large		1.49 sq ft
	Small		1.59 sq ft
	Total		3.08 sq ft
Area through large tubes as % of Total			48.4
Total free area as % of grate area			15.2
A/S ratio	- Large Tubes		1:302
	- Small Tubes		1:374
Steam pipe in boiler	- Bore		$5^1/_2$"
	- Cross sectional area		23.8 sq in
Regulator full open area			24.3 sq in
Superheater Elements Total Area			17.7 sq in
Steam pipes to Cylinders Total Area			31.8 sq in
Blast Pipe Cap diameter			$4^1/_2$"
Blast Pipe area			15.9 sq in
Chimney Throat	- diameter		1' 0 $^3/_4$"
	- area		0.89 sq ft
Chimney throat area as % of grate area			4.35
Height Blast Pipe Cap to Chimney Throat			2' 7"
Taper of Chimney			1 in 14

The above data applies to all members of the class when new except 82030/36-44. These ten engines were built to diagram SL/3VT/2, which had heavier tanks, increased bunker capacity and two less small boiler tubes.

The modified heating surface became:

Firebox (same)	118.4 sq ft
Tubes	923.54 sq ft
Total	1041.94 sq ft

Three different locomotive weights have been quoted. Note that all exceed the 16-ton axle load mentioned in Section 3.1.

Full	Estimated* Weight	Actual	82030/6-44
Leading Wheels	12t 18c	12t 13c	12t 8c
Leading Coupled Wheels	16t 4c	16t 6c	16t 10c
Centre Coupled Wheels	16t 5c	16t 6c	16t 10c
Trailing Coupled Wheels	16t 4c	16t 3c	16t 10c
Trailing Bogie Wheels	11t 19c	12t 13c	13t 2c
Total Full	73t 10c	74t 1c	75t 0c
Total Empty	60t 18c	61t 2c	
Water Capacity		1500galls	1500galls
Coal Capacity		3t 0c	3t 15c
Adhesion Factor		5.08	5.16

*(*Railway Magazine* 1951)

Features of the class were a). the use of Morganite Carbon bushes for the indicator arm of the tank capacity gauges (these eliminated surging problems during tank filling or heavy braking) and b). the cab-front windows were slightly inclined in an effort to eliminate reflections from the cab backplate.

The coupled wheelbase (15' 4") and the leading pony truck were similar to the Standard Class 4 2-6-4T design. The cylinders were cast steel from the pattern used for the LMS Class 4 2-6-0 design with cast iron liners. Unlike the Standard Class 4 2-6-4T design, no water was carried under the bunker, the entire water supply being held in the tanks. Smith-Stone electric light equipment was fitted in cabs.

3.3.1 Detail Alterations

Fluted coupling rods were fitted to 82000-19; whilst 82020 onwards were fitted with rectangular section rods (Figs. 99 & 100).

Swindon later fitted engines for use on the Western Region with a short hand-hold for the fireman filling the tanks as fitted to GWR 51xx 2-6-2T's and 56xx 0-6-2T's, just ahead of the dome on the boiler top (Fig. 101). The first engine to be so fitted was 82007 on 26th January 1957. Western Region engines were also fitted with the GWR ATC, but those working on other regions were in some cases fitted with the BR AWS system. 82019 was one so fitted in December 1959. Southern lamp irons were fitted to Southern Region locomotives and in latter days, a small yellow triangle was painted below the number to signify that the locomotive was fitted with the French TIA water-treatment system.

Earlier built members of the class had the Doncaster LNER pattern return cranks:- a square hole fitting on a square pin and held fast by two long vertical bolts. Later engines were fitted with the Derby LMS pattern return cranks:- four studs on a rounded face with four nuts securing the return crank pin.

The class seems to have suffered from the fore and aft oscillation problems seen with the pacifics but a remedy has not been recorded.

There were also several incidents involving splits in the side tanks (usually on the left hand side) with five occurrences reported by mid-August 1952. Possible causes were the pin jointed boiler tank stays fixed to the top plate and the use of $^3/_{16}$" plate for the tanks to keep the weight to a minimum. These splits were welded up but soon reappeared. Various sheds reported visible moving of the tank plates during tank

Fig. 99
82016 In Swindon Works yard with fluted coupling rods, 17th August 1952.
J.B. Arnold

Fig. 100 82038 at Swindon MPD after works overhaul 8 August 1957 with rectangular section rods. Note that although allocated to WR there is no handhold provided in front of dome. *G. Wheeler*

filling and whilst the engine was on the move.

Subsequent investigation revealed some irregularities in welding during construction and also that the steel plate used was under size.

In addition to the need to weld as originally shown on the drawings other proposed corrective actions were the use of ¹/₄" plate and the addition of a shallow gusset mid-way between the rear wash-plate and tank backplate on left hand side tanks, this having already been fitted to the right hand tanks.

A modification which should have been put in from new following experience with the other standard designs was the addition of 'wearing faces' to the main and pilot valves of the regulator to prevent jamming of these in the 'closed' position. Examination of 82001 in service showed that at least this engine was not so modified in late 1952.

Lot 393, built for the Southern Region, differed from the WR batch (Lot 392) in as much as steam for the atomiser was controlled by the cylinder cock gear instead of from the regulator handle and they also featured wide-pattern firehole doors with air louvres.

Of the second batch of locomotives, 82030/6-44, had their coal capacity increased by 15cwt by flattening the slope at the foot of the bunker. This final batch were probably built in this form which may well account for the transfer of 82000-9 from the South Wales area, as their coal capacity was insufficient for the normal Cardiff-Treherbert-Merthyr turns. It was also found that they fouled the coal chutes at Rhymney prior to being sent to Barry and Treherbert.

Fig. 101
82020 at Portmadoc with an up pick-up goods conveying three empty GWR steel sided gunpowder vans for Penrhyndeudraeth in July 1964. The hand-hold in front of the dome can be clearly seen as can the short length cut away from the running plate to allow easier access to the mechanical lubricator.

J.B. Arnold

After a while in service some members of the class had a short length cut away near the front of the running plate to allow easier access to the mechanical lubricators (Fig. 101).

3.4 Boilers

The boiler history of the class has been reconstructed from several sources and is thought to be reasonably complete despite the absence of several key documents.

Boilers 940-59, 1093-1107 and 1345-54 were fitted to the class. 1375-9 were built as spares and subsequently 1873 (1960). Cancelled engines 82045-62 would have had boilers 1577-62.

The following questions remain to be answered.

Spare boiler 1376 is not recorded in use. It is possible that this was the Darlington Works spare where boiler change details were not recorded. 82026-9 may have used this boiler together with swaps of 1099-1102.

82000 received a Heavy General overhaul at Crewe in October 1963. Either boiler 946 or 1350 is likely to have been fitted.

82007 was reboilered in October 1960 and 1348 is the likely candidate.

82009 received a Heavy General overhaul at Crewe in February 1964. Whichever of 946 or 1350 was not used for 82000 (above), or boiler 1375, is likely to have been fitted to 82009.

82025/33 both received overhauls in May 1961 at Eastleigh and Wolverhampton respectively. No boiler changes were recorded and no available boilers could be identified at this time. They may therefore have retained their existing boilers. It is known that boilers were transferred between Works, for example from Swindon to Eastleigh. 82036 was noted on 21st July 1963 with a boiler not fitted with GWR type hand-holds described in Section 3.3.1.

The boiler details known are as follows:-

82000 New 940, 1375 10.56, Off 10.63 replaced by 946 or 1350.
82001 New 941, 946 12.57, 1354 12.63
82002 New 942, 948 11.57, 943 8.60
82003 New 944, 940 5.57
82004 New 943, 1378 4.57, 949 12.61
82005 New 945, 941 6.58, 1873 6.60
82006 New 946, 943 8.57, 1353 1.60, 1352 11.60
82007 New 947, 1377 1.57, Off 10.60
82008 New 948, 944 10.57
82009 New 949, 947 5.57
82010 New 950, 1105 8.58, 1098 9.60
82011 New 951, 958 8.57
82012 New 952, off by 3.58 to 82017, replaced by 951
82013 New 953, 957 8.58
82014 New 954, 953 after 9.58
82015 New 955, off by 10.59 954 Undated
82016 New 956, 1345 by 3.59
82017 New 957, 952 3.58
82018 New 958, 959 3.57, 1095 4.61
82019 New 959, 1379 2.57, 956 (Spare) 4.64
82020 New 1093, 1351 7.61
82021 New 1094, 945 6.61
82022 New 1095, 1097 11.60
82023 New 1096, 956 3.59, 1105 3.63
82024 New 1097, 1105 10.60, 959 12.62
82025 New 1098, 1096 5.59
82026 New 1099
82027 New 1100
82028 New 1101
82029 New 1102
82030 New 1103, 955 10.59
82031 New 1104, 1346 8.61
82032 New 1105, 1351 3.58, 948 2.61
82033 New 1106
82034 New 1107, 945 9.58, 1353 12.60
82035 New 1345, 942 6.58, 1093 1.62
82036 New 1346, 941 2.61
82037 New 1347, 1378 5.62
82038 New 1348, 1103 1.60
82039 New 1349, 949 10.57, 1377 3.61
82040 New 1350, 950 1.59, 1104 4.62
82041 New 1351, 1349 11.57, 1094 12.61
82042 New 1352, 1350 7.59, 942 5.63
82043 New 1353, 1107 11.58
82044 New 1354, 1349 between 12.61 and 4.63

3.5 Livery

Unlike their Class 2 and 4 counterparts there were several livery variations within these 45 engines.

All started life in lined black with the original lion and wheel emblem. The pattern of lining was similar to that on the Class 4 tanks. The only change to those remaining in black livery was the substitution of the later BR totem after 1956, and a hybrid livery on 82044 which finished life with the number under the cab window - see Class 2 livery. Also 82027/9 had larger style bunker side numbers by 1962/3 (Fig 107) after repainting at Darlington North Road Works.

Green repaints seem to have started in 1957 and as might be expected it was the Western Region members of the class that were treated as they passed through Swindon Works. 82007 was noted at Swindon in January 1957 in unlined green livery, and later that year, on 3rd November, 82039 was noted ex-Works in green livery on the 12.38pm Andover-Swindon. Some later green repaints were carried out at Crewe.

There is some confusion over which engines were in lined green and those that were plain green. 82003 at least was lined green with the first lion and wheel totem despite its 1957 repaint date as was 82004. Some unlined green engines carried a larger version of the new type totem. Western Region examples also carried the 'yellow' route availability disc on the bunker side below the number.

82044 was noted at Shrewsbury ex-Crewe Works, 20th

Fig. 102 82001 outside Swindon Works when new in the first livery of lined black with small first crest April 1952. Power classification 3 above number. *G. Wheeler*

Fig. 103 82001 again outside Swindon Works following overhaul in lined green livery with the second crest and Power classification 3 above number also WR Yellow route indication disc below the number.

G. Wheeler

Fig. 104 82007 outside Swindon Works in unlined green livery with a large first crest 26 January 1957.   *G. Wheeler*

Fig. 105 82030 outside Swindon Works in lined green livery (as 82001 in Fig. 103) but with 2nd BR crest facing backwards 30 October 1959.
G. Wheeler

Fig. 106 82044 at Bristol Barrow Road MPD in 1965. This locomotive was the last of the class to be built. The livery from 4.63 was unique, being lined black except no lining of the coal bunker and the numbers were displayed below the cab windows.

David Tyreman collection

Fig. 107 82029 at Scarborough in lined black livery with second BR crest but with large numerals 4 September 1960.

F. Rowntree

April 1963 in lined black livery with cabside numerals. This repaint included the power classification '4' incorrectly above the number.

Livery Data

	Probable Green Paint Date	
82000	10.63	Probably lined.
82001	11.57	Lined by 11.57.
82002	4.58	Lined by 29.9.63.
82003	5.57 and 4.64	Lined. Second crest by 9.60.
82004	4.57	Lined by 8.58. Unlined large crest by 8.62.
82005	6.58	Lined by 9.62.
82006	8.57	Lined by 9.62. Unlined 'Economy Green' by 5.65.
82007	1.57	Unlined. Large first crest, later to second crest.
82009	5.57 and 4.64	Lined.
82020	9.58 and 7.61	Lined green 9.58. Plain green. Large emblem by 7.61.
82021	5.58 and 1961	Unlined green by 9.62 (possibly 1961).
82030	8.57 and 10.59	Lined.
82031	12.58	Unlined as at 1.62 - Large emblem.
82032	3.58 and 1961	Lined at 3.58 and lined by 5.65. (but unlined at 8.9.62 and 9.64)
82033	9.58	Unlined? 5.65. Reported lined on 16.11.58, and 30.9.64.
82034	9.58	Lined until at least 9.64, Unlined by 7.4.67.
82035	5.58	Unlined by 29.10.62.
82036	10.58	Lined.
82037	12.58	Lined.
82038	8.57	Lined.
82039	10.57 and 1961	Lined.
82040	1.59	Unlined green, large emblem by 6.62.
82041	12.57	Claimed as both lined and unlined/Observed lined at 4.58, 7.60, and 6.62 and 6.64 however.
82042	7.59	Lined green 29.10.62.
82043	1.59	Lined green.
82044	20.4.63*	Lined black and cabside numerals (black coal bunker sides) 20.4.63

*black paint date

3.6 Allocation and Duties

3.6.1 Distribution

For a relatively small class with a short life span these engines were allocated to a large number of sheds from as far south as Newton Abbot, the extremities of Wales (both North and South) and to the North East of England.
Specimen Allocations:-

December 1952

Tyseley	82000-9
Exmouth Jct.	82010-3/7-9
Eastleigh	82014-6

December 1954

Treherbert	82000
Barry	82001-9/30/1
Exmouth Jct.	82010/1/3/7-9/22-5
Eastleigh	82012/4-6
Nuneaton	82020/1
Kirkby Stephen	82026/7
Darlington	82028/9

December 1957

Shrewsbury	82000/7/31
Treherbert	82001/2/5/32-4
Barry	82003/35-7/9-44
Wellington	82004/6/9
Worcester	82008/30/8
Exmouth Jct.	82010/1/3/7-9/22-5
Eastleigh	82012/4/5/6
Wrexham Rhosddu	82020/1
Kirkby Stephen	82026/7
Darlington	82028/9

December 1959

Chester GW	82001-3/5/32/4/6
Bath Green Park	82004/41
Wellington	82006/9/30/8
Bristol Bath Road	82007/33/5/40/2-4
Worcester	82008
Exmouth Jct.	82010/1/3/7-9/22-5
Eastleigh	82012/4/5/6
Wrexham Rhosddu	82000/20/1/31/7
Scarborough	82026/8
Malton	82027/9
Templecombe	82039

December 1961

Machynlleth	82000/5/6/9/20/1/31/3/4
Templecombe	82001/2
Bristol Barrow Road	82003/35/7/9/40/3
Bath Green Park	82004/41
Bristol St.Philips Marsh	82007/38
Taunton	82008/30/42/4
Exmouth Jct.	82010/1/3/7-9/22-5
Eastleigh	82012/4-6
Scarborough	82026/7
Malton	82028/9
Shrewsbury	82032/6

December 1963

Machynlleth	82000/3/5/6/9/20/1/31-4
Taunton	82001/8/30/42/4
Exmouth Jct.	82002/40
Bath Green Park	82004/41
Bristol Barrow Road	82007/35-9/43
Nine Elms	82010-9/22-5
Bournemouth	82026-9

By 1st January 1966 there were only fourteen survivors allocated as follows:−

Patricroft	82000/3/9/31/4
Nine Elms	82006/18/9/23/4/6-9

The least moved engines of the class were 82010-4/7-9/22-5 all of which worked from three depots. 82030 had 14 different allocations during its working life, although this included a one month spell at Bristol (Bath Road) in April 1959 and a similar spell at Kidderminster in June 1959 during the period December 1955 to September 1959 when it was allocated to Worcester. The figure also included two spells at Bristol (Bath Road) and one at Bristol (Barrow Road) in

September 1960 following the transfer of the Bath Road allocation to Barrow Road.

It was originally intended to allocate the engines by Region as follows:- Southern 82000-9/20-9, Western 82010-9/30-54 and North Eastern 82055-62. When the order for 82045-62 was cancelled the plan was redrawn with 82000-9/30-44 scheduled to go to the Western Region, 82010-9 to the Southern and 82020-9 to the North Eastern. Even this plan was superseded as is shown in the following pages.

Fig. 108 82009 in light steam stands outside Machynlleth MPD. WR type lamp brackets are clearly visible.   *G.W. Sharpe & Co.*

Fig. 109 82014 at Eastleigh MPD 8 September 1956. There are visible signs of corrosion along the underside of the tank.   *E.W. Fry*

Fig. 110
82024 in Nine Elms Shed yard 5 May 1963. The yellow triangle under the number denotes that the locomotive has water treatment apparatus fitted.

Peter Groom

Fig. 111
82037 and two other unidentified Standard Class 3 locomotives are seen outside Bristol St. Philips Marsh MPD 13 July 1962.

Noel A. Machell

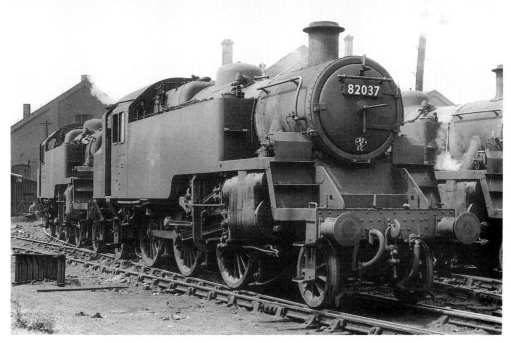

Fig. 112
82040 and 82044 at Taunton MPD 22 May 1964. A shed with a cramped layout set between two lots of running lines with bad underfoot conditions.

K.C.H. Fairey

3.6.2 London Midland Region

In the original allocation none of these engines were intended for the London Midland Region, but 82020/1 went, at first on loan and then permanently, to Nuneaton. They were newly turned out from Swindon Works in September and October 1954 and were, in fact, officially allocated to Exmouth Junction shed in line with the original plan prior to the cancellation of 82045-62. The change in plan meant that they were destined for the North Eastern Region and were allocated to Hull (Botanic Gardens) before the final decision to send them to Nuneaton.

Their main duties for 82020/1 were the Nuneaton - Coventry - Leamington Spa local passenger work, and were first noted in service at Coventry on 21st October 1954. This was not a class associated with the London Midland Region, and for many years they were the only examples of their class on the Region. Passenger services to Leamington from 2nd July 1956 were taken over by two-coach push-pull sets, using Ivatt Class 2 2-6-2T's based at Warwick (41227, 41228, 41285 and 41321) and Nuneaton (41226, 41322 and 41323). This made 82020/1 largely surplus to requirements at Nuneaton and they were transferred to the former GC shed at Wrexham Rhosddu. They only remained at Nuneaton for a little under two years; officially being transferred during the week ending 6th October 1956, although they did not leave Nuneaton until 15th October.

Other London Midland sheds to receive members of this class were Chester (LMS), following the closure of Chester (GW) shed, Bangor and Patricroft, although in the case of the last two sheds this was towards the end of steam working on British Railways. The former LMS sheds at Bristol (Barrow Road), Bath (Green Park) and Templecombe also received members of the class, but by this time these were under Western Region control.

During December 1961, the operation of seventeen of the two-car diesel multiple units at Bedford was suspended due to suspected flaws. Amongst a number of tank engines temporarily transferred there was 82029 from Malton shed, which was noted on Bedford - Hitchin and Bedford - Northampton workings. This engine was also noted on 14th September 1963 at Woodford Halse shed, on the former GC line, whilst being transferred from York to Guildford.

From September 1962, the responsibility for repairs of this class stationed on the Western Region, was transferred from Swindon to Crewe, which resulted in members of the class appearing in the Crewe area from time to time.

The three engines at Bangor, 82031/2/3, arrived in July 1964 from Machynlleth, but had little to do. By October 1964 they were in store, and 82033 had the legend 'spare' chalked on the bunker. A visit to Bangor on 20th April 1965 found 82032/3 present, although shortly afterwards 82033, along with 82031 were transferred from Bangor after a stay of only ten months; 82031 moved to Patricroft along with 82000/3/9/34, and 82033 moved to Nine Elms shed, where it joined other members of the class. However, its stay here was relatively short as it was withdrawn after a further five months, in September 1965. 82032 remained allocated to Bangor although it was seen at Willesden depot in steam on 25th April 1965, but was withdrawn on 1st May. It remained at Willesden until October 1965 when it was sold to Birds Commercial Motors at Morriston, near Swansea.

Besides 82031, Patricroft also received four other

Fig. 113 LNER J21 0-6-0 65033 running with A (Class 1) headcode hauling an RCTS railtour special past Stainmore signalbox 7 May 1960.
N.E. Stead

Fig. 114 LNER A5 4-6-2T 69838 at Stockton-on-Tees MPD in August 1956. *RAS Marketing*

members of the class, 82000/3/9/34, all ex-Western Region locomotives, and all transferred from Machynlleth depot. Again there was little work for them, although 82003 did work on the LCGB "Cotton Spinner" rail tour from Manchester Central on 16th April 1966, a rest from the regular duty as the Ordsall Lane pilot. All five were withdrawn at the end of 1966, 82009 in November, and the remainder in December. They were sold for scrap; 82009 to J.Cashmore, Great Bridge in February 1967 and the other four to J.Cashmore, Newport during April 1967. Their withdrawal removed all Standard tank classes from the London Midland Region.

3.6.3 North Eastern Region

As explained previously, of the ten locomotives originally allocated to the North Eastern Region, 82020-9, the first two were in fact sent to Nuneaton, and the next four went to the Southern Region, leaving only four available. A visit to Swindon Works on 17th October 1954 found 82026 nearing completion, and 82026/7 came out new from Swindon in November 1954 and went to Kirkby Stephen and 82028/9 were allocated new to Darlington in December 1954. All of these four remained on the North Eastern Region until they were transferred together to Guildford shed in September 1963.

When new their first duties were on the Darlington-Penrith trains which they worked until diesel multiple units took over on 6th January 1958. One such roster was the 2.55 pm Penrith to Darlington, a Darlington - Richmond - Darlington trip, and finally a return Darlington to Kirkby Stephen working at 10.30pm. These locomotives were well liked at both depots for duties on this exposed line and were a distinct improvement on the ageing ex-LNER J21 0-6-0's

previously used (Fig. 113). 82026/7 were also used on the Ulverston - Durham Miners Convalescent trains between Tebay and Durham on occasions.

82028/9 when not required for Stainmore line duties were used on Darlington - Saltburn/Crook/Tow Law and Richmond services, usually the haunts of A5's, A8's and L1's and ex-Works V1 and V3's (Figs. 114, 115).

On 24th May 1955 82026 was used by Kirkby Stephen to work a breakdown train to Smardale to re-rail Q6 0-8-0's 63355/73, which had run out of control on a Tebay - Kirkby Stephen goods train. 82028 was also seen on the 9.00am Sunderland - Newcastle local service on 3rd September 1956 (Fig. 116).

In January 1958 82026/7 were transferred to Darlington, but within the same month 82027 was transferred to West Hartlepool along with 82029. Here they worked local trains to Newcastle, Eaglescliffe and Northallerton. However, the stay was a relatively short one, as by September 1958 they had both been moved to Malton depot. Also in September 82026/8 moved from Darlington to Scarborough. Here they were used on station pilot duties, local passenger workings to Bridlington, Hull and Whitby, and on odd occasions one would be used on the morning goods to York and back.

On 19th January 1959 one of the worst sea fogs for 45 years made rails very greasy on the Scarborough - Whitby line. The following day 82028 carried out sanding operations from the Scarborough end with Fairburn 2-6-4T 42084 working from Whitby.

The Malton engines were popular with the men, and their power of acceleration was appreciated. As an example, on 4th April 1959, 82027 on the three-coach 4.00 pm from Malton, cleared Goathland summit in $11\frac{1}{4}$ minutes from the

Fig. 115
LNER A8 4-6-2T 69854 at Middlesbrough MPD on a date unknown.

S.J. Rhodes

Fig. 116 82026 at Smardale 24 May 1955 having worked the breakdown crane and tool vans from Darlington MPD in connection with the re-railing of Q6 0-8-0's 63355 and 63373. Note the crane-runner wagon has been set aside temporarily to facilitate re-railing operations.

J.W. Armstrong Trust

Levisham start, a very fast time. This, along with the 5.20am from Malton plus the 9.11am and 7.00pm from Whitby were the only remaining steam turns on the Whitby line. They were usually worked by 82027/9 from Malton shed, although Ivatt 2-6-2T's (41247/51/65) and 2-6-0's were used and on one occasion Stanier 2-6-4T 42553 from York appeared. The Class 3's were also used to assist Sunday Scenic Excursions between Whitby and Scarborough and vice versa following the closure of Whitby MPD on 6th April 1959. 82029 was noted piloting B1 61237 on one of these workings on 2nd June 1959, and on 14th June 82029 was noted again piloting another B1, 61383. They were also in use the following year as on 19th June 1960 82027 was seen with B1 61069 speeding up the 1 in 39 bank at Ravenscar.

On 2nd March 1960 82028 was sent on loan from Scarborough to Malton, but it was returned three days later with a badly cracked chimney, and was replaced by the other Scarborough Class 3, 82026. However, in June 1960 82027/9 were transferred to Scarborough, to join 82026/8 which were already there, so all four of the class allocated to the North Eastern Region were concentrated at the one depot. This situation prevailed until September 1961 when once again Malton depot received two members of the Class, 82028/9.

During their stay on the North Eastern Region, 82026-9 received overhauls at Darlington Works. The first occasion was in early October 1956 when 82029 was under repair. 82027 was noted there in May 1960, and 82029 in July of the same year.

At times there were problems with these engines. On 16th October 1961, 82028 (recently transferred to Malton shed from Scarborough) ran out of control whilst descending the two miles of 1 in 43 between Hawsker and Robin Hood's Bay with a ballast train. The train was turned into a dead-end siding at Robin Hood's Bay and demolished the buffer stops. The engine was running bunker first and came to rest with the leading brake van hard up against the smokebox door.

82027 brought the York breakdown crane the following day, but re-railing could not be achieved, and 82028 was left until possession of the single line could be obtained and two cranes used. The next re-railing attempt was the following Sunday 22nd October, when the line was specially opened to allow the York and Darlington breakdown cranes to reach the scene. Once the cranes were in position, the re-railing did not take long and 82028 was back on the rails by mid-day. It remained at Robin Hood's Bay until Wednesday 25th October when it was towed to Malton by BR Class 3 2-6-0 77013.

By the Autumn of 1962 there was little work left for 82026/7 at Scarborough, apart from pilot duties. However, 73168 dropped a fusible plug at Scarborough after working the 5.29am mail from York on 5th November 1962, so 82026 deputised on the pick-up goods to York and back. In November of that year 82026 was transferred to York on loan and 82027 was placed in store at Scarborough. On 2nd December 82026 was transferred to Low Moor shed at Bradford, although it had been intended originally that it should go to Sowerby Bridge shed near Halifax. In fact it was used for a week at Sowerby Bridge before being sent on to Low Moor. On 17th December 82027 was taken out of store and transferred back to Malton shed, from where it had been transferred to Scarborough some two and a half years earlier.

On 18th January 1963 all of the Birmingham Railway Carriage and Wagon Co. diesel multiple units on the Calder Valley services were withdrawn due to a number of fires in these units and 82026 was amongst various locomotives used on the replacement steam services.

Three days later there were heavy snow falls and 82027 was used to assist BR Class 3 2-6-0 77004 on snow-plough duties on the Scarborough - Whitby line. Amongst its other duties while at Malton, was its use on 26th February 1963 on a horse-box special from Malton as far as York, en route to Holyhead, and in April it was occupied with re-railing various locomotives at Scarborough, commencing on 16th April when D2103 was derailed in the Central Station yard. Three days later Class 5 45006 was derailed at Gallows Close Sidings and on 22nd April it assisted in the rerailing of B16 61448, also at Gallows Close.

Following the closure of Malton depot in April 1963, 82027-9 were transferred to York, although 82027 was actually working from Scarborough where it was noted later that month. When Scarborough shed closed in the following month, 82027 then moved to York to join 82028/9. At York they spent much of their time in store, although they were used from time to time on Officer's Specials. 82026 was also transferred in April from Low Moor shed to the former GNR shed at Copley Hill, Leeds, but by September 1963 all four engines were transferred to Guildford depot on the Southern Region. On 13th September 82027/8, both in steam, were noted running light through Doncaster, both showing large patches of rust, after their storage at York, and as already mentioned 82029 was in steam at Woodford Halse shed the following day. It also was en route to Guildford, and this may have been the only occasion of the class being seen on the former Great Central London extension.

3.6.4 Southern Region

Unlike the locomotives allocated to the Western and North Eastern Regions, which changed sheds frequently, some of the Southern Region locomotives were only stationed at two or three depots during the whole of their working life, particularly those at Eastleigh and Exmouth Junction.

82010-9 were turned out from Swindon Works between June and September 1952, and were originally all allocated to Exmouth Junction shed, where they replaced M7 0-4-4T's on the Exmouth and Bude branches and on local trains to Honiton and Axminster. One method of delivering them from Swindon was for the engine to work a Marston Sidings fish train to Newton Abbot and then to return the same day light engine to Exmouth Junction via Plymouth and Okehampton. 82011/2/4 all arrived at Exmouth Jct. shed in this manner. In addition to working local services, they also assisted the rostered station pilot at Exeter Central station on a Saturday and could be seen on other days banking the up evening freight trains from Exeter St. Davids to Central, turn and turn about with E1/R's 32124/35, 32695/7.

82014/5/6 moved to Eastleigh for use on the Fawley line goods duties after a short stay at Exmouth Junction and were joined in February 1953 by 82012. On Saturday 13th September 1952, the 2.25pm express from Plymouth Friary to Exeter Central comprised seven well-loaded corridor coaches and was hauled throughout by 82017, arriving about ten minutes late. Other cases are on record of this class of

Fig. 117 82027 with a local passenger train at Barnard Castle in March 1955. Note the timber supporting the signal gantry!

J.W. Armstrong Trust

locomotive being substituted for a West Country Pacific class locomotive on these trains.

The next batch of engines, 82020-5 were intended for the North Eastern Region, but when 82020/1 were turned out from Swindon in September and October 1954, they were re-allocated to the London Midland Region and worked from Nuneaton shed, to relieve a shortage of engine power there, as described in section 3.6.2 The remainder of the batch, 82022-5 went to Exmouth Junction shed in October and November 1954, in exchange for Fairburn 2-6-4T's 42072/3/93/4, which went to the North Eastern Region.

An unusual working was noted on 7th February 1955, when 82012 ran light from Eastleigh shed to Netley via Bevois Park and then entered the Royal Victoria Hospital sidings, where it picked up three War Department Ward Cars and a passenger brake-van provided by Netley. It left with these for Eastleigh via Bevois Park at 1.10pm.

The locomotives allocated to the Southern Region usually went to Eastleigh Works for repairs, 82017 was noted there in late September 1956, although in May 1955 82016, an Eastleigh engine, was noted at Newton Abbot Works.

On 16th April 1955, Battle of Britain class pacific 34058 caught fire at North Tawton. It was working the 8.20am

Plymouth Friary to Exmouth Junction freight, double-headed with another member of the class, 34057. 82022 came to the rescue and after the local fire brigade had dealt with the fire, 34057 proceeded with the train and 82022 brought the damaged locomotive forward to Exeter. On 7th August 1955 82014 (from Eastleigh) arrived at Nine Elms light engine and on 10th August 1955 was sent round to Bricklayers Arms repair shop for attention. It was noted at Brighton on 9th August 1955 and 12th August 1955 when it worked the 4.36pm to Tunbridge Wells West, probably the first visit of the class to the Uckfield line.

The class was sometimes used on excursion work, and on Whit-Monday 1958 82010 and 82019, both Exmouth Junction engines, were in the yard at Seaton, having brought excursions from Yeovil and Taunton down the branch from Seaton Junction. Another unusual turn was noted on 9th August 1958 at Shawford, when 82014, an Eastleigh engine, piloted U1 2-6-0 31613 on the three-coach 2.56pm Oxford to Southampton Terminus train.

During 1959 the Eastleigh members of the class continued to do stalwart work on freight trains on the Fawley branch. The 12.30 pm Fawley to Bevois Park freight presenting a stirring sight when worked double-headed by two 82xxx

106

Fig. 118 82027 with large numerals approaching Scarborough with a pick-up goods train on a date unknown.

David Tyreman Collection

Fig. 119 82028 making a spirited departure from Whitby passing Bog Hall signalbox with a train bound for Malton on a date unknown.

N.E. Stead collection

Fig. 120
82029 on the East Coast main line leaving Darlington with a Richmond train on a date unknown.

RAS Marketing

Fig. 121
82029 leaving Levisham with 4pm Malton to Whitby train 13 October 1961. The signal which is slotted in the foreground is of North Eastern Railway origin and is a two way signal giving access to and exit from Levisham Goods Yard. This location is now part of the North Yorkshire Moors Railway. *Hugh Ballantyne*

Fig. 122
A busy scene at Kirkby Stephen as 82029 pulls away with the 10.10am Darlington Bank Top to Penrith stopping passenger train on a date unknown.

David Tyreman Collection

locomotives with up to fifty loaded wagons (Fig. 129). By 1962 diesel locomotives had begun to infiltrate the Fawley line, and on 5th June that year 82014 was seen piloting D6505 on the 6.55pm Eastleigh - Fawley freight. They also worked Andover to Swindon Town MSWJR duties.

On the passenger side, good work was still being done by members of the class from Exmouth Junction shed. On 4th August 1962, 82025 worked the Bude portion of the "Atlantic Coast Express" and the 5.32pm Bude to Halwill Junction local.

In November 1962, several members of the class were transferred to Nine Elms depot in south London, and were used on Waterloo - Clapham Junction empty carriage workings replacing M7 0-4-4T's and E4 0-6-2T's (Fig. 72). Apart from the ECS workings, their duties also included local goods work and van trains to Reading.

Following this initial allocation, other members of the class followed during 1963, 1964 and 1965, not only from Southern Region sheds but also from the Western and North Eastern Regions. On 11th May 1963, a total of eight members of the class, 82010/4/5/7-9/22/5, were noted at Clapham Junction during a four hour period. A visit to Nine Elms depot on 19th April 1964 found 82010-2/4/5/7/8/23/5 in residence. By April 1965 some withdrawals had taken place, but the following members of

the class were allocated to Nine Elms; 82005/6/18-24/26-9/33, a total of fourteen locomotives out of a remaining class total of thirty-two!

Not all of the class finished up at Nine Elms however, for instance 82001, resplendent in lined-green livery, ex-Crewe Works, arrived at Exmouth Junction shed in August 1963 having been transferred from Hereford depot on the Western Region. As an ex-Western Region engine it still retained its WR style lamp irons so that the Southern discs had to be hung instead of mounted.

In September 1963, 82026-9 were transferred from the North Eastern Region to Guildford, where they only remained for a short time before moving on to Bournemouth at the end of 1963. Here their duties were to replace the ageing M7 0-4-4T's on the Bournemouth West and Brockenhurst via Ringwood service. This passenger service was withdrawn on 2nd May 1964, and the last train, the 7.08pm from Bournemouth and 8.56pm return from Brockenhurst were worked by 82028. However, their work in the area continued on the Swanage and Lymington branches, again former M7 duties.

May 1964 saw the withdrawal of the first of the class from the Southern Region, 82012/4 from Nine Elms depot, followed in June by 82013 from the same depot. However, all were still working in early August, although 82014 at least was

Fig. 123 82019 eases into London Waterloo station with empty milk tanks from Vauxhall 4 August 1965. A main line locomotive will then come onto the other end for the journey back to the West of England.
Courtney Haydon

Fig. 124 82005 with a train of empty vans for Clapham Junction carriage sidings leaving London Waterloo station 14 May 1965. *Peter Groom*

stopped by 14th, but 82013 was still shunting at Raynes Park on 31st of the month!

Three condemned locomotives from the Western Region (no doubt providing spare parts for working members of the class) were cut up at Eastleigh Works during May and June 1964, 82002/8/43, 82008 having had the dubious honour of being the last steam locomotive to be cut up at the Works by British Railways.

During the Autumn of 1964, 82030/5/9/42/4, also ex-Western Region locomotives, spent some time at Exmouth Junction shed, which by now was a Western Region shed following boundary changes in January 1963.

The last steam working on the Romsey - Andover line, an enthusiasts special, on 6th September 1964, was hauled by 82029 an ex-North Eastern Region engine. The train started at Winchester Chesil, and running via Southampton Central, Romsey and Andover Junction, terminated at Ludgershall.

82024/8 were on loan to Redhill shed from September 1964 and worked various duties to Tonbridge, Eastbourne and Heathfield, and 82024 even arrived at Hastings on 17th December, possibly the first of the class to appear there.

A visit to Nine Elms depot on 21st March 1965 found eleven members of the class on shed viz. 82010/6-9/22/4/6-9; on the same day Feltham shed contained 82023. In May 1965 82005/6/33 were transferred to Nine Elms; the first two from Machynlleth and the other from Bangor shed, and they joined the other class members in the ECS workings to and from Clapham Junction also transferring milk tanks to and from Vauxhall.

During 1965 and 1966 withdrawal of the class continued

Fig. 125 82010 with empty carriages from an up express passing Vauxhall en route from London Waterloo to Clapham Junction carriage sidings 7 August 1963. The Houses of Parliament can be seen in the distance.
Peter Groom

Fig. 126 (above)
Activity at Clapham Junction, 82010 waiting to leave with empty stock for London Waterloo whilst 82023 approaches with empty coaches from Waterloo station 10 August 1964.

Courtney Haydon

Fig. 127
82014 shunting empty coaching stock at Southampton Central 28 February 1959. *E.W. Fry*

Fig. 128
82015 passing Southampton Central with a Fawley branch goods train 21 April 1956. *E.W. Fry*

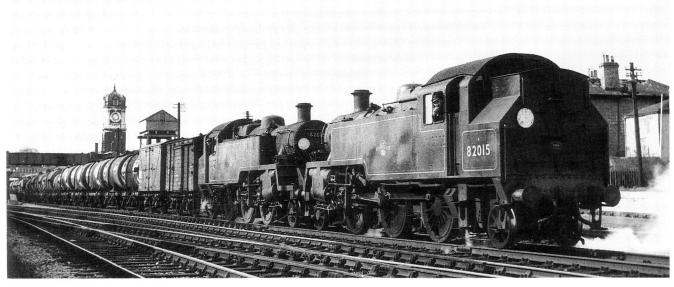

Fig. 129 82015 and 82016 working the loaded 12.30pm Fawley, consisting of Esso tanks, to Bevois Park yard through Southampton Central station 3 March 1960.
Courtney Haydon

Fig. 130 Another photograph of the 12.30pm Fawley to Bevois Park goods train passing Southampton Central 31 May 1960. This time it is hauled by 82014 and 82012. The third locomotive is WD 0-6-0ST 106 (formerly 75040) being transferred from the Marchwood Military Port Railway to the Longmoor Military Railway. Coupling rods have been removed for the journey.
Courtney Haydon

Fig. 131
82028 at Corfe Castle with a Wareham to Swanage train 18 August 1964.   *Brian Hilton*

Fig. 132 82027 on the Swanage branch with a Wareham to Swanage train passing under Holme Lane bridge, 18th May 1964.

Rodney Lissenden

Fig. 133
82013 leaving Exeter Central station with the 6.12pm train to Exmouth, Sunday 9 July 1961
David Tyreman collection

Fig. 134 82017 leaving Exmouth for Exeter Central 13 October 1959.

R.C. Riley

Fig. 135 82030 leaving Padstow with the 11.05am train to Okehampton 19 September 1964.

Courtney Haydon

apace, although 82023 met with a sudden end on 28th September 1966 when it ran into a 2-HAL electric unit No. 2626, which was standing at signals between Waterloo and Vauxhall. Luckily the electric unit was empty so there were no casualties. 82023 managed to run under its own steam to Nine Elms depot, but it had sustained a fractured steam pipe at the right-hand front end in the collision, and was condemned a few days later.

The few survivors of the class hung on at Nine Elms, their last duties included week-end ballast trains from Wimbledon, but their main job to the end was the empty stock workings. By 1967 only 82019/29 remained in service, and on 24th June 82019 even made it to Marylebone station for a filming contract, and worked the 4.38pm Kensington Olympia to Clapham Jct. on 7th July 1967 (The last day of steam operation on this service). 82029 bowed out on the 7.18 am Waterloo-Salisbury on 8th July, and the following day both locomotives were withdrawn and were noted in store at Salisbury on 29th of the month.

3.6.5 Western Region

82000-2 were turned out from Swindon Works in April 1952, work having started on 82001 in December 1951. They were allocated to Tyseley depot in Birmingham, and were followed by 82003-7 in May 1952 and by 82008/9 in June. Their work in the Birmingham area was mainly on the Moor Street to Stratford-on-Avon service, some being shedded at

Stratford, which was a sub-shed of Tyseley. They were also used on Snow Hill tunnel end pilot duties.

82000 first ran to Dauntsey on 4th April 1952. It was handed over for traffic duties on 8th April acting as Swindon shed pilot but the next day ran a scheduled passenger service to Didcot and back, but was returned to the Works on 17th April to have a firehole deflector plate fitted.

When newly out of works these engines performed running-in turns in the Swindon area. 82004 was noted on the 6.02pm Didcot-Swindon on 19th and 20th May 1952 having worked a stopping train from Bristol Temple Meads to Weston-super-Mare on 10th May. 82002/3/5 were also noted on the 5.45pm Bristol-Swindon via Badminton on various dates in May 1952. On 16th May 82003 worked the 9.25am Swindon to Bristol Temple Meads and the 1.10pm return, both via Bath. By this time 82002 had already completed its running in work being noted at Banbury.

In the event the class did not stay in the Birmingham area for long. In September 1953 82000-9 were transferred to South Wales where they were allocated to Barry and Treherbert depots for working the Barry-Penarth-Cardiff-Rhondda Valley passenger services. They were replaced at Tyseley by ex-GWR 0-6-2T's 6614/20/68/9 and 51xx 2-6-2T's.

The final fifteen locomotives in the class, 82030-44, were also destined for the Western Region. Swindon turned out the first two of this order in December 1954 and the final engine of this batch and the class was put into service in

Fig. 136
82010 and 82017 bank a London Waterloo bound express away from Exeter St. Davids station for the steep gradient of 1 in 37 to Exeter Central Date Unknown.

David Tyreman collection

August 1955. Eleven of this batch, 82030-2/5/6/39-44, joined the other members of the class at Barry for use on the South Wales even interval services and the allocation was further increased by 82037 which had been initially allocated to Swansea Victoria when delivered in April 1955 but had moved to Barry a few months later. 82033/4 went new to Newton Abbot in January 1955 and were joined there by new 82038 in May.

Even this early in their history transfers were taking place and 82004/9/31 moved to Newton Abbot to join other members of the class where they were mainly employed on Torquay line trains, which changed engines at Newton Abbot. However some worked throughout from Exeter to Kingswear, for example 82009 was noted on an Exeter St. Davids-Kingswear duty in the summer of 1955. They were also employed on Dainton banking duties and soon after their arrival in Devonshire they were regularly employed on the Moretonhampstead branch in place of 51XX 2-6-2T's. On August bank holiday in 1955 the passenger trains were worked by 82002/34 with 82009 on the goods on this branch line. 82033 was noted working the Kingsbridge branch trains on 7th May 1955. These were normally 45XX 2-6-2T duties (Fig. 137).

On 26th March 1955 82009 had the honour of being the first standard type seen on the Calne branch when working a service to Chippenham, probably following a visit to Swindon Works.

In August 1955 Sugar Loaf tunnel, on the Central Wales line, was closed for repairs and a shuttle service operated between Llanwrtyd Wells and Craven Arms. 82030/1 from Shrewsbury shed and 82037 from Swansea Victoria appeared on this duty although by now the latter was allocated to Barry.

By mid-1956 the Newton Abbot allocation consisted of nine members of the class. Of these, 82001/2/5/32/3 moved to Treherbert in exchange for 51XX 2-6-2T's, and 82004/6/9/34 moved to Wellington. The transfer of 82004

in July 1956 was the first of the class to be allocated there; this was shortly joined by 82006/9/34 and between them they worked the Much Wenlock branch and local services to Wolverhampton, Crewe and Shrewsbury. 82034 was only briefly at Wellington, as in September 1956 it joined other members of the class at Treherbert.

Locomotives allocated to Shrewsbury shed worked the Severn Valley services to Bridgnorth, Bewdley and Kidderminster, and 82030 was also noted on a local working from Banbury to Oxford on 29th April 1956. The Worcester locomotives, 82030/8, had turns on Gloucester locals and later worked between Oxford and Kingham. They were also noted on the Midland line on Worcester (Shrub Hill) to Gloucester services. In September 1957 82008 was transferred from Kidderminster to Worcester to join 82030/8, although it was briefly sent back to Kidderminster in November before being officially transferred to Worcester again in December.

82000 was in Swindon Works on 12th August 1956, and in early 1957, on 24th February, 82007 was noted at the Works in green livery and fitted with a Great Western style hand rail on the top of the boiler in front of the dome. Although engines allocated to the Western Region usually went to Swindon Works for overhaul, light repairs were also carried out at Barry Works. For example 82043 in May 1957 and 82002 in June of that year, and several of the class received attention there until the works ceased locomotive repairs on 24th December 1959. The responsibility for the repair of all Western Region examples passed to Crewe Works from September 1962.

During 1958 diesel multiple units started to appear in South Wales and some of these displaced 82XXX engines from Barry shed, these moving to Valley sheds north of Cardiff. Many of these were soon moved to Bristol (Bath Road) shed and at the end of May 1958 were seen on shed. In June 1958 the final members of the class, 82040-4 left the South Wales area for Bristol (Bath Road), having been

Fig. 137
GWR Churchward 2-6-2T 4577 stands in the 'Middle Road' at Torquay station 13 August 1955.

R.K. Taylor

replaced by DMUs, less than five years since their allocation to the area for the even interval services.

Duties included the Cheddar Valley branch and several other local turns in the Bristol area, including Wells services. They also strayed further afield with duties such as the 7.48am Bristol (Temple Meads) to Taunton, 10.28am Taunton to Minehead and the 12.20pm Minehead-Taunton, which operated in the 1958 Winter timetable. However, some only stayed briefly, as 82001/2/3/5/32/4/6 moved to Chester (GW) shed after only two months at Bristol. One of the Bristol engines, 82009, was noted passing Reading on an early morning freight on 15th June 1960, the first time that a member of the class had been recorded there since the new allocations in 1954.

Wolverhampton Works also dealt with members of the class prior to its closure, as did other ex-GWR works. On 1st March 1959, 82004 was receiving attention at Wolverhampton, and in October of that year 82005/44 were also present. 82030 was being repaired at Caerphilly in October 1960, and 82020 was noted under repair in the former Cambrian Railways Works at Oswestry in November 1960.

Although allocated to Bristol Barrow Road depot 82042 was seen on a stopping train between Swansea and Port Talbot in October 1960. In September 1961 this locomotive was transferred to Neyland shed in company with 82008/44 where they displaced ex-GWR 45XX 2-6-2T's on local passenger and freight duties in West Wales. Another member of the class to work in West Wales was 82003, which was allocated to Carmarthen shed for a short time in March 1962.

The Cambrian line (transferred to LMR control January 1963) was another haunt of the class, 82005/6/31/3/4 being sub-shedded at Portmadoc, but when this depot closed on 10th August 1963 the class operated from Pwllheli, the residents by then being 82003/9/20/1/33.

The main sphere of operation was between Machynlleth and Pwllheli with stopping trains on three-day cyclical rosters. With an overall speed limit of 55mph, 19 stations and 12 halts in 57 miles, this was exactly the type of work that the class had been designed for. They also had freight and Talerddig

banking duties having been drafted in to replace the Dukedog 4-4-0's and 45XX 2-6-2T's, but they also ousted the Standard Class 2 78XXX series from this line and the ex-GWR 54XX and 74XX 0-6-0PT's on Aberystwyth pilot duties.

Taunton engines worked the Barnstaple services in 1962 whilst the turntable on the branch was out of action. By the middle of that year the Somerset & Dorset line stopping passenger trains were being worked by 82001/2 from Templecombe shed and 82004/41 from Bath Green Park. In October 1961, 82044 (returned from Neyland depot in West Wales), moved to Taunton and was working Yeovil trains; this duty remaining with the class until 1964 with 82035 from Yeovil shed also participating.

The Bristol engines worked various services, and on 21st July 1963, 82036 worked the RCTS Gloucestershire rail tour. A regular summer Saturday working in 1963 was the 1.07pm Calne to Weston-super-Mare, worked throughout, 82040 being noted on this turn on 7th September.

By 1964 Exmouth Junction shed had become part of the Western Region and examples of the class working from there were 82042 on the 7.43am Exmouth - Exeter St. Davids on 8th July 1964 and 82035 with the 6.20pm Padstow - Okehampton the following day, whilst 82040 was noted on the 6.40am Barnstaple - Taunton and 11.25am return, also on 8th July.

The first Western Region withdrawals also took place in 1964 with 82002 (Exmouth Junction), 82008 (Taunton) and 82043 (Bristol Barrow Road) all being condemned in February, and 82007, also from Bristol Barrow Road, being withdrawn in June. Despite these withdrawals new opportunities were opened up for the heavier final batch with authorisation being given in 1964 for them to work the Portishead branch.

A visit to Bristol Barrow Road shed produced 82001/36-8 on 17th January 1965, Exmouth Junction was host to 82030/9/40/2 on 8th May of that year, shortly before they were moved to Gloucester (Horton Road) depot where they spent most of their time in store. 82030 was condemned on 2nd August 1965, but was reinstated to Bath Green Park shed

Fig. 138 82031 assisting GWR Manor Class 4-6-0 7819 with an up express train near Talerddig in August 1963.   *Real Photographs Ltd*

Fig.139 82022 with Down pick-up goods train approaching Towyn station 16 July 1962.   *Rodney Lissenden*

on 22nd November, only to be withdrawn again on 3rd January 1966. 82044, withdrawn at the same time as 82030, was reinstated, again to Bath Green Park, on 20th September, but lasted only until replaced by the reinstatement of 82030. Throughout this time 82041 remained active being noted on the 10.10am Bath Green Park to Bristol service on 1st January 1966, although officially notified as withdrawn in December 1965.

Cambrian line duties had continued, 82006 coupled to 75002 worked the 12.07pm Morfa Mawddach - Dovey Junction three-coach train on 31st December 1964. On 10th April 1965 Aberystwyth shed (a sub-shed of Machynlleth by that time) closed, but remained as a signing-on point. Shunting duties there were still performed by an 82xxx which ran light from Machynlleth each day. However with the introduction of diesel multiple units on the line 82005/6/20/1 were transferred to the Southern Region in May 1965.

By the end of 1965 all the remaining members of the class on the Western Region had been officially withdrawn and sold as scrap to contractors for cutting up, the working of 82041 noted above probably being a final duty for the class.

Fig. 140 82006 pauses at Minffordd station with 8.20 Dovey Junction to Pwllheli 3 August 1964. The Ffestiniog Railway crosses the BR line
by the bridge over the train's second coach.
Courtney Haydon

Fig. 141 82033 shunting goods wagons at Afon Wen station in July 1963.   *J.B. Arnold*

Fig. 142 82000 taking water at Leamington Spa General station on an unknown date at the head of a Birmingham Division local passenger train.   *David Tyreman Collection*

3.6.6 Storage

Several of the class also spent periods in store. Those recorded officially in store are as follows:-

82001 22.1.61 - 9.4.61, 22.11.65 - 29.11.65
82002 22.1.61 - 7.4.61
82003 22.1.61 - 9.4.61
82005 22.1.61 - 9.4.61
82020 17.9.63 - 11.10.63
82030 31.7.65 - 14.8.65
82031 8.11.64 - 21.3.65, 3.11.65 - 10.12.66
82032 12.3.61 - 7.4.61, 1.11.64 - unknown
      (Withdrawn 1.5.65)
82033 1.11.64 - unknown (Withdrawn 19.9.65)
82034 22.1.61 - 9.4.61, 1.11.65 - unknown
      (Withdrawn 10.12.66)
82035 5.10.63 - 28.12.63, 19.6.65 - 6.8.65
82036 12.3.61 - 7.4.61
82039 12.6.65 - 2.7.65
82040 5.10.63 - 30.11.63, 19.6.65 - 2.7.65
82042 12.6.65 - 3.9.65
82044 31.7.65 - 14.8.65

3.6.7 Allocation Summary

82000 4.52 Tyseley, 7.53 Barry, 9.53 Treherbert, 11.55 Shrewsbury, 2.59 Wrexham (Rhosddu), 1.60 Machynlleth, 3.65 Patricroft.

82001 4.52 Tyseley, 9.53 Barry, 6.55 Newton Abbot, 9.56 Treherbert, 3.58 Bristol (Bath Road), 7.58 Chester (GW). P4.60 Chester (LMS), 4.61 Templecombe, 8.62 Hereford, 4.63 Exmouth Jct., 12.63 Taunton, 5.64 Exmouth Jct., 5.64 Bristol (Barrow Road), 11.65 Bath (Green Park).

82002 4.52 Tyseley, 9.53 Barry, 6.55 Newton Abbot, 9.56 Treherbert, 4.58 Bristol (Bath Road), 7.58 Chester (GW). P4.60 Chester (LMS), 4.61 Templecombe, 9.62 Hereford, 4.63 Exmouth Jct.

82003 5.52 Tyseley, 9.53 Barry, 3.58 Bristol (Bath Road), 7.58 Chester (GW), P4.60 Chester (LMS), 4.61 Bristol (Barrow Road), 2.62 Bristol (St. Philips Marsh), 3.62 Carmarthen, 6.62 Machynlleth, 3.65 Patricroft.

82004 5.52 Tyseley, 9.53 Barry, 4.55 Newton Abbot, 7.56 Wellington, 6.59 Shrewsbury, 8.59 Wellington, 10.59 Bath (Green Park).

82005 5.52 Tyseley, 9.53 Barry, 6.55 Newton Abbot, 8.56 Treherbert, 5.58 Bristol (Bath Road), 7.58 Chester (GW). P4.60 Chester (LMS), 4.61 Shrewsbury, 7.61 Machynlleth, 10.61 Shrewsbury, 11.61 Machynlleth, 4.65 Nine Elms.

82006 5.52 Tyseley, 9.53 Barry, 6.55 Newton Abbot, 7.56 Wellington, 1.60 Bristol (Bath Road), 9.60 Bristol (Barrow Road), 2.61 Machynlleth, 4.65 Nine Elms.

82007 5.52 Tyseley, 9.53 Barry, 6.55 Treherbert, 11.55 Shrewsbury, 5.58 Leamington, 6.58 Wellington, 7.58 Wrexham (Rhosddu), 8.58 Worcester, 9.58 Bristol (Bath Road), 9.60 Bristol (Barrow Road), 2.61 Bristol (St. Philips Marsh), 10.62 Bristol (Barrow Road).

82008 6.52 Tyseley, 9.53 Barry, 8.55 Kidderminster, 8.57 Worcester, 11.57 Kidderminster, 12.57 Worcester, 7.61 Machynlleth, 9.61 Neyland, 10.61 Taunton.

82009 6.52 Tyseley, 9.53 Barry, 4.55 Newton Abbot, 8.56 Wellington, 6.59 Shrewsbury, 8.59 Wellington, 1.60 Bristol (Bath Road), 9.60 Bristol (Barrow Road), 10.60 Bristol (St. Philips Marsh), 2.61 Machynlleth, P4.65 Patricroft.

82010 6.52 Exmouth Jct., 9.62 Eastleigh, 11.62 Nine Elms.

82011 7.52 Exmouth Jct., 9.62 Eastleigh, 11.62 Nine Elms.

82012 7.52 Exmouth Jct., 3.53 Eastleigh, 12.62 Nine Elms.

82013 7.52 Exmouth Jct., 9.62 Eastleigh, 11.62 Nine Elms.

82014 8.52 Exmouth Jct., 8.52 Eastleigh, 12.62 Nine Elms.

82015 8.52 Exmouth Jct., 10.52 Eastleigh, 12.62 Guildford, 3.63 Nine Elms.

82016 8.52 Exmouth Jct., 10.52 Eastleigh, 12.62 Guildford, 3.63 Nine Elms.

82017 8.52 Exmouth Jct., 9.62 Eastleigh, 11.62 Nine Elms.

82018 9.52 Exmouth Jct., 9.62 Eastleigh, 11.62 Nine Elms.

82019 9.52 Exmouth Jct., 9.62 Eastleigh, 11.62 Nine Elms.

82020 9.54 Hull (Botanic Gardens), 9.54 Nuneaton (on loan), P11.54 Nuneaton, P10.56 Wrexham (Rhosddu), 1.60 Shrewsbury, 3.60 Machynlleth, 4.65 Nine Elms.

82021 10.54 Hull (Botanic Gardens), P10.54 Nuneaton (on loan), P11.54 Nuneaton, P10.56 Wrexham (Rhosddu), 1.60 Shrewsbury, 3.60 Machynlleth, 6.64 Bangor, 6.64 Machlynleth, 4.65 Nine Elms.

82022 10.54 Exmouth Jct., 9.62 Eastleigh, 11.62 Nine Elms.

82023 10.54 Exmouth Jct., 9.62 Eastleigh, 11.62 Nine Elms.

82024 10.54 Exmouth Jct., 9.62 Eastleigh, 11.62 Nine Elms.

82025 11.54 Exmouth Jct., 9.62 Eastleigh, 11.62 Nine Elms.

82026 11.54 Kirkby Stephen, 1.58 Darlington, 9.58 Scarborough, 12.62 Low Moor, 3.63 Copley Hill, 9.63 Guildford, 1.64 Bournemouth, 9.64 Nine Elms.

82027 11.54 Kirkby Stephen, 1.58 Darlington, 1.58 West Hartlepool, 9.58 Malton, 6.60 Scarborough, 12.62 Malton, 4.63 York, 9.63 Guildford, 1.64 Bournemouth, 9.64 Nine Elms.

82028 12.54 Darlington, 9.58 Scarborough, 9.61 Malton, 4.63 York, 9.63 Guildford, 1.64 Bournemouth, 9.64 Nine Elms.

82029 12.54 Darlington, 1.58 West Hartlepool, 9.58 Malton, 6.60 Scarborough, 9.61 Malton, 4.63 York, 9.63 Guildford, 1.64 Bournemouth, 9.64 Nine Elms.

82030 12.54 Barry, 5.55 Shrewsbury, 12.55 Worcester, 4.59 Bristol (Bath Road), 5.59 Worcester, 6.59 Kidderminster, 7.59 Worcester, 10.59 Wellington, 1.60 Bristol (Bath Road), 9.60 Bristol (Barrow Road), 10.61 Taunton, 6.64 Exmouth Jct., 6.65 Gloucester (Horton Road), Withdrawn 2.8.65, Reinstated 22.11.65, 11.65 Bath (Green Park).

82031 12.54 Barry, 1.55 Laira, 2.55 Newton Abbot, 5.55 Shrewsbury, 1.59 Wrexham (Rhosddu), 1.60 Machynlleth, P7.64 Bangor, P4.65 Patricroft.

82032 1.55 Barry, 6.55 Newton Abbot, 9.56 Treherbert, 3.58 Cardiff (Cathays) located Radyr, 4.58 Bristol (Bath Road), 7.58 Chester (GW), P4.60 Chester (LMS), 4.61 Shrewsbury, 8.61 Machynlleth, 11.61 Shrewsbury, P11.62 Machynlleth, P7.64 Bangor.

82033   1.55 Newton Abbot, 9.56 Treherbert, 3.58 Cardiff (Cathays) located Radyr, 4.58 Bristol (Bath Road), 9.60 Bristol (Barrow Road), 12.60 Machynlleth, 7.64 Bangor, 4.65 Nine Elms.

82034   1.55 Newton Abbot, 8.56 Wellington, 9.56 Treherbert, 3.58 Cardiff (Cathays) located Radyr, 4.58 Bristol (Bath Road), 7.58 Chester (GW), P4.60 Chester (LMS), 4.61 Machynlleth, 4.65 Patricroft.

82035   3.55 Barry, 4.58 Bristol (Bath Road), 9.60 Bristol (Barrow Road), 2.62 Bristol (St. Philips Marsh), 10.62 Bristol (Barrow Road), 3.64 Exmouth Jct., 9.64 Yeovil.

82036   4.55 Barry, 3.58 Cardiff (Cathays) located Radyr, 4.58 Bristol (Bath Road), 7.58 Chester (GW), P4.60 Chester (LMS), 4.61 Machynlleth, 11.61 Shrewsbury, 7.62 Bristol (St. Philips Marsh), 10.62 Bristol (Barrow Road).

82037   4.55 Swansea (Victoria), 6.55 Barry, 6.56 Abercynon, 7.56 Barry, 4.58 Cardiff (Cathays) located Radyr, 4.58 Bristol (Bath Road), 6.58 Bath (Green Park), 2.59 Wrexham (Rhosddu), 1.60 Bristol (Bath Road), 9.60 Bristol (Barrow Road), 2.62 Bristol (St. Philips Marsh), 10.62 Bristol (Barrow Road).

82038   5.55 Newton Abbot, 9.55 Shrewsbury, 11.55 Worcester, 9.59 Wellington, 1.60 Bristol (Bath Road), 9.60 Bristol (St. Philips Marsh), 10.62 Bristol (Barrow Road).

82039   5.55 Barry, 4.58 Bristol (Bath Road), 2.59 Templecombe, 9.60 Bristol (Barrow Road), 2.62 Bristol (St. Philips Marsh), 10.62 Bristol (Barrow Road), 3.64 Exmouth Jct., 5.65 Gloucester (Horton Road).

82040   5.55 Barry, 6.58 Bristol (Bath Road), 9.60 Bristol (Barrow Road), 2.62 Bristol (St. Philips Marsh), 10.62 Bristol (Barrow Road), 10.63 Exmouth Jct., 7.65 Gloucester (Horton Road).

82041   6.55 Barry, 6.58 Bristol (Bath Road), 3.59 Bath (Green Park).

82042   6.55 Barry, 7.58 Bristol (Bath Road), 10.60 Bristol (Barrow Road), 9.61 Neyland, 10.61 Taunton, 6.64 Exmouth Jct., 5.65 Gloucester (Horton Road).

82043   6.55 Barry, 6.58 Bristol (Bath Road), 9.60 Bristol (Barrow Road), 1.62 Taunton, 2.62 Bristol (St. Philips Marsh), 10.62 Bristol (Barrow Road).

82044   8.55 Barry, 6.58 Bristol (Bath Road), 9.60 Bristol (Barrow Road), 9.61 Neyland, 10.61 Taunton, 6.64 Exmouth Jct., 5.65 Gloucester (Horton Road), Withdrawn 2.8.65, Reinstated 20.9.65, 10.65 Bath (Green Park).

Fig. 143 82004 stands in Stratford-on-Avon at the head of a stopping train to Birmingham Moor Street 22 May 1952.   *NRM York*

Fig. 144 82004 with a local train of Bulleid SR Stock at Mangotsfield 17 March 1962   *G.W. Sharpe & Co.*

Fig. 145 82009 cresting the summit of 1 in 75 climb westwards out of Cranmore hauling the 3.28pm from Witham to Yatton 23 April 1960. The rear carriage is a former GWR slip coach.   *Hugh Ballantyne*

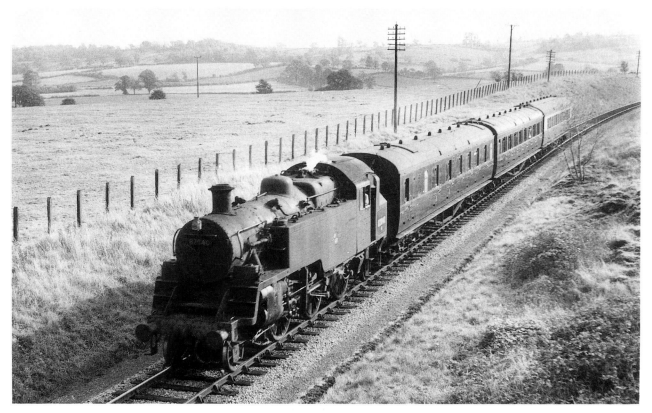

Fig. 146 82040 with the 10.50am Frome to Bristol Temple Meads via Radstock seen between Clutton and Pensford. This route was known as the North Somerset line. 31 October 1959.   *Hugh Ballantyne*

Fig. 147 82040 in a quiet rural setting passes Whitchurch Halt located between Brislington and Pensford working the same train on same day seen in Fig. 146. Note the 'Pagoda' shelter which was GWR Standard design for halts.   *Hugh Ballantyne*

Fig. 148 82042 passes Pensford and Bromley Collieries Signalbox 13 September 1959 with 4.50pm (Sundays) Bristol Temple Meads to Frome. The sidings were disused by this date and the train was photographed on the last Sunday before the line was closed which was in the pre-Beeching era. *Hugh Ballantyne*

Fig. 149 82042 leaving Yeovil Town station with the 4.25pm from Taunton bound for Yeovil Pen Mill 1 June 1963. *Courtney Haydon*

3.7 Service Performance

No logs of performance have been found relating to runs with members of this class. Within the section on the Class 4 tanks there is a short note comparing the fastest start to stop time on the Chester to Birkenhead line which shows 82xxx to have a fair turn of speed (Page 63).

During the running-in tests with these engines 82000 was reported as achieving a speed of 69 mph on the 9.28am Swindon - Gloucester on 5th June 1952 with 72 mph on the return (load 200 tons), whilst 76 mph was reached on 17th July when working a test special to Stoke Gifford during investigations into excessive for and aft oscillation.

However, more typically the class were found on rural branch lines and an excerpt from an article in the June 1960 Trains Illustrated by R.C.Riley describes some of a days duty for a member of this class.

'From Exmouth I continued my journey on the 9.52am to Tipton St. Johns, consisting of four corridor coaches, two of which were through coaches for Waterloo. The engine was Class 3 2-6-2 tank 82013, with Driver Sampson (Exmouth Junction) and its roomy draught-free cab was a striking contrast to the spartan comfort offered on the Drummond M7 tank.

Immediately after the signalbox, where the token was collected, the branch curves away from the Exeter line, climbing at 1 in 50 on a long viaduct that carries it across the back of the town. At Littleham, a pleasant little station with three camping coaches, the token was exchanged. From here to the summit the line is relatively straight, with the grade gradually hardening from 1 in 126 to 1 in 50. After the main road overbridge the line enters woodland and the engine quietly coasts down a 1 in 50 grade with frequent brake applications to keep speed below the 40 mph permitted maximum.

Budleigh Salterton, five miles from Exmouth, is another crossing station, and in common with most stations on the Devon branches it is clean and tidy, and has a well-kept garden. The line continues falling at 1 in 50 through rolling downland, then after a short level stretch there is an easy climb to East Budleigh. In this delightful country setting two camping coaches were in the siding and three miles on at Newton Poppleford there were two more. Between these two stations the line climbs at grades varying from 1 in 100 to 1 in 300, and for the whole distance it is close to the River Otter, crossing it twice (and, incidentally, three times more before the main line is reached). Beyond Newton Poppleford the Sidmouth line can be seen across the valley as it falls sharply towards Tipton St. Johns. The Budleigh branch climbs a brief stretch of 1 in 150 to the junction of the two lines immediately south of the platform.

At Tipton St. Johns 82013 ran round the train and then hauled it back to the branch, leaving the up platform clear for the train from Sidmouth. This consisted of another 82xxx Class 3 2-6-2 tank and four coaches, two of which would work through to Exeter, the other two being for Waterloo. As soon as this train came to rest, No. 82013 shunted the two Exmouth - Waterloo coaches on, and then ran into the down platform, whence it would take its remaining two coaches back to Exmouth'

3.8 Modifications as a result of Service Experience

Data from engine record cards shows other less obvious modifications than those referred to earlier.

Lamp Brackets.

82000-9/30-44 were recorded with GW-type lamp brackets from new. 82020/1 although on the Western Region for a while were not modified.

82000 was noted on 18th November 1965 with all brackets to Standard pattern except the front central one.

82010-9/22-5 were fitted with the Southern Railway pattern lamp brackets, and 82026-9 were modified to this type after transfer from North Eastern to Southern Regions in late 1963.

AWS

This appears to have been fitted during service rather than being new on any engine. Reported were:-

Undated.	82010-4/6-8/22-33/5-8/40-4.
12.59	82019.
9.60	82015.
	82029 subsequently had AWS removed, date unknown.

Two Extra Washout Plugs fitted
Undated. 82010/2-4/8/22/4.

Briquette feeder fitted
Undated. 82010-8/22-5/8/9.

UK Piston Rod Packing (Mod No. 8895)

Undated.	82000/3/7/12/3/23/30.
1.57	82024.
3.57	82018/9.
5.57	82025.
9.57	82011.
5.59	82022.

Injector Overflow Pipe modification
Undated. 82012/3/22/4/7/8.

Fitting of Safety Clips to Brake Hanger Pins

12.56	82015.
3.57	82018.

Weather shield fitted
Undated. 82001.

Speedometer
Thought to be fitted new from 82022 onwards.

9.62	82003.
Fitted to 82020 by 8.61.	
Undated.	82001/21.

82029 reported as not fitted when withdrawn.

Continuous Blowdown Apparatus

2.56	82020/1 when allocated to Nuneaton.
Undated.	82029/38/9.

Cylinder Cock Gear controlled atomiser steam
82010-34/7/8/40-4.

G&C Atomiser with lower ball check valve removed
Undated. 82000-4.

Two Southern Region fusible plugs, tool iron brackets and tank lifting brackets
1.57 82024 only.

Fig. 150 82000 outside Swindon Works after attention with GWR County Class 4-6-0 1001 21 October 1956.

Philip J. Kelley

Ejector Isolating Elements, two start thread spindles
Undated.   82030/8/9.

3.9 Running Costs and Maintenance

The only details available, and then only to 1957, on maintenance costs appeared in the book in 1966 by E.S.Cox on the Standard Locomotives which quoted 6.73d/mile for the engine as a whole and 0.99d/mile for the boiler.

Except for the Western Region, locomotives were dealt with at Crewe, Darlington and Eastleigh Works, which continued to work to their long-established practices.

The Western Region initially dealt with 82000-9/20/1/30-44. It used its full range of workshops with engines recorded as visiting Barry, Caerphilly, Newton Abbot, Oswestry, Swindon and Wolverhampton (Stafford Road) Works. Swindon was the only Works to carry out heavy general overhauls, but boilers were changed at Wolverhampton, and also, in the case of 82037, at Caerphilly.

Locomotives allocated to the Southern Region always went to Eastleigh Works for attention. As noted in section 3.4 dealing with boilers this component was on occasions moved from one works to another for refitting.

82026-9 received all their heavy maintenance at Darlington but did visit Eastleigh for light repair upon transfer to the Southern Region.

Swindon's final dealings with the class for heavy maintenance appears to have been 82040 in 1962 whilst Wolverhampton ceased work with 82033 in May 1961. Thereafter Crewe took up the maintenance of the non-Southern Region allocated engines with 82000/1/3/5/6/

9/30/4/6/8/42/3/4 being recorded, 82043 being the first on 9th September 1962 and 82000 noted in the Erecting Shop on 10th November 1963.

Mileages to Heavy General overhauls varied considerably, but some very high figures were recorded.

82001	191,301	82017	232,570
82002	189,442	82018	178,647
82003	180,574	82019	169,415 and 280,000 approx.
82005	188,117	82020	187,948
82010	255,049	82021	196,278
82011	208,897	82023	196,756
82013	256,335		

The highest individual yearly mileage noted on the scant records was 51,533 for 82005 in 1957.

The Southern Region engines appear to have run the highest mileages with 82010/1/3/7/8 being around 420,000 miles at the end of 1963. 82019 was at 453,000 at its heavy general overhaul at the end of 1964, and with three years of service still ahead of it, a total of 500,000 miles was almost certainly achieved.

82020 however clearly led a different life with only approximately 200,000 miles to its credit at the end of 1963 with a likely final total of around 250,000. This is partly due to the fact that during its first two years, when allocated to Nuneaton, there was little regular work, and it spent some of its time as shed pilot, which entailed relatively low mileages.

82030 was another low mileage engine having covered only 216,309 miles at December 1963, and 82038 had run just 201,403 miles at that time.

3.10 Construction, Withdrawal and Disposal Information

Class totals were as follows:–

12.52 and 12.53	20
12.54	32
12.55 to 12.63	45
12.64	35
12.65	14
12.66	2
12.67	nil

Withdrawal commenced in February 1964 with 82002/8/43 from Exmouth Jct., Taunton and Bristol (Barrow Road) respectively, and the class was rendered extinct on 9th July 1967, which was also the end of steam operation on the Southern Region, when 82019/29 were withdrawn from Nine Elms shed.

The engine with the shortest life span was 82043 (only 8 years 8 months) and 82019 the longest with 14 years 10 months.

None of the class survived into preservation although 82003/31/4 remained at Cashmore's Yard at Newport until October 1968 before being cut up.

Fig. 151 82014 is in a poor run down state at Nine Elms MPD 17 July 1964. A shunter's pole is seen on the front buffer beam which indicates it had been used on freight work or shunting locomotive coal wagons at the shed.

Peter Groom

Fig. 152 82001 bereft of smokebox numberplate and in a disgraceful condition at Bristol Barrow Road MPD on 9 October 1965.

Courtney Haydon

Disposal Details

Loco	New	With drawn	Sold	Contract No	Cut Up
82000	4.4.52	10.12.66		4.67	J.Cashmore, Newport. Ex-Patricroft 19.4.67 with 82003/31/4
82001	18.4.52	31.12.65	2.2.66	17/230/522T/190	J.Cashmore, Newport. Ex-Bath
82002	28.4.52	2.64			Eastleigh Works from WR w/e 23.5.64
82003	2.5.52	10.12.66		4.67	J.Cashmore, Newport 5.67. Ex-Patricroft 19.4.67 with 82000/31/4. Cut up 10.68
82004	14.5.52	1.10.65	9.11.65	16/230/522T/160	Birds Commercial Motors, Bridgend. (R.&S. Hayes) Ex-Bath (Green Park) at Severn Tunnel Jct. 11.2.66
82005	16.5.52	19.9.65	12.65		Birds Commercial Motors, Risca 2.66. Ex-Nine Elms, at Severn Tunnel Jct. 11.2.66
82006	27.5.52	18.9.66	12.66		J.Buttigieg, Newport. Ex-Nine Elms
82007	30.5.52	29.6.64	29.9.64	230/522T/17	J.Cashmore, Newport. Ex-Bristol (Barrow Road) 12.64
82008	5.6.52	2.64			Eastleigh Works week ending 13.6.64. Ex-Taunton
82009	13.6.52	5.11.66	2.67		J.Cashmore, Great Bridge 2-3.67
82010	25.6.52	24.4.65	8.65		Birds Commercial Motors, Morriston 8-9.65. Ex-Nine Elms
82011	1.7.52	30.8.64	11.64		George Cohen, Cransley Sidings, Kettering. Ex-Nine Elms 11.64
82012	4.7.52	31.5.64	11.64		George Cohen, Cransley Sidings, Kettering. Ex-Nine Elms 11.64

Disposal Details continued

Loco	New	With drawn	Sold	Contract No	Cut Up
82013	9.7.52	14.6.64	11.64		George Cohen, Cransley Sidings, Kettering. Ex-Nine Elms 11.64
82014	1.8.52	31.5.64	11.64		George Cohen, Cransley Sidings, Kettering. Ex-Nine Elms 11.64
82015	13.8.52	6.12.64	2.65		J.Cashmore, Newport 4.65. Ex-Nine Elms
82016	21.8.52	25.4.65	10.65		Birds Commercial Motors, Morriston 10.65. Ex-Nine Elms
82017	8.8.52	25.4.65			Birds Commercial Motors, Morriston 8.65. Noted 31.7.65 at Bristol Barrow Road Shed en route to South Wales
82018	8.9.52	10.7.66			J.Buttigieg, Newport 8-9.66. Ex-Nine Elms, at Swindon Works Yard 7.10.66
82019	26.9.52	9.7.67			Birds Commercial Motors, Risca 11.67-3.68.
82020	29.9.54	19.9.65			Birds Commercial Motors, Risca 1.66
82021	6.10.54	17.10.65			J.Buttigieg, Newport 1-3.66. Ex-Nine Elms
82022	15.10.54	17.10.65			J.Buttigieg, Newport At yard 8.4.66. Ex-Nine Elms
82023	22.10.54	2.10.66			J.Cashmore, Newport 2-3.67. Ex-Nine Elms
82024	29.10.54	30.1.66			George Cohen, Morriston 5.66
82025	5.11.54	9.8.64			George Cohen, Cransley Sidings, Kettering 12.64
82026	12.11.54	26.6.66			J.Buttigieg, Newport 10.66 Ex-Nine Elms 9.66, at Swindon 6.10.66
82027	23.11.54	9.1.66			Cox and Danks, Park Royal 2-4.66. Ex-Nine Elms
82028	2.12.54	4.9.66			J.Cashmore, Newport 12.66-2.67. Ex-Nine Elms
82029	13.12.54	9.7.67			Birds Commercial Motors, Risca 11.67-1.68
82030	21.12.54	31.12.65★	11.2.66	17/230/522T	J.Cashmore, Newport 2-4.66. Ex-Bath (Green Park)
82031	30.12.54	10.12.66			J.Cashmore, Newport 4-6.67. Ex-Patricroft
82032	1.1.55	1.5.65			Birds Commercial Motors, Morriston 10.65. Ex-Willesden
82033	13.1.55	19.9.65			Birds Commercial Motors, Risca 12.65-2.66
82034	28.1.55	10.12.66			J.Cashmore, Newport 4.6.67. Ex-Patricroft
82035	3.3.55	6.8.65	6.9.65	16/230/522T/136	J.Cashmore, Newport 10-11.65. Ex-Yeovil
82036	1.4.55	21.7.65	25.8.65	16/230/522T/130	J.Cashmore, Newport 10-11.65. Ex-Bristol (Barrow Road)
82037	20.4.55	25.8.65	24.9.65	16/230/522T/142	J.Cashmore, Newport 10.65. Half cut up 1.11.65. Ex-Bristol (Barrow Road)
82038	4.5.55	6.9.65	6.6.65	16/230/522T/136	Birds Commercial Motors, Bridgend (R.&S. Hayes) 10.65. Ex-Bristol (Barrow Road)
82039	10.5.55	2.7.65	25.8.65	16/230/522T/130	Birds Commercial Motors, Long Marston 10.65. Ex-Gloucester
82040	19.5.55	2.7.65	25.8.65	16/230/522T/130	Birds Commercial Motors, Long Marston 10.65. Intact 14.11.65 Ex-Gloucester
82041	17.6.55	31.12.65	11.2.66	17/230/522T/190	J.Cashmore, Newport. On site 7.5.65. Ex-Bath (Green Park)
82042	20.6.55	6.9.65	6.6.65	16/230/522T/136	Birds Commercial Motors, Bridgend (R. & S. Hayes) 10.65-2.66. Ex-Gloucester.
82043	27.6.55	2.64			Eastleigh Works w/e 9.5.64. Ex-Bristol (Barrow Road)
82044	12.8.55	18.11.65~	30.12.65	16/230/522T/179	J.Buttigieg, Newport 1-2.66. Ex-Bath (Green Park)

★ 82030 was withdrawn on 2.8.65 and reinstated on 22.11.65 to Bath (Green Park)

~ 82044 was withdrawn on 2.8.65 and reinstated on 20.9.65 to Bath (Green Park)

4.   CLASS 2   2-6-2T   84000-29

Fig. 153 84000 after overhaul seen in Crewe Works yard 29 August 1960.

Courtney Haydon

4.1 Purpose

At the time of railway nationalisation in 1948 there were still a large number of country branch lines worked by push-pull trains. The principle of this method of working is that the locomotive remains at the same end of the train regardless of direction of travel and when pushing is controlled from the "cab" at the end of the leading coach, such trains were, in some areas, referred to as auto-trains or motor trains. To work in this manner locomotives and coaches had to be fitted with suitable remote control apparatus. Some trains worked with the locomotive in the middle with a "driver's cab" at each end.   Three control systems were in use on British Railways using respectively vacuum, compressed air and mechanical linkage. Locomotives equipped to operate push-pull trains were referred to as motor or auto-fitted.

The motive power for many of these services was frequently a pre-grouping 0-4-4, 0-4-2, 2-4-2 or 0-6-2 tank engine. The Great Western 0-4-2T was designed for such work. The Southern Railway employed 0-4-4T's of LSWR and SECR origin and LBSCR 0-4-2T's. The LNER also had various elderly motor-fitted tank engines.

Only on the LMS had an attempt been made to build a modern branch line locomotive although even on that system there were still a great many ex-Midland and Caledonian Railways 0-4-4T's to be seen. However, H.G.Ivatt, who had been appointed CME of the LMS in February 1946, introduced a small modern 2-6-2 tank engine for light duties,

this being derived from his class 2-6-0 tender design which incorporated a large number of labour saving devices. 130 of these locomotives were constructed between 1946 and 1952, all having been built at Crewe except the final ten which were constructed at Derby. The class was numbered 41200-41329 (Fig. 154).

Once the motive power types for the Standard range had been decided the team led by R.A.Riddles selected the Ivatt 2-6-2 tank design as the basis for their Standard Class 2.

4.2 Construction

The parent office for the design was Derby with work on specific parts being carried out by Brighton, Doncaster and Swindon. The Ivatt design was changed to incorporate the various standard fittings, such as boiler feed clack valves in place of the LMS type top-feed, on the type BR8 boiler. External regulator rodding was employed. As with earlier designs a self cleaning smokebox was fitted as well as a rocking grate and self emptying ashpan. A speedometer was fitted on all locomotives from new but not AWS.

Vacuum-controlled push-pull gear was fitted to all locomotives. This operated through auxiliary regulator valves fitted in each steam pipe from the superheater header to the cylinders. These were single seated poppet valves and were operable from a compartment at the opposite end of the train via supplementary train pipes and controls.

84000-19 were fitted with Downs sanding gear.

Fig. 154 LMS Ivatt 2-6-2T 41285 at Leamington shed 8 July 1962. The Standard 84XXX Class had many similarities with these locomotives.

Noel A. Machell

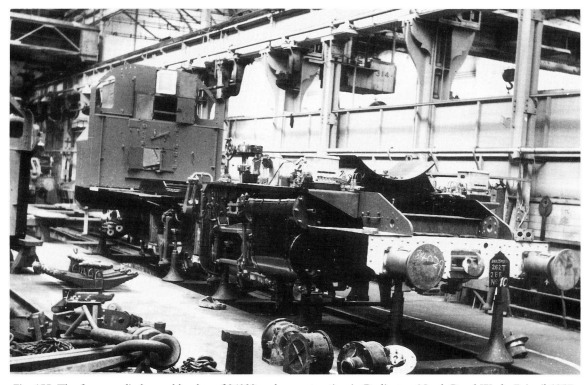

Fig. 155 The frames, cylinders and bunker of 84029 under construction in Darlington North Road Works 7 April 1957.

D.B. Swale

Photographic evidence suggests that 84000-19 were built with fluted coupling rods and that 84020-9 were built with rectangular rods.

The cab layout was as originally proposed for all of the Standard classes.

Construction was in two batches, namely

1953 84000-19 Crewe (originally scheduled for Darlington).

1957 84020-9 Darlington.

84029 was the last tank engine to be constructed and was also the last steam engine built at Darlington North Road Works (Fig. 155).

Various costs of construction have been quoted. Official figures give an estimated cost for the Crewe-built engines of £9575 with an actual figure of £13104, whilst the Darlington construction was costed at £9350 with an actual figure of £17924. E.S.Cox quotes actual costs of £12246 and £16511 for Crewe and Darlington respectively whilst the Engine History Cards quote 84000-17 at £12750, 84018/9 at £12751 and 84020-9 at £16570.

84000-19 were built under Lot No. 229, Order authority RE5262 of 4th January 1951 to diagram SL/2VP/1, the boilers were to diagram SL/2VT/1.

The frames for the first engines were laid out at Crewe Works in February 1953, 84000/1 being noted complete in No. 9 shop in mid-July of that year. 84000-19 went new to the London Midland Region and 84020-9 to the Southern Region.

4.3 Dimensions and Data

Information not shown on the diagram (Fig. 156) is as follows:-

Piston Swept Volume (1 cylinder)	5,132 cu in
Piston Valves (Walschaert)	8" diameter
steam lap	1⁵/₁₆"
maximum travel	5.92"
lead	¹/₄"
exhaust clearance	nil
Maximum Cut-off	78%
Travel at 20% cut-off	3.23"
Clearance Volume as % of piston swept volume	Not quoted by E.S.Cox
Maximum Piston thrust	42,765 lbs
Steam Chest volume between valve heads	Not quoted by E.S.Cox
Steam Chest volume as % of piston swept volume	Not quoted by E.S.Cox
Revolving Masses-weight per cylinder	1,172lbs
Reciprocating Masses - total weight/cylinder	564lbs
- percentage balanced	50
- unbalanced weight/cyl	282lbs
Ratio unbalanced weight/cylinder to total engine weight	1:526
Firebox Volume	83 cu ft
Heating surface	101 sq ft
Water Surface at half glass	63 sq ft
Volume steam above half glass	53 cu ft
Heating surface tubes	924 sq ft
Total heating surface including firebox	1025 sq ft
Superheater surface area	124 sq ft
Free area through tubes	Large 0.98 sq ft
	Small 1.76 sq ft
	Total 2.74 sq ft

(The diagram shows a Total figure of 2.77 sq ft)

Area through large tubes as % of Total	36.5
Total free area as % of grate area	15.9
A/S ratio - Large Tubes	1:343
- Small Tubes	1:369

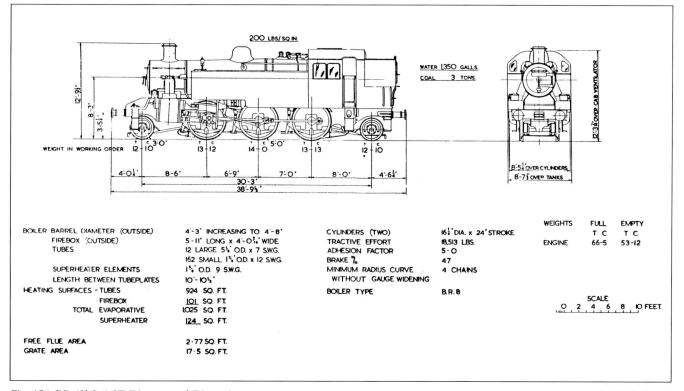

Fig. 156 BR '2' 2-6-2T Diagram and Dimensions.

British Railways

Steam pipe in boiler - Bore		5"	
Cross sectional area		19.6 sq in	
Regulator full open area		21.5 sq in	
Superheater Elements Total Area		11.1 sq in	
Steam pipes to Cylinders Total Area		22.1 sq in	
Blast Pipe Cap diameter		4 $^1/_8$"	
Blast Pipe area		13.4 sq in	
Chimney Throat	- diameter	1' 0"	
	- area	0.79 sq ft	
Chimney throat area as % of grate area		4.4	
Height Blast Pipe Cap to Chimney Throat		2' 5$^1/_2$"	
Taper of Chimney		1 in 14	
Tractive Effort at 85% Boiler Pressure		18513 lbs	

Weights	Planned	Actual as per diagram
Full		LD/9/14/6
		dated 27 June 1961
Leading Wheels	12t	12t 10c
Leading Coupled Wheels	13t	13t 12c
Centre Coupled Wheels	13t 10c	14t 0c
Trailing Coupled Wheels	13t	13t 13c
Trailing Bogie Wheels	12t	12t 10c
Total Full	63t 10c	66t 5c
Total Empty	50t 8c	53t 12c
Adhesion Factor	4.7	5.0

4.4 Boilers

The idea of interchangeability of parts was practised with this class in as much as some boilers were exchanged with those built for the Class 2 (78XXX) tender engines (Fig 187). The BR8 boiler was common to both classes.

Boilers 1107-27 and 1355-64 were built for the engines with 1369 and 1501/2 constructed as spares. However, at least 1272/94/7 also appeared on the class.

Although the level of records is better for this class than the other tank designs, they are also incomplete and other boiler changes are likely to have taken place.

Those known are as follows:-

84000	New	1108,	1297	1.9.60
84001	New	1109,	1369 (Spare)	4.12.57
84002	New	1113,	1120 (06)	2.9.58
84003	New	1110,	1114 (13)	4.1.61
84004	New	1116,	1118 (05)	17.4.59
84005	New	1118,	1127 (19)	12.9.58
84006	New	1120,	1502 (Spare)	3.4.58
84007	New	1119,	1501 (Spare)	26.9.58
84008	New	1121,	1116 (04)	13.2.60
84009	New	1111,	No record of change	
84010	New	1122,	1294	13.10.60
84011	New	1124	No record of change	
84012	New	1117,	1108 (00)	21.10.60
84013	New	1114,	Removed by 10.60	
84014	New	1112,	1122 (10)	11.11.60
84015	New	1115,	1123 (16)	10.1.61
84016	New	1123,	1117 (12)	28.11.60
84017	New	1125,	1272	30.5.60
84018	New	1126,	1112 (14)	22.12.60
84019	New	1127,	1109 (01)	17.7.58
84020-9	New	1355/64 in sequence with no changes recorded.		

4.5 Livery

The livery was the standard lined black BR livery. The Crewe built engines received the Lion and Wheel crest when new (Fig 157), but the Darlington-built engines always carried the later type of BR totem (Fig 158). It is thought that all the early build received the later type as they passed through works.

Unlike the 80XXX and 82XXX classes the lining out was not applied to the bunker side, the number being applied beneath the cab window similar to the LMS Ivatt 2MT 2-6-2T's.

84015 was noted in unlined black following a late repaint and it is possible that others also were turned out similarly.

4.6 Allocation and Duties

4.6.1 Distribution

The main spheres of activity for the class were on the London Midland Region in Lancashire, North Wales and around the Burton/Leicester area, also the Eastern Division of the Southern Region. The North Eastern Region gained a locomotive because of boundary changes with 84009 at Royston and the former Western Region depot at Oswestry also received members of the class, but none was ever allocated to the Scottish or Eastern Regions.

Specimen Allocations:-

December 1954

Wrexham Rhosddu	84000-4
Bedford	84005
Burton-on-Trent	84006-8
Royston	84009
Lees (Oldham)	84010/2/5
Low Moor	84011/3/4
Fleetwood	84016-9

December 1956

Birkenhead	84000/3
Chester Northgate	84001
Bletchley	84002/4
Bedford	84005
Burton-on-Trent	84006-8
Royston	84009
Rose Grove	84010/1
Bank Hall	84012
Lees (Oldham)	84013/4/9
Fleetwood	84015-8

December 1958

Birkenhead	84000/3
Chester Northgate	84001
Bletchley	84002/4
Bedford	84005
Burton-on-Trent	84006-8
Royston	84009
Lower Darwen	84010-2
Lees (Oldham)	84013/4
Skipton	84015
Fleetwood	84016-8
Bolton	84019
Ashford	84020-4
Ramsgate	84025-9

Fig. 157
84000 not very clean but in lined black livery displaying the first BR crest at Birkenhead MPD when allocated there. The bunker is unlined.
David Tyreman collection

Fig. 158
84021 when new recently outshopped from Darlington North Road Works stands outside Darlington shed 31 March 1957. It is strange that the former NER A8 4-6-2T recently repainted during overhaul sports the first BR crest whilst 84021 displays the second type of crest which was introduced in 1956. *Brian Hilton*

December 1960	
Birkenhead	84000/1/3
Bletchley	84002/4
Bedford	84005
Wellingborough	84006-8
Hull Dairycoates	84009
Fleetwood	84010/6-8
Lower Darwen	84011/2
Bolton	84013/4/9
Skipton	84015
Ashford	84020-9

December 1962	
Warrington	84000
Bletchley	84002/4
Rhyl	84003

Kentish Town	84005/29
Annesley	84006/7/27
Leicester	84008
Llandudno Jct.	84001/9/20
Fleetwood	84010-2/6/7/8
Bolton	84013/4/9/25/6
Skipton	84015/28
Crewe Works	84021-4

84018 held the record for the least moved member of the class having only two homes. It was allocated new to Bury in November 1953, moving to Fleetwood in May 1954 where it remained until its withdrawal in April 1965. 84005 moved the most times with eleven transfers involving five different depots, including three spells each at Bedford and Wellingborough. (The full class allocations are shown at 4.6.4.)

4.6.2 London Midland Region

After a short initial allocation to Crewe North depot, for running in, mainly on Northwich push-pull turns, 84000/1/2 were transferred to Plodder Lane shed (Bolton) for local passenger work between Bolton Great Moor Street-Manchester Exchange and Kenyon Jct. 84003/4 were turned out from Crewe in September 1953 and joined the first three at Plodder Lane. 84005 was also placed into traffic in September at Bedford. The next three, 84006/7/8, went to Burton-on-Trent depot for use on the "Tutbury Jenny", as the Burton-Tutbury push and pull was called; they were also used on Burton-Leicester trains. 84009 was allocated to Royston replacing MR 0-4-4T 58066 (Fig. 159) and was normally used on the Cudworth-Barnsley Court House services, also Sheffield Midland push-pull turns, sharing with Ivatt 2-6-2T's 41281/2.

The next six locomotives 84010-5 went to Low Moor depot when new in September and October 1953, working to Leeds Central and Halifax, and the remaining four locomotives of the Crewe-built batch, 84016-9, arrived at Bury shed in October. All of these were used on various secondary passenger duties in East Lancashire including Bury-Bacup push-pull services.

84000-3 were moved from Plodder Lane to Wrexham GC in March 1954, initially shown as on loan, with 84004 following in October. This was due to the withdrawal of passenger services from Bolton (Great Moor Street) to Manchester (Exchange) and Kenyon Junction lines, and the subsequent closure of the former LNWR shed at Plodder Lane on 10th October 1954. In May 1954 84016-9 were transferred to Fleetwood from Bury, for work on local services between Blackpool North, Poulton and Fleetwood sharing duties with Ivatt 2-6-2T's 41260/1/2/80. 84019 was exhibited at the International Railway Congress at Willesden in the same month following repairs to collision damage at Crewe Works.

84010/5 moved to Lees (Oldham) in September 1954 from Low Moor, and 84012 followed in October for working the Greenfield and Delph services. With the closure of Plodder Lane and Bacup MPD's in October the remaining allocation of both these sheds went to Patricroft, but 84004 was shown as being allocated to Denbigh, a sub-shed of Rhyl, and 41287 moving to Patricroft in exchange. However, this may have only been a temporary assignment as 84004 was shown officially as allocated to Wrexham (Rhosddu) in the same month.

The Bedford engine 84005 was often used on the push-pull service between Bedford and Hitchin and from Bedford to Northampton. In June 1956, due to engine shortages, it was used as a pilot engine to Black 5 45137 on the 8.05am express from Bedford to Luton and London St. Pancras, and it was also noted being used as pilot to Ivatt 2-6-2T 41269 on a heavy goods on the Hitchin branch.

Fig. 159 Former Midland Railway 0-4-4T 58068 employed as a Station Pilot at Sheffield Midland Station on a date unrecorded.

David Tyreman collection

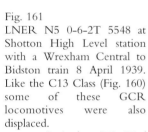

By July 1956 the first engines of the class 84000/1/2/4 had left Wrexham, and were at Chester Northgate and Birkenhead sheds, where they worked trains on the Wirral lines. 84000/3 were regular performers on the Hooton-Ellesmere Port-Helsby push-pull trains in the autumn of 1956. 84003 moved to Birkenhead in August 1956, and at the same time 84002/4 were transferred to Bletchley. Here they worked the push-pull services to Buckingham, where they connected with diesel single units 79900/1, which had started working the service to Banbury Merton Street on 13th August 1956, and also the Wolverton - Newport Pagnell branch trains. 84004 also worked to London replacing electric multiple units between Watford and Harrow on Sundays due to engineering works during September 1956.

84012 was noted working as the station pilot at Liverpool Exchange on 24th December 1956 whilst allocated to Bank Hall shed.

This class of locomotive was particularly suitable for railtours, and on 24th September 1955, 84006 of Burton shed, was used for the RCTS East Midlands Branch rail tour from Nottingham to Kegworth and Kingston-upon-Soar. Again on 27th April 1957, the same engine worked a three-coach push-pull set on an SLS special train from Nottingham which toured the Nottinghamshire coalfield (Fig. 162).

The Crewe-built locomotives normally went to Crewe for overhaul in their early days and in March 1957 84003 was undergoing repair, including new cylinders, for serious damage sustained in an accident on the Wirral.

When 84009 was allocated to Skipton in 1955 it was utilised on Worth Valley services on at least one occasion and was noted again at Haworth in June 1957.

84009, allocated to Royston shed, changed ownership from the London Midland to the North Eastern Region when boundary changes were made in 1957. It was subsequently moved from Royston to Hull Dairycoates shed where it shared Paragon Station pilot duties with an Ivatt Class 2 2-6-2T 41262. During its time on the NER its maintenance was the responsibility of Darlington Works where it was noted outshopped on 4th December 1960. It is believed to be the only one of the first batch to visit Darlington.

Fig. 162
84006 at Ollerton Colliery stopped during the SLS Notts. Coalfield tour 27 April 1957. Detraining at such a location would certainly be frowned upon today!

R.J. Buckley

Fig. 163
Former LYR 2-4-2T 50714 at Ilkley station 30 August 1952.
J.W. Armstrong Trust

Fig. 164
84013 at the head of a local train on a very wet and murky day at Oldham Clegg Street.
Brian Hilton

Fig. 165
84005 entering Piddington station with a Northampton Castle to Bedford Midland push-pull train 15 February 1962. *K.C.H. Fairey*

By April 1957, the first of the Darlington-built engines had been turned out and although destined for Ashford, 84020 arrived ex-Works at Bedford on 14th April and was promptly put to work on the Bedford to Bletchley push-pull service. After two weeks at Bedford, it resumed its journey to Ashford via Stewarts Lane.

In May 1957, 84011/2 which had been for some time at Rose Grove working push-pull services to Colne, having replaced former LYR 2-4-2T's (Fig. 163), were transferred to Lower Darwen and took over shunting duties in the goods yards. They were also used on the Sunday push-pull trains from Blackburn to Clitheroe and Hellifield. 84015/6 were transferred from Fleetwood to Lancaster at the end of June 1957 and were put to work on the Lancaster Castle to Morecambe Euston Road push-pull service. 84013 of Lees MPD was noted on the 6.04 pm Stockport Edgeley to Oldham Clegg Street service on 10th August 1957 (Fig. 164).

By 1958 many branch lines were being worked by the then new diesel multiple units and railbuses but there were often cases of failure in their early days, particularly at Bedford, where 84005 had to take over with a push-pull set (Fig. 165).

In February 1959, 84007/8 were transferred to Wellingborough from Burton-on-Trent in exchange for ex-LMS Ivatt 2-6-2T's 41277 and 41328. Once at Wellingborough they were used on the Higham Ferrers branch during its last days. They were also used on the Wellingborough - Northampton push-pull service along with Ivatt 2-6-2T's, and were also to be seen working local trains to Kettering. The Higham Ferrers branch closed to passenger traffic on 13th June 1959 and 84007/8 worked the trains on the last day, the mid-afternoon trains had 84007 sandwiched between two coaches in front and two behind, well filled with passengers making their final journey (Fig. 166).

In November 1959 84004 was still working from Bletchley to Buckingham with the two coach push-pull service, but the Banbury - Buckingham - Bletchley services were scheduled for closure on 31st December 1960, and on that day 84002 worked the final passenger service over these lines. However, in January 1961 both 84002/4 could still be

seen on the 7.28 am Leighton Buzzard to Luton and the 8.20 am return, although the Hatfield to Dunstable service was by then totally operated by diesels.

One of the Wellingborough engines, usually 84006, was to be found at Seaton shed, where it worked the branch line to Uppingham. Seaton had been a sub-shed of Peterborough Spital Bridge and when this closed, of Market Harborough, which in turn subsequently became a sub-shed of Leicester.

In the latter part of 1961, the ten Darlington-built engines 84020-9 were transferred from the Southern Region to the London Midland Region in exchange for Ivatt 2-6-2T's 41320-9.

During December 1961, seventeen of Bedford's two-car diesel sets were taken out of service due to suspected flaws, and during this time 84005 was amongst a number of engines which shared the Hitchin and Northampton branch work from Bedford. 30th December 1961 was the last day of the Bedford - Hitchin service. Apart from the first round trip, the service was worked by 84005 plus two auto coaches, M15863M and M24319M. In January 1962 84006 was briefly allocated to Bedford MPD, and was working the Bedford - Northampton service along with Ivatt Class 2 41224.

In April 84002 was used as the Bletchley station pilot, and on 30th June 1962, it was in charge of the morning Leighton Buzzard to Dunstable train on the last day of its passenger service. However, by August of the same year it was noted stored out of use at Bletchley, together with eight LNWR 0-8-0's.

If this class of engine had any claim to fame, it must have been for working the last train on country branch lines and several examples have been noted in this text.

84000, allocated to Warrington Dallam shed, worked alongside Ivatt 2-6-2 tanks on stopping trains such as Manchester Oxford Road to Warrington Bank Quay and Liverpool Lime Street prior to withdrawal of passenger services on the line in 1962. On Easter Saturday 1962 84001 was noted on the 4.19pm Manchester Oxford Road to Broadheath and Liverpool Lime Street service.

On 15th July 1962 84021-4 became works shunters at Crewe, these being amongst the ten engines transferred from the Southern Region. 84003 was seen at Llandudno Jct. on

Fig. 166
84007 working a push-pull train, sandwiched between two sets of coaches, on the last day of passenger services over the Higham Ferrers branch 13 June 1959. It is seen at Wellingborough station.

L. Hanson

Fig. 167
A panoramic view of Wellingborough station 29 June 1961. 84006 has arrived from Northampton Castle, deposited its passengers and will now cross over into platform 3 which is the bay platform at the far end of the station prior to returning to Northampton.

K.C.H. Fairey

Fig. 168
84007 stands at the head of a local train in Northampton Castle station 15 August 1959.

L. Hanson

Fig. 169 84008 approaches Stamford Town station with a push-pull train on a wintry afternoon 23 January 1965.　　*Courtney Haydon*

Fig. 170 84008 with a Northampton bound train in Kettering station 2 July 1960.　　*D. Trevor Rowe*

Fig. 171
84004 stands at the head of a local train at Buckingham 4 May 1959.

F.A. Blencowe

Fig. 172
84004 leaving Oswestry with a train for Gobowen during the period it was allocated to Oswestry.

David Tyreman collection

6th August 1962 working the "Welsh Dragon" service complete with headboard. During November 1962, 84005/8/29 were stored in the shed at Kentish Town, but by February 1963, 84005 had re-appeared on local trip work from Bedford. It had been briefly re-allocated to Bedford in early 1963 before moving on to Wellingborough. In February 1963 84002/4 were noted on the 'dead' road at Bletchley, stored out of use. A little later 84002 was seen in steam, although by 18th May it was noted dead again this time inside Bletchley shed. By now 84004 (Fig. 172) had joined 84000 at Oswestry for use on motor workings to Gobowen and Wrexham replacing GW 0-4-2 Tanks and auto coaches from week ending 21st July 1963 but as no push-pull sets had arrived in the area, the engines had to run round at each end. 84000 was noted shunting in Gobowen Goods Yard on 21st November 1964.

During the summer of 1963, 84026 had become works shunter at Horwich and 84019 was used on the Horwich-Blackrod push-pull trains, where it was noted on 10th July

working the 4.51pm from Horwich. 84006/7/27 were transferred to Annesley shed in early 1962 for use on the 'Dido' workmens trains which ran between Bulwell Common and Annesley, but shortly after their arrival, this working was taken over by a bus service, so consequently they were little used and were in a semi-derelict condition by September 1962. 84027 was withdrawn from Annesley in May 1964, having been in store from March 1962, probably without further use. 84007 was shown as stored from September 1962 until December 1963 when it was then transferred to Wellingborough. However, as it was withdrawn in January 1964 it is doubtful if it actually worked from Wellingborough shed, but it was reported stored there from March to October 1964. 84006 also went to Wellingborough for a second spell in August 1964 but after two months was transferred to Leicester. It was not withdrawn until the end of 1965.

84012 was the first of the class to be withdrawn in October 1963 from Southport MPD. Between May and November 1963 the four which had been Crewe Works

Fig. 173 84003 with a push-pull set in Llandudno Junction station on an unknown date.
W.A. Camwell/A. Gosling Collection

Fig. 174
84018 with a local passenger train from Fleetwood at Kirkham and Wesham station 8 September 1962.
B.W.C. Brooksbank

shunters, 84021-4 were taken out of use and remained in a derelict condition there, until their withdrawal in September 1964. In January 1964 84007 was withdrawn from Wellingborough, but remained there until 16th September, when it was hauled to A. Looms (Scrap Merchant) at Spondon for scrapping, where it was noted still intact on 17th October.

In late March 1964 84002 was back in steam and was noted at Bletchley in use as the station pilot where it was still working in early July. On 10th May that year 84026 was seen awaiting attention at Crewe Works whilst 84019 was outside the Electric Traction shop. A visit to Crewe Works on 14th June 1964 found 84021/3/4/5/8 stored in the Arrival Sidings, 84022 on the Scrap Road intact, while on the same day 84027 was on Crewe South shed. On a subsequent visit on 30th August 84021 had joined 84022 on the Scrap Road, 84015

was in the Arrival Sidings with 84023/5 and 84028 had moved to the Stripping Shop. By 4th October 84015/28 were in the Erecting Shop, 84025 was in the Erecting Shop yard and 84024 was the only member still present in the Arrival Sidings.

Although further members of the class were withdrawn in 1964, a number were still in use. 84003/9 from Llandudno Junction MPD were at Bangor shed in October, although 84009 was temporarily out of use due to an accident which had damaged the top of the right-hand cylinder casing and the bottom of the tank on the same side. Prior to this, during their brief stay at Croes Newydd, from March to June, they had worked to Bala. For example, 4th April found 84003 working from Bala to Bala Junction and 84009 on the 4.00 pm from Wrexham General to Bala.

84026 was in steam at Bolton MPD on 11th October and

Fig. 175 84014 stands at Blackrod station with a train to Chorley on a date unknown.   *A. Gosling*

Fig. 176 84028 approaches Skipton with an empty three coach set 31 July 1965.   *Courtney Haydon*

on 29th October 84015 ex-shops in unlined black was banking at Manchester Victoria. By this time the Lytham services were in the hands of diesel units, but steam still deputised on occasions. On 20th October, a few days prior to the closure of Blackpool Central on 1st November 1964, 84018 from Fleetwood shed was seen working the 1.08 pm Kirkham - Blackpool Central. This engine was noted at Skipton early in November 1964 and was used on the daily passenger duty to Garsdale and on the Barnoldswick pick-up goods. Prior to this 84011, also from Fleetwood shed, had been working the morning train to Garsdale, and the Barnoldswick pick-up goods, but by 22nd October Ivatt 2-6-2T 41251 had arrived from Malton NER to replace it.

1965 was the last year for this class. On 16th January 84000 was the station pilot at Oswestry, the last day of working there. The depot closed the following evening and 84000 moved on to Croes Newydd depot at Wrexham. In February 84005 was the lonely occupant of Wellingborough shed; it was used on the daily parcels train to Northampton. 84008 was still at Seaton Junction for working the Luffenham and Stamford locals, which were the last steam push-pull services in the country. It was joined in May 1965 by 84013 from Stockport, but this locomotive returned to Stockport in July, after only two months of working the Seaton services. 84002, which had been dead at Bletchley for some months, was withdrawn in April 1965, and although the shed closed on 5th July it remained dumped there until November. At one time it was stated that this engine was earmarked for possible use on the Isle of Wight.

84019 and 84025 from Bolton shed were used on the Blackrod and Chorley auto-trains until these were withdrawn on 11th December (Fig. 175). 84005/6/8 were the only locomotives remaining allocated to Market Harborough MPD, which had become a sub-shed of Leicester. They remained there until the push-pull services from Seaton ceased in September 1965, but were in store at Leicester on 22nd August, the Ivatt 2-6-2T's having taken over the service in the final weeks. Earlier in the year, on 10th May, a depot visit found 84006 at Leicester and 84008 at Wellingborough. 84003 was in steam at Llandudno Junction on 19th July. The last passenger train down the Barnoldswick branch from Skipton ran on 25th September and consisted of five coaches hauled by 84015. This engine together with 84028 were then placed in store at Skipton MPD. 84011/8 from Fleetwood were sold for scrap during November to Hughes Bolckow of Blyth.

At the end of 1965 a proposal to use this class on the Isle of Wight was again mooted, (see section 4.6.3). The engines concerned were 84010/3-7/9/25/6/8, which were surplus to requirements on the LMR. They were to be sent direct to Fratton for the transfer to the island, the modifications to be carried out at Ryde. On the LMR transfer list for the week ended 27th November 1965 they were shown as being transferred to the Southern Region, but the transfer list of the following week, 4th December 1965, showed them as returned to the LMR. In fact 84010/5/6/28 were dumped at Lostock Hall MPD during November, each labelled "Dead engine to Fratton, Portsmouth", 84015/28 having been moved from Skipton on 16th November 1965. 84011/8 were dead at Fleetwood and 84019/25 at Bolton until mid-November, one of which had received the attention of a humorist, who had painted a 70H shed code, and RYDE on

the buffer-beam. The only engine which is known to have arrived on the Southern Region is 84014, which had a hot box at Basingstoke where it was stopped on shed. It did however reach Eastleigh in December 1965 and was still present in February 1966. 84010/5/6/28 were hauled away dead from Lostock Hall on 10th November, but never arrived at Fratton; they were dispersed with the remainder of the class to Springs Branch and Stockport sheds, and were all withdrawn in December, although many could still be seen during 1966 dumped, awaiting despatch to scrap merchants.

4.6.3 Southern Region

Work commenced on the Darlington-built engines in January 1957 and these were placed in traffic on the following dates:-

84020	23.3.57
84021/2	30.3.57
84023	5.4.57
84024	10.4.57
84025	16.4.57
84026	18.4.57
84027	16.5.57
84028	15.5.57
84029	11.6.57

They were run-in on push-pull services between Middleton-in-Teesdale and Darlington and were sub-shedded at Middleton-in-Teesdale replacing NER G5 0-4-4T 67305 (Figs. 177 & 178).

84020-4 went to Ashford depot and 84025/6 to Ramsgate, all were turned out in the standard black lined livery, with the then new second BR crest on the tank sides. The remaining three 84027/8/9 all went to Ramsgate MPD, 84027/8 in May and 84029 in June 1957.

At both Ramsgate and Ashford the class replaced SECR H 0-4-4 tanks (Fig. 179) on secondary passenger duties, van trains and station shunting at Canterbury West and carriage shunting at Margate. Duties worked by both Ramsgate and Ashford engines included:-
Ashford to Maidstone East, Ashford to Rye, Ashford to Hastings and Ashford to Margate via Canterbury West. Some specimen diagrams are shown in Appendix D.

It was rather unfortunate that these new engines could not be used on Southern Region push-pull trains, because their equipment worked on the vacuum system, whereas the Southern trains used the compressed air system. The tanks were therefore used on local trains that did not involve push-pull working.

With the advent of further electric and diesel services in the South East of England and the closure of Ramsgate shed in June 1959, other work had to be found for these ten engines, which were now allocated to Ashford. 84028 made several trips over the Brighton to Horsham line during early November 1959 and Eastleigh MPD often borrowed these engines when they had been to Works. 84020/1/5/7/9 were all in Eastleigh Works between early November 1959 and the end of January 1960, and 84020 was again present in April 1960.

On 8th January 1960 84021 worked the 7.13am van train from Southampton Terminus to Fareham, and the 9.07am from Fareham to Netley. This is believed to have been the first working of the class over the Netley line. It distinguished itself by becoming involved in a minor collision with some empty vans at Netley. Other engines of the class often gave a

Fig. 177 84028 when new was 'run in' from Middleton-in-Teesdale (being a sub-shed of Darlington) where it is taking water prior to working to Darlington Bank Top station in May 1957.

J.W. Armstrong Trust

Fig. 178 LNER G5 0-4-4T 67323 on a Blyth push-pull train at Monkseaton on unknown date. This station is now part of the Tyne and Wear metro system.

E.E. Smith

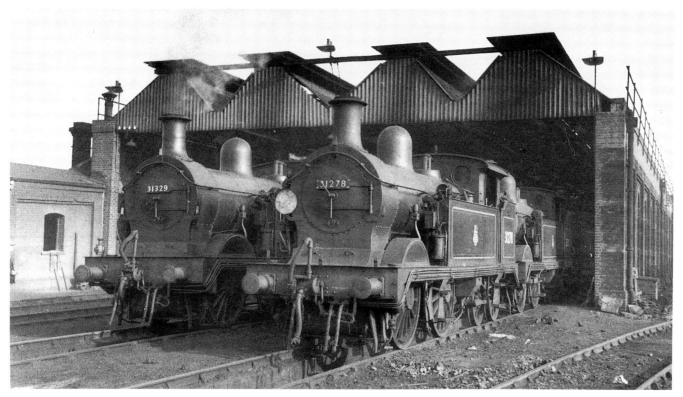

Fig. 179 SECR H 0-4-4T's 31329, 31278 and 31310 at Tunbridge Wells West MPD 11 November 1956. These locomotives were replaced by 84XXX 2-6-2T's in East Kent. *R.K. Taylor*

Fig. 180 84029 at Ramsgate MPD in rather dirty condition 1 June 1959. This was the last engine of the class. *Courtney Haydon*

helping hand with freight traffic on the Fawley branch after visits to Eastleigh Works.

Ashford Works also repaired members of the class, 84026 was present in late November 1959.

In March 1960 a plan was put forward to modify three of these engines for use on the Isle of Wight to replace the ageing LSWR 02 0-4-4T's. Alterations required were:-
1). Fitting a new chimney, 6 $\frac{1}{2}$" shorter than the original.
2). Reducing the height of the dome casing by 2$\frac{1}{16}$"
3). Lowering the cab roof by 1"
4). Removing the cab side windscreens.
5). The substitution of compressed air equipment for vacuum train braking. (The engine steam brake to be retained)

In July of that year, 84022 arrived at Eastleigh Works for these modifications, although they were never carried out. The locomotive was still at Eastleigh in early August where it was on view at the Open Day on 3rd August. This plan was revived again in 1965 (previously described in section 4.6.2). A decision was taken later to electrify, using the third rail, the remaining part of the Isle of Wight system with former London Transport Underground tube rolling stock. The new service commenced 20th March 1967.

In November 1960 84020 was used on the 6.05pm Brighton - Tonbridge train and also appeared on the Uckfield lines, and in June of the following year 84024-7 were transferred to Brighton MPD where they were used on the local passenger services to Horsham. 84020-3 went to Exmouth Junction shed where they were used on the Exeter - Exmouth branch, Exeter - Honiton locals and station shunting at Exeter Central, all tasks being previously performed by LSWR M7 0-4-4T's which they replaced. They also shared banking duties between Exeter St Davids and Central stations. The remaining two Eastern section engines were transferred to Eastleigh, where they performed carriage shunting duties, empty stock working to Southampton Terminus, local goods and parcels turns and were used as Locomotive Works pilot.

Towards the end of their days on the Southern Region five of the class worked in the London area, 84020 was at Stewarts Lane and 84021-4 were at Bricklayers Arms prior to their move in May 1961. Here they were employed on ECS working between Clapham Jct. and Waterloo and van trains to Woking and to Guildford. 84024 was frequently used on the unadvertised passenger service between Clapham Jct. and Kensington Olympia when this was not diesel operated.

As already mentioned, all of the Darlington-built locomotives 84020-9 were transferred to the London Midland Region towards the end of September 1961. On 9th October 84025 put in a final appearance on the Southern Region when it was present at the centenary celebrations of the Steyning line. It hauled the 10.19am to Horsham before departing light engine for the London Midland Region. 84029 lingered on the Southern Region even longer. On 25th October it was still working from Eastleigh depot, although officially allocated to Bedford depot, and was noted on the 3.30pm Eastleigh - Southampton Terminus empty stock working.

The arrival of the ten Class 2 2-6-2T's had little impact on the Southern Region as by the time they had arrived, the Region's thoughts were on electrification, so they were performing mundane duties almost from their arrival.

4.6.4 Allocation Summary

84000 7.53 Crewe North, 8.53 Plodder Lane, 3.54 Wrexham Rhosddu, 7.56 Birkenhead, P6.61 Warrington (Dallam), 4.63 Oswestry, P1.65 Croes Newydd.

84001 7.53 Crewe North, P8.53 Plodder Lane, 3.54 Wrexham Rhosddu, P10.55 Chester Northgate, P1.60 Birkenhead, P6.61 Warrington (Dallam), P12.62 Llandudno Jct.

84002 8.53 Plodder Lane, 3.54 Wrexham Rhosddu, 10.55 Chester Northgate, P8.56 Bletchley.

84003 8.53 Plodder Lane, 3.54 Wrexham Rhosddu, 7.56 Birkenhead, 9.61 Rhyl, P2.63 Llandudno Jct., P3.64 Croes Newydd, P6.64 Llandudno Jct.

84004 8.53 Plodder Lane, 10.54 Wrexham Rhosddu, P7.56 Birkenhead, P8.56 Bletchley, P4.63 Oswestry, P1.65 Croes Newydd.

84005 8.53 Bedford, 6.61 Neasden, 12.61 Bedford, P3.62 Neasden, P7.62 Kentish Town, P1.63 Wellingborough, 1.63 Bedford, 2.63 Wellingborough, P2.64 Leicester, 5.64 Wellingborough, 9.64 Leicester.

84006 8.53 Burton-on-Trent, P1.59 Wellingborough, 12.61 Neasden, P1.62 Bedford, P3.62 Neasden, P4.62 Annesley, 7.64 Wellingborough, 9.64 Leicester.

84007 9.53 Burton-on-Trent, P2.59 Wellingborough, P3.62 Annesley, P12.63 Wellingborough.

84008 9.53 Burton-on-Trent, P2.59 Wellingborough, 6.61 Neasden, P7.62 Kentish Town, 12.62 Leicester. P5.63 Wellingborough, P2.64 Leicester, 5.64 Wellingborough, 9.64 Leicester.

84009 9.53 Royston, P1.55 Skipton, P7.55 Royston, 6.59 Hull Dairycoates, 12.62 Llandudno Jct., P3.64 Croes Newydd, P6.64 Llandudno Jct.

84010 9.53 Low Moor, 9.54 Lees, P5.56 Rose Grove, P6.57 Lower Darwen, P13.59 Fleetwood, 11.65 To Eastleigh SR (for I of W), 12.65 Returned to Fleetwood LMR (for immediate withdrawal).

84011 9.53 Low Moor, P1.55 Bank Hall, P5.56 Rose Grove, P5.57 Lower Darwen, P3.61 Fleetwood.

84012 9.53 Low Moor, 9.54 Lees, P6.55 Rose Grove, 9.55 Bank Hall, P5.57 Lower Darwen, P3.61 Fleetwood, P2.63 Southport.

84013 9.53 Low Moor, P1.55 Bank Hall, 11.55 Lees, 4.59 Bolton, 12.64 Stockport, P5.65 Leicester, P7.65 Stockport, 11.65 To Eastleigh SR (for I of W), 12.65 Returned to Stockport LMR (for immediate withdrawal).

84014 9.53 Low Moor, P1.55 Bank Hall, P4.55 Southport, 11.55 Lees, 2.59 Bolton, 12.64 Stockport, 11.65 To Eastleigh SR (for I of W), 12.65 Returned to Stockport LMR (for immediate withdrawal).

84015 10.53 Low Moor, 9.54 Lees, P6.55 Rose Grove, 9.55 Fleetwood, P7.57 Lancaster, 7.58 Skipton, 11.65 To Eastleigh SR (for I of W), 12.65 Returned to Skipton LMR (for immediate withdrawal).

84016 10.53 Bury, P5.54 Fleetwood, P7.57 Lancaster, 11.58 Fleetwood, P6.65 Stockport, 6.65 Fleetwood, 11.65 To Eastleigh SR (for I of W), 12.65 Returned to Fleetwood LMR (for immediate withdrawal).

84017 10.53 Bury, P5.54 Fleetwood, 10.63 Southport, 6.64 Bolton, P6.65 Stockport, 11.65 To Eastleigh SR (for I of W), 12.65 Returned to Stockport LMR (for immediate withdrawal).

84018 10.53 Bury, P5.54 Fleetwood.

84019 10.53 Bury, 6.54 Fleetwood, 11.55 Lees, P4.58 Bolton, 11.65 To Eastleigh SR (for I of W), 12.65 Returned to Bolton LMR (for immediate withdrawal).

84020 3.57 Ashford, 2.61 Stewarts Lane, 6.61 Exmouth Jct., 9.61 Llandudno Jct.

84021 3.57 Ashford, 2.61 Bricklayers Arms, 6.61 Exmouth Jct., 9.61 Llandudno Jct., P7.62 Crewe Works.

84022 3.57 Ashford, 2.61 Bricklayers Arms, 6.61 Exmouth Jct., 9.61 Llandudno Jct., P7.62 Crewe Works.

84023 4.57 Ashford, 2.61 Bricklayers Arms, 6.61 Exmouth Jct., 9.61 Lancaster, P1.62 Widnes, P7.62 Crewe Works.

84024 4.57 Ashford, 1.61 Bricklayers Arms, 6.61 Brighton, 9.61 Warrington Dallam, P1.62 Widnes, P7.62 Crewe Works.

84025 4.57 Ramsgate, 6.59 Ashford, 6.61 Brighton, 9.61 Newton Heath, 11.61 Bolton, 11.65 To Eastleigh SR (for I of W), 12.65 Returned to Bolton LMR (for immediate withdrawal).

84026 4.57 Ramsgate, 6.59 Ashford, 6.61 Brighton, 9.61 Newton Heath, 11.61 Bolton, 5.63 Horwich Works, 12.63 Bolton, 12.64 Stockport 11.65 To Eastleigh SR (for I of W), 12.65 Returned to Stockport LMR (for immediate withdrawal).

84027 5.57 Ramsgate, 6.59 Ashford, 6.61 Brighton, 9.61 Newton Heath, 10.61 Bolton, 1.62 Wellingborough, P3.62 Annesley.

84028 5.57 Ramsgate, 6.59 Ashford, 6.61 Eastleigh, 9.61 Newton Heath, 9.61 Skipton, 11.65 To Eastleigh SR (for I of W), 12.65 Returned to Skipton LMR (for immediate withdrawal).

84029 6.57 Ramsgate, 6.59 Ashford, 6.61 Eastleigh, 9.61 Bedford, P1.62 Neasden, P7.62 Kentish Town, P1.63 Wellingborough, P2.63 Leicester.

Fig. 181 84008 in Wellingborough Roundhouse in company with Standard 9F 2-10-0 92224 14 July 1963. *Courtney Haydon*

Fig. 182 84015 stands outside Skipton shed 31 July 1965.   *Courtney Haydon*

Fig. 183 84022 in Ashford MPD yard in June 1958.   *RAS Marketing*

Fig. 184 84025 outside Bolton MPD 11 April 1965.　　　　　　　　　　　　　　　　　*Courtney Haydon*

Fig. 185 84028 at Eastleigh MPD 30 October 1959.　　　　　　　　　　　　　　　　　*L. Elsey*

4.6.5 Storage

Many of the class also spent considerable periods in store. Those recorded on the engine history cards are as follows - U denotes unserviceable.

84000	9.9.62 - 4.4.63, 16.7.65 - 30.10.65
84001	9.9.62 - 29.11.62
84002	9.7.62 - 3.12.62
84003	15.9.63 - 15.3.64, 10.8.65 - 2.10.65 U
84004	3.9.62 - 4.4.63, 15.7.65 - 30.10.65
84005	14.11.60 - 30.6.61, 7.5.62 - 14.1.63
	24.5.65 - 30.10.65 U
84006	30.10.60 - 10.4.61, 8.10.62 - 13.4.64
	24.5.65 - 30.10.65 U
84007	10.9.62 - 4.12.63
84008	10.4.61 - 21.6.61, 19.6.62 - 24.12.62
	21.6.65 - 30.10.65 U
84009	15.9.63 - 15.3.64
84010	1.11.64 - 29.10.65 U from 5.7.65
84011	1.11.64 - Unknown (Withdrawn 4.65)
84013	23.11. 64 - Unknown (Withdrawn 12.65)
84014	23.11.64 - Unknown (Withdrawn 12.65)
84015	28.9.62 - 19.1.63, 26.9.65 - 2.11.65
84016	1.11.64 - 14.6.65, 5.7.65 - 29.10.65 U
84017	23.11.64 - 1.2.65, 17.5.65 - 14.6.65
	9.10.65 - 23.10.65 U
84018	11.10.64 - Unknown (Withdrawn 4.65)
84019	24.10.55 - 7.11.55, 11.5.59 - 10.8.59
	12.6.65 - Unknown (Withdrawn 12.65)
84025	6.11.61 - 22.4.63, 5.5.63 - 24.6.63
	27.9.65 - 23.10.65
84026	3.10.61 - 22.4.63, 23.12.63 - 9.3.64
84027	16.10.61 - 22.1.62, 26.3.62 - 13.4.64
84028	26.9.65 - 2.11.65
84029	19.6.62 - 14.1.63, 18.3.63 - 6.4.64

4.7 Modifications as a result of Service Experience

The class appear to have received fewer modifications than the other tank engine classes with the following being recorded:-

E3329 Modification of Piston for Continuous Blowdown Valve, same as for 80xxx. The cost for the 84xxx class appeared to be 17s 6d (87.5p)

26.1.57	84003	28.12.57	84001/11/2
25.1.58	84015	22.2.58	84008
22.3.58	84010	22.5.58	84013
9.8.58	84019	4.10.58	84002/5
10.9.60	84000	3.12.60	84014/6/8

E4341 Removal of Downs Sanding Gear. This modification was carried out in conjunction with R5151 which has not been identified. The cost of the two modifications varied from £80 10s 0d (£80.50p) to £86 6s 11d (£86.35p).

12.12.57	84001	19.4.58	84006
9.8.58	84019	6.9.58	84002
4.10.58	84005/7	27.2.60	84008
18.6.60	84017	10.9.60	84000
5.11.60	84010/2	31.12.60	84011/4/6/8
28.1.61	84003		

Fig. 186 84006 along with other members of the class in store unserviceable at Leicester 3 October 1965.   *Courtney Haydon*

E4361 Fitting of revised pony truck lifeguards. The cost was £6 2s 0d (£6.10p)

19.5.56	84005	16.6.56	84014
28.6.56	84002	11.8.56	84009
8.9.56	84001	6.10.56	84018
26.1.57	84000/3	23.3.57	84004
20.4.57	84016/7	28.12.57	84010/1/2
25.1.58	84015	22.2.58	84008/13
19.4.58	84006	9.8.58	84019
4.10.58	84007		

E4983 Fitting of AWS. Cost £302 9s 0d (£302.45p)

12.60	84009	26.1.63	84003
23.2.63	84001		

Documentation exists on a further modification, this being the provision of an additional footstep on the sloping part of the foot framing at the front end on each side on LMR engines at a cost of £40 each. This note was dated 24th February 1954. This could be modification R5151.

Engines observed with front footsteps:-

84003	7.62	84020	20.7.59
84005	4.11.61	84022	11.4.60
84006	1960	84026	26.1.61
84015	25.9.65	84029	22.4.61

There are no records of modifications to 84020-9, other than E4983, all the others were first noted prior to the start of production of the second batch so it is probable that these locomotives were built with the modified design incorporated.

Injectors.
84000-19 appear to have been fitted with right and left hand side Davies and Metcalfe injectors.
Changes recorded were (all undated):-
To WR type   84000/2/3/4
Subsequent GW to LMR type Gresham & Craven 84003
Davies and Metcalfe to Gresham and Craven   84005
At least one other locomotive had Davies and Metcalfe injectors but both on the right hand side. 84027/9 (at least) of the second batch were recorded with 2 x 8mm live steam injectors from new.

Other Modifications
Fitting of Gresham and Craven Graduable Brake Valve for operating the engine only, plus Gresham and Craven Ejector for train:-
84000/2-5/7/8/9
Coal bunker access doors fitted:- 84000/2/4-7/9
Weather Shield fitted:- 84000
Smoke deflector plate fitted:- 84002
Heating surface (cards missing for several locomotives):-
    84000-8 - 1025.5 sq. ft.
    84009   - amended from 1025.5 to 1149
    84027/9 - 1149 from new.
Push-pull apparatus inoperative on 84027 - undated.
SR lamp bracket on sides of smokebox door:-
                84021 by 5.57

4.8 Running Costs and Maintenance

Data on running costs is scarce, the only quoted source being E.S.Cox who gave figures of 8.46d/mile for the engine and 0.43d/mile for the boiler. These figures were for 1957 when none of the engines had visited works for heavy repairs and the oldest engine had only seen four years service. As age took its toll these figures could well have increased.

Crewe Works was responsible for the maintenance of the first batch, 84000-19. Darlington carried out non-classified repairs to some of the 84020-9 batch after running in before despatch to the Southern Region where Eastleigh looked after the engines, although four of the class are recorded as having visited Ashford Works. No cost details are available for those engines overhauled by the Southern Region.

The records show that 84020-9 received Light Intermediate repairs at Eastleigh or Ashford between approximately 77,000 miles (84024/5) and 98,000 miles (84020/2). There is no record of any of the final batch receiving a heavy repair.

Of the earlier locomotives the normal overhaul pattern was a Light Intermediate followed by a heavy general overhaul. However five engines (84002/5/8/13/8) had a heavy intermediate overhaul. Exactly what defined the difference cannot be seen but the heavy overhaul of 84005 actually cost less at £1,744 than most of the light overhauls.

The average mileage to the Intermediate overhaul was 95,620 and the cost £2,029. A Heavy General overhaul followed after a further 57,360 miles at an approximate cost of £3,000.

The maximum mileage to a Light Intermediate was 112,749 by 84000, the lowest 66,895 by 84014. Going on to a Heavy General overhaul 84003 ran the highest mileage at 75,013, 84001 the lowest at 41,004. There is no record of 84013/5/6 ever receiving a Heavy General overhaul.

84006/7/19 did not receive an Intermediate overhaul, running 83,851, 90,762 and 104,874 miles respectively to a Heavy General overhaul.

84018 ran to 97,754 miles for a Heavy Intermediate overhaul. This was followed by a light classified overhaul at 39,235 miles costing £1,057. It then ran only 14,194 miles before it was given a Heavy General overhaul.

4.9 Construction Withdrawal and Disposal information

The first of the class to be withdrawn was 84012 on 12th October 1963 with the final batch, 84010/3-7/9/25/6/8 all being condemned on 11th December 1965.

84000 had the longest life of 12 years 3 months and 84027 the shortest lasting just 6 years 11 months.

Year end class totals were	1953 - 56	20
	1957 - 62	30
	1963	29
	1964	20
	1965	Nil

Mileage information was not recorded beyond 1960. It is estimated that 84001 probably ran the highest mileage, about 260,000 with 84000/17 at about 250,000. 84007/14/9 probably ran the lowest mileage of the first batch at about 170,000. 84020-9 put in very high mileages whilst on the Southern Region, 84028 may have topped 200,000 with 84025/7/9 at the other end of the scale with 160,000 total miles run. 84008 has the highest recorded single year mileage with 54,921 in 1960.

None of the locomotives survived their sale for scrap.

However there is a proposal to build a 'new' member of the class, with the conversion of Class 2 2-6-0 78059 to 84030, no doubt influenced by the fact that there is no tender available for this engine. 78059 came from Barry Docks to the Bluebell Railway on 23rd May 1983 having been purchased on 4th May for £7,500. Many other parts besides the tender were also missing from this engine and will have to be replaced. In mid-1994 the engine had been stripped and the wheelsets were reprofiled at Swindon Works and a new trailing truck built. Work was underway on the frames and 90% of the motion and fittings made or acquired. Boiler BR8 1841 is with this locomotive. (Fig. 187).

Fig. 187 Standard Class 2 2-6-0 78022 looking very smart in preservation at Ingrow, KWVR on 24th April 1993. 78059 of this class which has no tender is a potential candidate to be converted to a Standard Class 2 2-6-2T and numbered 84030. *J.B. Arnold*

Summary

	Date New	Date Withd'n	Disposal Details
84000	4.7.53	30.10.65	J.Buttigieg, Newport. 2.66 ex-Shrewsbury.
84001	6.7.53	31.10.64	Hughes Bolckow, North Blyth. Sold 12.64 ex-Llandudno Jct. Cut up 1.65.
84002	7.8.53	17.4.65	J.Buttigieg, Newport. Sold 12.65 ex-Bletchley. At yard 8.4.66, remains in evidence 23.9.66.
84003	10.8.53	2.10.65	J.Cashmore, Great Bridge. 2.66 ex-Llandudno Jct.
84004	19.8.53	30.10.65	J.Buttigieg, Newport. Arrived 4.66 ex-Shrewsbury. Cut up 6.66.
84005	24.8.53	30.10.65	J.Buttigieg, Newport. Sold 1.66. At yard 7.1.66 ex-Leicester LMS. Still intact 14.8.66.
84006	26.8.53	30.10.65	J.Buttigieg, Newport. Sold 1.66. At yard 7.1.66 ex-Leicester LMS. Still intact 14.8.66.
84007	31.8.53	18.1.64	A.Looms, Spondon. Sold 9.64. At yard 17.10.64 ex-Wellingborough.
84008	31.8.53	30.10.65	J.Buttigieg, Newport. Sold 1.66. At yard 7.1.66 ex-Leicester LMS. Still intact 14.8.66.
84009	3.9.53	20.11.65	J.Cashmore, Great Bridge. 1.66 ex-Llandudno Jct.
84010	8.9.53	11.12.65	Central Wagon Co., Ince. At yard 18.2.66 ex-Lostock Hall. Cut up 2.66.
84011	18.9.53	24.4.65	Hughes Bolckow, North Blyth. Sold 11.65 ex-Fleetwood. Still intact 28 12.65.
84012	17.9.53	12.10.63	Crewe Works, cut up 10.63.
84013	21.9.53	11.12.65	Arnott Young, Parkgate and Rawmarsh. Sold 3.66 ex-Stockport 17.3.66.
84014	22.9.53	11.12.65	J.Cashmore, Newport. 4.66 ex-Eastleigh.
84015	2.10.53	11.12.65	Central Wagon Co., Ince. Cut up 2.66 ex-Lostock Hall.
84016	7.10.53	11.12.65	Central Wagon Co., Ince. Cut up 2.66 ex-Lostock Hall.
84017	13.10.53	11.12.65	Arnott Young, Parkgate and Rawmarsh. Sold 2.66 ex-Stockport. Cut up 3.66.
84018	23.10.53	24.4.65	Hughes Bolckow, North Blyth. Cut up 11.65 ex-Fleetwood.
84019	31.10.53	11.12.65	Arnott Young, Parkgate and Rawmarsh. Sold 3.66 ex-Stockport 3.3.66. Cut up 3.66.
84020	27.3.57	31.10.64	Hughes Bolckow, North Blyth. Sold 12.64 ex-Llandudno Jct. Cut up 1.65.
84021	30.3.57	5.9.64	Crewe Works, cut up 10.64.
84022	30.3.57	5.9.64	Crewe Works, cut up 10.64.
84023	5.4.57	5.9.64	Crewe Works, cut up 10.64.
84024	10.4.57	5.9.64	Crewe Works, cut up 10.64.
84025	16.4.57	11.12.65	Arnott Young, Parkgate and Rawmarsh. Sold 3.66 ex-Stockport 3.3.66. Cut up 3.66.
84026	18.4.57	11.12.65	Arnott Young, Parkgate and Rawmarsh. Sold 3.66 ex-Stockport 3.3.66. Cut up 3.66.
84027	16.5.57	2.5.64	Crewe Works, cut up 7.64 ex-Annesley.
84028	15.5.57	11.12.65	Central Wagon Co., Ince. Sold 1.66 ex-Lostock Hall. Cut up 2.66.
84029	11.6.57	13.6.64	J.Cashmore, Great Bridge. 10.64 ex-Leicester LMS.

5. BIBLIOGRAPHY AND ACKNOWLEDGEMENTS

Bibliography

Roger P. Bradley	The Standard Steam Locomotives of British Railways, David and Charles 1984
E.S. Cox	British Railways Standard Steam Locomotives, Ian Allan 1966, 1973
H.C.B. Rogers	The Last Steam Locomotive Engineer, R.A. Riddles, CBE, George Allen and Unwin 1970
E. Talbot	A Pictorial Record of British Railways Standard Steam Locomotives, Oxford Publishing Co., 1982
	Railway Magazine
	Railway Observer
	Steam World
	Trains Illustrated

Acknowledgements

80064 Loco Fund
Project 78
80080 Locomotive Co. Ltd.
The Brighton Standard 4 Tank Fund
80104 Locomotive Fund
The Wales Railway Centre
80154 Locomotive Company
Keighley and Worth Valley Railway
Bury Standard 4 Group

John Baker	Eric Fry
Geoffrey Bird	Andrew Lait
Reg Bond	David Monk-Steel
Mike Burnett	Raymond Rourke
Alan Clothier	Brian Sullivan
Chris Cubitt	David Tyreman
Peter Cupper	Robert Urie
Ken Davies	John Ward

APPENDIX A

Extracts from Engine Working Programmes
Southern Region – Eastern District for Class 4 2-6-4T's
Summer 1954 and Winter 1958 Schedules

Central District Engines working over Eastern District—WEEK-DAYS

TUNBRIDGE WELLS WEST DUTY No. 670.
2 P.T. (L.M.R. Class.)

SATURDAYS EXCEPTED.

**	Eastbourne Loco. ...	9.45 p.m. ▼
	Eastbourne ... ...10.	9 p.m. ▼
	(8.30 p.m. ex St. Leonards)	
11.16 p.m.	Haywards Heath...	12.42 a.m. ▼
1.46 a.m.	Eastbourne	** ‖
**	Eastbourne Loco.	

Eastbourne Men.
S.X.—Prepare for 9.45 p.m. ‖.

St. Leonards Men.
S.X.—Off No. 408, relieve 9.45 p.m., work and change with No. 411, at Eastbourne 1.50 a.m., work and relieved in depot.

Eastbourne Men.
M.X.—Off No. 411 change over at Eastbourne 1.50 a.m., work and dispose.

BRIGHTON DUTY No. 732.
7 P. (W.C. Class.)

MONDAYS EXCEPTED.

1.31 a.m.	London Bridge ...	1.50 a.m.
1.55 a.m.	Cannon St. ...	1.56 a.m.
2. 0 a.m.	Ewer St. ...	2.45 a.m.
2.51 a.m.	London Bridge ...	3.25 a.m.
	and as shewn.	

SUNDAY MORNING.

12.26 a.m.	London Bridge ...	1. 0 a.m.
1. 4 a.m.	Cannon St. ...	1. 5 a.m.
1. 8 a.m.	Ewer St. ...	4. 0 a.m.
4. 6 a.m.	London Bridge ...	4.45 a.m.
	and as shewn.	

Brighton Men.

BRIGHTON DUTY No. 737.
4 P.T. (B.R. Class.)

SATURDAYS ONLY.
30th July until 4th September.

	Eastbourne	6.41 a.m. P
	(11.40 p.m. ex Manchester)	
7.14 a.m.	Hastings	7.30 a.m. ‖
7.35 a.m.	Ore	** ‖ E
**	St. Leonards Loco.	11.40 a.m. E
11.52 a.m.	Ore	12.15 p.m. E
12.19 p.m.	Hastings	12.30 p.m. P
1.43 p.m.	Brighton	** ‖
**	Loco. Yard	

Eastbourne Men.
S.O.—Off No. 667 work to St. Leonards Loco. Dispose and home as ordered.

St. Leonards Men.
S.O.—On duty 10.40 a.m. work to Brighton get engine of No. 667 work 3.10 p.m. ‖. etc. to Eastbourne, change to No. 405 at 4.15 p.m., work and dispose.

Central District Engines working over Eastern District—WEEK-DAYS

TUNBRIDGE WELLS WEST DUTY No. 663.
4 P.T. (L.M.R. Class.)

As shewn in Central District Workings.

	Eastbourne Loco. ...	9.50 a.m. =
**	Eastbourne ... ...10.	3 a.m. P
	(9.25 a.m. Hastings).	
10.40 a.m.	Brighton	** ‖ =

SATURDAYS EXCEPTED.

	Brighton Loco. ...	1. 0 p.m.
	and as shewn by Central District.	

Eastbourne Men.
S.X.—Off No. 670, change at 9.5 a.m., work, change to No. 405 at 10.0 a.m., work to Depot, dispose and relieved in depot.

St. Leonards Men.
S.X.—Off No. 405, change over at Eastbourne at 10.0 a.m. work and relieved Brighton at 10.55 a.m., passenger per 11.11 a.m. to Eastbourne relieve No. 411 at 12.5 p.m. relieved at Polegate at 1.0 p.m. home Passenger per 4.19 p.m.

Other Duties.
As shewn Central District.

TUNBRIDGE WELLS WEST DUTY No. 667.
4 P.T. (B.R. Std.)

SATURDAYS EXCEPTED.

**	Loco. Yard	7.15 a.m. P
8.58 a.m.	Eastbourne	7.33 a.m. P
9.25 a.m.	Tunbridge Wells W. ...	9. 8 a.m. P
10.10 a.m.	Tonbridge	9.32 a.m. P
10.26 a.m.	Redhill	10.20 a.m.
**	Loco. Yard ...	11.58 a.m.
	Redhill	12. 7 p.m.
	(9.45 a.m. ex Reading)	
12.47 p.m.	Tonbridge	1. 4 p.m. P
1.22 p.m.	Tunbridge Wells W. ...	1.56 p.m. ** =
3.13 p.m.	Eastbourne ...	

SATURDAYS ONLY.
3rd July until 4th September.

**	Brighton Loco. ...	3.10 a.m. P
	Brighton	3.28 p.m. P
	(11.5 a.m. ex Walsall)	
4. 6 p.m.	Eastbourne	** ‖ E
**	Loco. Yard ...	

S.X.—As shewn in Central District.

3rd July until 4th September.

St. Leonards Men.
S.O.—Off No. 738 relieve at 3.10 p.m. work and change with No. 405 at Eastbourne 4.15 p.m. work and dispose.

Eastbourne Men.
S.O.—Off No. 405 change over at Eastbourne and work to Loco.

Central District Engines working over Eastern District—WEEK-DAYS

TUNBRIDGE WELLS WEST DUTY No. 662.
4 P.T. (B.R. Class.)

SATURDAYS EXCEPTED.
As shewn in Central District.

	Eastbourne	6.37 a.m. P
8.22 a.m.	Tunbridge Wells West ...	8.27 a.m. P
	(M.X. double headed by No. 324)	
8.42 a.m.	Tonbridge	8.59 a.m. P
**	West Yard ... ...11.	10 a.m. F
**	East Yard ... ...12.	12 noon F
**	West Yard	** ‖ P
	Tonbridge Loco. ...	3.55 p.m.
4.14 p.m.	Tunbridge Wells West	4.35 p.m.
6.12 p.m.	Eastbourne ...	—
	and as shewn in Central District.	

SATURDAYS ONLY.

9.37 a.m.	Redhill	12.10 p.m. =
	Redhill	12.50 p.m. P
12.14 p.m.	Loco. Yard	1. 5 p.m. = P
1.44 p.m.	Redhill	** ‖ =
**	Loco. Yard	4. 0 p.m. P
**	Tonbridge ...	4.29 p.m. P
4.47 p.m.	Tunbridge Wells West	—
	C—Shunting 5.0 p.m. to 5.40 p.m.	
**	Tunbridge Wells West	5.55 p.m. =
7.18 p.m.	Eastbourne ...	** ‖
**	Loco. Yard	—

TUNBRIDGE WELLS WEST DUTY No. 660.
4 P.T. (B.R. Class.)

SATURDAYS EXCEPTED.
As shewn in Central District.

9.44 a.m.	Tunbridge Wells West 10.31 a.m. P	
10.47 a.m.	Tonbridge ... ...11.10 a.m.	** ‖ F
**	West Yard ... ...12 noon	F
**	East Yard	** ‖
**	West Yard	** ‖ P
	Tonbridge Loco. ...	3.55 p.m.
4.14 p.m.	Tunbridge Wells West	4.35 p.m. P
6.12 p.m.	Eastbourne ...	—
	and as shewn in Central District.	

SATURDAYS ONLY.

5.45 p.m.	Tunbridge Wells West	6.26 p.m. P
6.46 p.m.	Tonbridge ...	7.49 p.m. P
8.14 p.m.	Tunbridge Wells West	** ‖
	Loco. Yard	—

Central District Rosters.
S.X.—Until 10.15 a.m.

Tonbridge Men.
S.X.—Off No. 291, relieve at Tunbridge Wells West at 10.20 a.m., work and relieved in depot.
S.X.—No. 2 P. & D. men dispose.
S.X.—P. & D. men prepare for 3.55 p.m. ‖.
1st set (S.X.) on duty 3.40 p.m. change with No. 291 at Tunbridge Wells West at 4.20 p.m. relieved at 6.10 p.m., relieve No. 309 at 6.20 p.m. work and relieved in depot.

Central District Rosters.
S.X.—From 4.20 p.m.

Central District Rosters.
S.X.—From 6.15 p.m.

Tunbridge Wells West Men.
S.O.—Off No. 625 dispose.

Central District Rosters.
From 7.18 p.m.

Eastbourne Men.
1st set (S.X.) on duty 5.5 a.m., relieved at Tunbridge Wells West 8.22 a.m., relieve No. 635, 8.31 a.m. work and dispose.
1st set (S.O.) on duty 5.5 a.m., relieved 8.22 a.m., relieve No. 635 8.45 a.m. ‖ prepare for 12.15 p.m. ‖, and as ordered.

Tunbridge Wells West Men.
1st set (S.X.) on duty 8.5 a.m., relieve 8.22 a.m. relieved Redhill 10.50 a.m., relieve No. 667 11.5 a.m., relieved 11.17 a.m. relieve No. 664 2.21 p.m., work and dispose.

Redhill Men.
S.X.—Off No. 646, relieve 10.50 a.m. work relieved Redhill 12.50 p.m.

Tonbridge Men.
S.X.—Off No. 341 (E), work 12.50 p.m. ‖
S.X.—No. 2 P. & D men dispose.
1st set (S.X.) on duty 3.0 p.m. relieved Eastbourne 7.18 p.m. pass. 7.24 p.m. to Brighton, work No. 253 (E.) 9.5 p.m. ‖ etc., relieved in depot.

Central District Roster.
From 7.18 p.m.

Central District Engines working over Eastern District—WEEK-DAYS

BRIGHTON DUTY No. 738.
4 P.T. (B.R. Class.)

SATURDAYS ONLY.

As shewn in Central District.

**	Brighton	6.52 p.m.	P
8. 1 p.m.	Tunbridge Wells West	8. 6 p.m.	P
8.23 p.m.	Tonbridge	8.34 p.m.	P
9.14 p.m.	Redhill	9.33 p.m.	P
9.37 p.m.	Loco. Yard	11. 0 p.m.	P
**	Redhill	11.11 p.m.	P
11.50 p.m.	Tonbridge	**	‖
	Loco. Yard		

(Stable for No. 738 Sunday)

Brighton Men.

3rd set (S.O.) on duty 5.28 p.m. relieve at Brighton at 5.53 p.m. relieved at Tunbridge Wells West at 8.1 p.m. and as shewn in Central District.

Tonbridge Men.

S.O.—Off No. 306 (E.) relieve at Tunbridge Wells West at 8.1 p.m. work and relieved in depot.

S.O.—No. 4 P. & D. men dispose.

BRIGHTON DUTY No. 740.
4 P.T. (B.R. Standard.)

SATURDAYS EXCEPTED.

—	Brighton	5.44 p.m.	P
7.17 p.m.	Tonbridge	7.30 p.m.	P
—	Loco. Yd. (West End)	9. 0 p.m.	
—	Tonbridge	9.23 p.m.	P
10.54 p.m.	Brighton	—	

Central District Men.

BRIGHTON DUTY No. 745.
4 P.T. (B.R. Standard.)

SATURDAYS EXCEPTED.

9.13 a.m.	Eastbourne	8. 0 a.m.	P
9.38 a.m.	Eridge	9.28 a.m.	P
9.56 a.m.	Tunbridge Wells West	9.41 a.m.	P
11.16 a.m.	Tonbridge	10.38 a.m.	‖
11.36 a.m.	Redhill	11.30 a.m.	P
**	Loco. Yard	1.55 p.m.	‖B
	Redhill	2.11 p.m.	P

(12.5 p.m. ex Reading)

BRIGHTON DUTY No. 745—continued

2.18 p.m.	Tonbridge	2.51 p.m.	P
3. 9 p.m.	Tunbridge W. W. ...	3.37 p.m.	P
3.54 p.m.	Tonbridge	4.11 p.m.	P
4.52 p.m.	Redhill	5.18 p.m.	‖
5.23 p.m.	Loco. Yard	5.55 p.m.	P
	Redhill	6. 9 p.m.	P
6.50 p.m.	Tonbridge	6.53 p.m.	P
7.11 p.m.	Tunbridge Wells West	7.39 p.m.	P
8.50 p.m.	Brighton	**	‖

(B)—Engine to be well coaled.

SATURDAYS ONLY.

As shewn in Central District until.

9.13½ a.m.	Eridge	9.28 a.m.	P
9.56 a.m.	Tonbridge	**	
**	Loco. Yard	12. 5 p.m.	P
12.49 p.m.	Tunbridge Wells West	12.31 p.m.	—

C. Chunting 1.0 p.m. to 1.45 p.m.

And as shewn in Central District.

Brighton Men.

1st set (S.X.) on duty 4.20 a.m. relieved at Tunbridge Wells West at 9.38 a.m. then as shewn by Central District.

Tonbridge Men.

S.X.—Off No. 295 relieve at Tunbridge Wells West at 9.38 a.m. work and relieved at Tonbridge at 4.10 p.m.

1st set (S.X.) on duty 3.50 p.m. relieve at Tonbridge at 4.10 p.m. relieved at Tunbridge Wells West at 7.10 p.m. relieve No. 635 at 7.30 p.m. relieved at Tonbridge at 8.25 p.m. relieve No. 315 in depot at 9.30 p.m. work and relieved in depot.

Brighton Men.

S.X.—Off No. 733, relieved 7.10 p.m. work and dispose.

Central District Rosters.

S.O.—Until 9.39 a.m.

Redhill Men.

S.O.—Received at Tonbridge at 9.56 a.m. relieve No. 296 in depot at 10.15 a.m. work and dispose.

Tonbridge Men.

S.O.—P. & D. men relieve at Tonbridge at 9.56 a.m. and dispose.

1st set (S.O.) on duty 11.5 a.m. work and change with No. 660 at Tunbridge Wells West at 6.15 p.m. work and relieved at Tonbridge at 7.45 p.m.

Central District Rosters.

S.O.—From 6.15 p.m.

[continued.

738—745

TUNBRIDGE WELLS DUTY No. 667.
¼ PT./¼ FT. (B.R. Class.)

```
  **         Loco. Yard  ...    7.10 a.m.   =P
             Tunbridge Wells West 7.30 a.m.  P
  7.40 a.m.  Eridge ...   ...    8.15 a.m.   P
  8.48 a.m.  Tonbridge ...  ...  8.59 a.m.   P
  9.37 a.m.  Redhill ...   ...    —
      C—Shunting 9.45 a.m. to 10.15 p.m.
             Redhill ...   ...   10.30 p.m.
  **         Loco. Yord ...  ...  1.55 p.m.
  10.58 a.m. Redhill ...   ...    2.11 p.m.  P
  2.48 p.m.  Tonbridge ...  ...   4.10 p.m.  P
  6.4 p.m.   Eastbourne ...  ...  6.20 p.m.**||
        and as shewn Central District.
```

Tunbridge Wells Men.

(1) As shewn Central District, relieved at Tonbridge at 8.55 a.m., relieve No. 291 at 9.41 a.m. work and as shewn in Central District.

Redhill Men.

(2) Off No. 635, relieve at Tonbridge at 8.55 a.m., work and relieved in depot, dispose, and as ordered

Tonbridge Men.

(3) No. 346, relieve in Redhill Depot, perform requirements for 1.55 p.m. ||, work and relieved at Tonbridge at 3.30 p.m.

Eastbourne Men.

(4) Off No. 741, relieve at Tonbridge at 3.30 p.m. and as shewn Central District.

BRIGHTON DUTY No. 735.
¼ PT./¼ FT. (B.R. Class.)

```
As Central District until
  **         Eastbourne ...  ...  9.45 a.m.  P
  11.25 a.m. Tonbridge ...  ...  12.10 p.m.  P
  1.41 p.m.  Brighton ...   ...    2.45 p.m.
      C—Shunting 1.55 p.m. to 2.45 p.m.
             Brighton ...   ...    2.45 p.m.
  2.50 p.m.  Loco. Yard ...  ...   3.40 p.m.
  **         Brighton ...   ...    3.55 p.m.  P
  5.32 p.m.  Tonbridge ...  ...    5.45 p.m.  E
  6.3 p.m.   Edenbridge ...  ...   6.55 p.m.  P
  7.22 p.m.  Tunbridge Wells Ctl. 7.24 p.m.  P
  8.41 p.m.  Brighton ...   ...    8.56 p.m.
  **         Brighton Loco. ...     —
```

Tunbridge Wells West Men.

As shewn Central District until 11.7 a.m.

(1) Off No. 705 relieve at Tunbridge Wells West at 11.7 a.m.. relieved at Brighton at 2.5 p.m.. relieve No. 291 in depot at 2.25 p.m. work and relieved at Tunbridge Wells West at 4.10 p.m.

Brighton Men.

(2) Off No. 766 relieve at Brighton at 2.5 p.m., work and relieved at Brighton at 3.50 p.m.

Tonbridge Men.

(3) Off No. 736 relieve at Brighton at 3.50 p.m., work and relieved at Tonbridge at 5.40 p.m.

BRIGHTON DUTY No. 736.
¼ PT./¼ FT. (B.R. Class.)

```
  **         Loco. Yard  ...    7.30 a.m.   =P=
  **         Brighton ...  ...   7.55 a.m.   P=
  9.25 a.m.  Tonbridge ...  ...  9.32 a.m.   P
  10.10 a.m. Redhill ...   ...  10.20 a.m.
          (coupled to No. 622 (M.X.))
  10.26 a.m. Loco. Yard ...  ... 11.58 a.m.
  **         Redhill ...   ...   12. 4 p.m.  P
  12.42 p.m. Tonbridge ...  ...   1.10 p.m.  P
  2.41 p.m.  Brighton ...   ...    —
      C—Shunting 2.55 p.m. to 3.50 p.m.
        And as shewn in Central District.
```

Central District Rosters.

Until 9.7 a.m.

Tonbridge Men.

(1) Off No. 295, relieve at Tunbridge Wells West at 9.7 a.m., work and relieved at Tonbridge at 9.25 a.m.

(2) 1st set on duty 9.5 a.m., relieve at Tonbridge at 9.25 a.m., relieved at Tonbridge at 12.55 p.m., relieve No. 306 in depot, work and perform requirements for 4.45 p.m. ||.

(3) 2nd set on duty 12.35 relieve at Tonbridge at 12.55 p.m., relieved at Brighton at 3.40 p.m., relieve No. 735 in depot at 3.50 p.m., work and relieved at Tonbridge at 5.40 p.m. and as ordered

(4) 1st set (M.O.) on duty 5.20 p.m. relieve at Tonbridge at 5.40 p.m., relieved in Brighton Loco. relieve No. 294 at 9.45 p.m. work and dispose.

Brighton Men.

(5) No. 4 P. and D. men dispose.

159

BRIGHTON DUTY No. 737.
4 PT./4 FT. (B.R. Class.)

MONDAYS EXCEPTED.

As shewn by Central District until—

1.40 a.m.	East Croydon ...	1.13 a.m.	Y
	Victoria Central ...	1.50 a.m.	Y
		(Trip)	=
**	Victoria (E.) ...	2. 5 a.m.	
**	Victoria Central ...		
C—Shunting 2.10 a.m. to 4.0 a.m.			
	Victoria Central...	4. 0 a.m.	—
4.40 a.m.	Stewarts Lane Loco. ...		

Central District Men.

BRIGHTON DUTY No. 738.
4 PT./4 FT. (B.R. Class.)

As shewn in Central District until—

9.50 a.m.	Brighton Loco. ...	10.40 a.m.	=P
**	Brighton ... z	10.55 a.m.	P
12.27 p.m.	Tonbridge ...		—
**	Loco. Yard ...	2.30 p.m.	**
**	Tonbridge ...	2.54 p.m.	E
3. 6 p.m.	Tunbridge Wells Ctl. Goods		
3.25 p.m.	Tunbridge Wells Ctl. ...	3.2? p.m.	E
4.41 p.m.	Brighton ...	4.56 p.m.	P
5. 7 p.m.	Loco. Yard ...	5.50 p.m.	==
and as shewn in Central District.			

Tonbridge Men.

(1) Off No. 293, relieve at Brighton Depot at 10.35 a.m. work and perform requirements for 2.30 p.m. ||.

(2) 1st set on duty 2.15 p.m. relieved at Tonbridge at 2.54 p.m., relieve No. 312 in depot at 3.25 p.m. work and relieved in depot.

Brighton Men.

(3) Off No. 295, relieve at Tonbridge at 2.54 p.m. work to Brighton and as shewn in Central District.

Other Men.

As shewn in Central District.

BRIGHTON DUTY No. 739.
4 PT./4 FT. (B.R. Class.)

As shewn in Central District until—

**	Eastbourne Loco. ...		
6.18 p.m.	Eastbourne ...	6.15 p.m.	P
8.25 p.m.	Tonbridge ...	6.43 p.m.	P
10.41 p.m.	Brighton ...	9.10 p.m.	P
**	Loco. Yard ...	10.50 p.m.	=

Rosters as shewn in Central District until—

Eastbourne Men.

(1) 1st set on duty 5.0 p.m., relieve in depot, work and relieved at Tunbridge Wells West 8.7 p.m., relieve No. 675 at 8.15 p.m., work and dispose.

Brighton Men.

(2) Off No. 659, relieve at 8.7 p.m., work and dispose.

BRIGHTON DUTY No. 741.
4 PT./4 FT. (B.R. Class.)

**	Loco. Yard ...	5.30 a.m.	=P
**	Brighton ...	6. 5 a.m.	P
7.27 a.m.	Tonbridge ...	8.23 a.m.	P
9. 2 a.m.	Redhill ...	9.20 a.m.	P
9.25 a.m.	Loco. Yard ...	10. 5 a.m.	
**	Redhill ...	10.18 a.m.	P
10.53 a.m.	Tonbridge ...	11.10 a.m.	=
1. 0 p.m.	Eastbourne ...	1.12 p.m.	
1.15 p.m.	Loco. Yard ...	1.35 p.m.	
1.38 p.m.	Eastbourne ...	1.45 p.m.	
3.25 p.m.	Tonbridge ...		**
**	Tonbridge ...	4.45 p.m.	**
**	Brighton ...	5.12 p.m.	=P
6.41 p.m.	Brighton ...		—
C—Shunting 6.55 p.m. to 7.5 p.m.			
7.10 p.m.	Brighton ...	7. 5 p.m.	P
**	Top Table ...	7.41 p.m.	P
**	Brighton ...	7.55 p.m.	P
9.27 p.m.	Tonbridge ...	10.10 p.m.	P
11.49 p.m.	Brighton (S.R.E.) ...		—
C—Shunting 11.55 p.m. to 12.10 a.m.			
**	Brighton ...	12.10 a.m.	=
12.15 a.m.	Loco. Yard ...		

Brighton Men.

(1) 1st set on duty 4.30 a.m., relieved at Tonbridge at 8.20 a.m., relieve No. 635 at 8.40 a.m. work and relieved at Brighton at 11.50 a.m.

Tonbridge Men.

(2) 1st set on duty 8.0 a.m. relieve at Tonbridge at 8.20 a.m., relieved at Tonbridge at 11.5 a.m., relieve No. 670 at 11.58 a.m., work and relieved at Tonbridge at 3.58 p.m.

Tunbridge Wells West Men.

(3) Off No. 668, relieve at Tonbridge at 11.5 a.m., work and relieved at Tunbridge Wells West at 11.29 a.m.

Eastbourne Men.

(4) Off No. 674, relieve at Tunbridge Wells West at 11.29 a.m., work and relieved in depot.

(5) 1st set on duty 1.20 p.m., work and relieved Tonbridge 3.25 p.m., relieve No. 667 at 3.30 p.m., and as shewn Central District.

Tonbridge Men.

(6) No. 2 P. and D. men assist with requirements for 4.45 p.m. ||.

[continued

BRIGHTON DUTY No. 741—continued.

Tonbridge Men.

(7) 2nd set on duty 3.5 p.m., relieve at Tonbridge at 3.25 p.m., relieved at Brighton at 6.41 p.m., relieve No. 299 at 7.11 p.m., work and dispose.

Brighton Men.

(8) 2nd set on duty 5.20 p.m. as ordered, relieve at 6.41 p.m., work and dispose.

BRIGHTON DUTY No. 744.
4 PT./4 FT. (B.R. Class.)

As shewn in Central District until—

4. 8 p.m.	Brighton ...	4.25 p.m.	=
4.30 p.m.	Loco. Yard ...	5.24 p.m.	P
**	Brighton ...	5.55 p.m.	P
7.29 p.m.	Tonbridge ...	8.10 p.m.	P
	(7.35 p.m. Sevenoaks)		
9.41 p.m.	Brighton ...		=
C—Shunting 10.0 p.m. to 10.55 p.m.			
**	Brighton ...	10.55 p.m.	
**	Loco. Yard ...		

Central District Rosters.

Until 4.10 p.m.

Brighton Men.

(1) 1st set on duty 3.45 p.m. relieve 4.10 p.m. work and relieved in depot.

(2) No. 5 P. and D. men dispose.

APPENDIX B
Instruction regarding the removal of Downs Sanding gear
from Locomotives 80034-53

21.
British Railways,
C.M.& E.E.Dept.,
Loco.Works,
Derby.

WDL.158/16/19.PF1.

Order No.X.1071
Sheet No.1

12th August,1957.

Job 5777.Removal of "Downs" Sanding Gear from
B.R.Std.Locomotives. B.R.Std.Cl.4.2-6-4 Tank
Engines 80034-80053.

The "Downs" sanding gear is to be removed from
20 B.R. Standard Class 4, 2-6-4 Tank Engines Nos.80034-80053 which are
maintained by Derby Locomotive Works. This order covers the removal
of the equipment from the second 10 engines and its replacement by
ordinary sand trap and ejector.

An estimate number EE1094 has been prepared for
this scheme and only those documents issued by the Production Office
should be used.

On completion of this order a further order will
be issued.

The Production Office will issue documents.

Authority. C.M.& E.E.'s letter ref.LG43/G/2/31 of 17.2.55 in lieu of
Job instruction and New Works authority which is to be issue
later.

Source of mat'l supply. Derby Loco.

Drawing No. See specification.

Heat treatment reqd.

Inspection. W.I.D.

Work to be carried out.   The engines are to be dealt with as they pass
through the works for general repair only.

Reports to be made.   The individual numbers of the engines so
fitted to be advised in weekly returns to the
Locomotive Repairs Office by No.8 shop.

No.8 shop to report completion to the Progress Section of the
Production Office.

The Production Office will report completion to the Accountant.

F.F.B.Simpson.

Messrs.Mear (6) Reade(2) Birchall, Beech(3) Parker (3) L.D.O.

Shops: 1(3) 5,8(3) 9(3) 12(2) 14,18(3) 19(3)

I.E. 8 & 9 shops.
Ratefixers: 8 & 9 shops.

MATERIALS SOLD BY
BRITISH RAILWAYS BOARD

ADVICE OF DESPATCH

Scottish Region/Workshops

Adviser's Reference *ME/STATS/L/4*

Date of this Advice *28th May 1969*

Serial No. of this Advice *1*

Contract Reference: | 1 | 7 | / | 2 | 3 | 0 | / | 5 | 2 | 2 | / | 4 | 6 | 8 | / | | |
14 ... 31

Item No. | | | |
32 ... 34

Date of Contract *18th March 1969*

COPY No. I TO:— (Name and POSTAL address of Purchaser)
Keighley & Worth Valley
Railway Preservation Society
4 Milton Drive
Poynton, Stockport, Cheshire

DESPATCHED/~~COLLECTED~~ FROM *Chief Mech & Elec Engr* Department

Eastfield Works/Depot

TO (Name of Consignee) *Keighley & Worth Valley Railway Preservation Society*

Destination station or siding *Keighley*

* ~~Carriage charges payable by purchaser. Consignment note passed to Goods Agent.~~

* Carriage paid by B.R. Free Invoice/Waybill passed to Goods Agent.

* Delete whichever is inapplicable.

CATALOGUE No.

MATERIAL *Condemned locomotive*

Date of Despatch or Collection	WAGON			ACTUAL QUANTITY DESPATCHED/COLLECTED (Estimated weights must NOT be inserted)											
	Prefix Letter	No.	No. of Articles	Gross				Tare				Net			
				T	C	Q	lb.	T	C	Q	lb.	T	C	Q	lb.
20·5·69		80002													
TOTALS (If more than one entry):—															

Signature _____ For General Manager

aah **British Railways Board**

The Railway Technical Centre
London Road
Derby DE2 8UP
Derby 42442 Extn ЈАЭ Ꮿ
Telex 37367   Supplies Manager

- Ainsworth Esq
273 Otley Road
West Park
LEEDS 16

y/r
o/r 17/230/522/468   5 Mar 69

Dear Sir

SALE OF LOCOMOTIVE NO 80002

With reference to your telephone conversation on
5 Mar, wherein you confirmed that you wish to
purchase locomotives 80002 standing at Eastfield
for the sum of £2,700, delivered to Keighley, in
the condition as at date of your agreement to
purchase.

Your offer is confirmed, subject to being unsold on
receipt of your official application.

The sale would be in accordance with the attached
terms and conditions, 2 copies of which are enclosed
together with 2 copies of indemnity form and should
you decide to purchase, it will be necessary for
you to sign and return one copy of each document before
the sale can be implemented.

Yours faithfully

for P B HOFF

WILL YOU HELP RESTORE

80064 TO WORKING ORDER

80064 LOCO FUND

Please will you help us to restore ex BR Standard Class 4 2-6-4T No. 80064 so that it can return to working order on the Paignton-Kingswear section of the Dart Valley Railway ? Most of the missing fittings have now been obtained for 80064. It is intended that 80064 will be restored as near as possible to its 1953 condition and livery, and is now being returned to full working order by some members of the Dart Valley Railway staff at Buckfastleigh Station.

80064 was one of the 155 2-6-4 tanks built to the BR Standard design under the direction of the CME Mr. R.A. Riddles and constructed at Brighton, Derby and Doncaster between 1951 and 1956. The design was derived from the Fowler, Stanier and Fairburn varieties of L.M.S.R. 2-6-4 tanks, introduced from 1930 onwards.

The BR locos were extremely successful and were found on all Regions of British Railways. 80064 was completed at Brighton in June 1953 and allocated to Watford Junction with 9 other members of the class to work the outer London surburban services between Euston, Tring and Bletchley and perform shunting duties at places like Berkhamsted and Tring. Due to the introduction of deisels, 80064 was transferred to the Southern Region at the end of 1959. First to Ashford and then Tonbridge.

In 1962 it was transferred to Exmouth Junction to work services in Devon. 80064 remained at Exmouth Junction when the depot was transferred to the Western Region in January 1963. In June 1965 it was transferred to Bristol Barrow Road MPD for possible use on local services to Bath and on the Somerset and Dorset, but due to the water capacity of the loco it was placed in store at Bristol Barrow Road MPD until September 1965 when 80064 was withdrawn from service as being surplus to requirements after a mere 12 years service and sold to Woodham Brothers at Barry Docks, South Wales.

80064 was purchased in December 1972 with the help of a loan and was moved to Buckfastleigh Station in February 1973. Money is urgently required to help with restoration work and to repay the loan needed to purchase 80064. Donations towards the purchase and restoration of 80064 should be sent to the Treasurer of the Fund who will record and acknowledge all donations.

To: The Treasurer, 80064 Loco Fund, 18 Hilton Road, Newton Abbot, Devon.

I enclose a donation of £_____ towards the restoration of 80064.

Name (Block letters) _____

Address _____

Signed _____   Date _____

WILL YOU HELP SAVE

80064 at Whitstone & Bridgerule 27.7.63

photo by M.J. Vinton

80064 LOCO FUND

Will you help save ex BR Standard Class 4 2-6-4T No.80064 so that it can return to Devon to work on the Paignton-Kingswear section of the Dart Valley Railway? Most of the missing fittings have now been obtained for 80064. It is intended that 80064 will be restored as near as possible to its 1953 condition and livery and be returned to full working order by some members of the Dart Valley Railway staff in Devon.

80064 was one of 155 2-6-4 tanks built to the BR Standard design under the direction of the CME Mr. R.A. Riddles and constructed at Brighton, Derby and Doncaster between 1951 and 1956. The design was derived from the Fowler, Stanier and Fairburn varieties of L.M.S.R. 2-6-4 tanks, introduced from 1930 onwards.

The BR locos were extremely successful and were found on all Regions of British Railways. 80064 was completed at Brighton in June 1953 and allocated to Watford Junction with 9 other members of the class to work the outer London surburban services between Euston, Tring and Bletchley and perform shunting duties at places like Berkhamsted and Tring. Due to the introduction of diesels 80064 was transferred to the Southern Region at the end of 1959. First to Ashford and then Tonbridge.

In 1962 it was transferred to Exmouth Junction to work services in Devon. 80064 remained at Exmouth Junction when the depot was transferred to the Western Region in January 1963. In June 1965 it was transferred to Bristol Barrow Road MPD for possible use on local services to Bath and on the Somerset and Dorset, but due to the water capacity of the loco it was placed in store at Bristol Barrow Road MPD until September 1965, when 80064 was withdrawn from service as being surplus to requirements after a mere 12 years service and sold to Woodham Brothers at Barry Docks S. Wales.

The fund is already progressing well but a considerable amount of money is still urgently required. Any promises, shares or donations whether in full or spread over a period by bankers order, would be greatly appreciated. They should be sent to the Treasurer of the Fund who will record and acknowledge all donations, and only if the fund fails will donations be returned in full. The cost of 80064 and movement to Devon will be approximately £4000.

INVOICE № 4517

Registered Office :
No. 1 DOCK
BARRY, SOUTH GLAM.
CF6 6UD

ESTABLISHED 1892

.... 1st March ....19.83.

Mr. R. Hunter (80080 Loco Holdings),.......................................

54 Parkhill Grove, Eastmoor, Wakefield, Yorkshire.

Dr. to ...

WOODHAM BROS.

Proprietor :
D. L. V. Woodham, B.E.M.

IRON AND METAL MERCHANTS
V.A.T. Reg. No. 289 0553 27

Telephone :
BARRY (0446) 733136/7

	Rate	Price	Rate	VAT Amount	Total Amount
To sale of locomotive 80098		9000.00	15%	1350.00	£10350.00

APPENDIX D

Extracts from Engine Working Programmes
Southern Region – Eastern District for Class 2 2-6-2T's
Winter 1958 Schedules

ASHFORD DUTY No. 361.
2 P.T./2 FT. (Standard Class.)

MONDAYS ONLY.

—	Ashford Loco.	... 4. 0 a.m.	=
4.30 a.m.	Canterbury West...	—	

F—Shunting 4.30 a.m. to 6.50 a.m.
(includes 10 minutes coaching shunting)
F—Shunting 7.10 a.m. to 9.30 a.m.
G—Shunting 10.0 a.m. to 10.30 a.m.

—	Canterbury West...	...10.30 a.m.	=

and as shewn below.

MONDAYS EXCEPTED.

(Off No. 362 previous day)

2.50 a.m.	Ramsgate Loco.	... 2.20 a.m.	—

C—Shunting 3.0 a.m. to 3.30 a.m.
F—Shunting 4.0 a.m. to 6.0 a.m.
F—Shunting 7.10 a.m. to 9.30 a.m.
C—Shunting 10.0 a.m. to 10.30 a.m. ‖

—	Canterbury West	...10.30 a.m.	=
11.20 a.m.	Ashford Loco.	...10.30 a.m.	
**	Ashford...	...12. 2 p.m.	P
12.40 p.m.	Maidstone East	... 1.45 p.m.	P
2.28 p.m.	Ashford...	... 3.13 p.m.	P
	(1.40 p.m. Margate)		
3.44 p.m.	Maidstone East	... 4.35 p.m.	P
5.16 p.m.	Ashford...	... 6.12 p.m.	P
6.37 p.m.	Rye	... 6.45 p.m.	E
7. 8 p.m.	Ashford	... 7.25 p.m.	P
8. 4 p.m.	Maidstone East	... 8.32 p.m.	P
9.12 p.m.	Ashford	...	P

C—Shunting (Down Side) 9.20 p.m. to 9.50 p.m. ‖

—	Ashford	... 9.50 p.m.	=
9.53 p.m.	Loco. Yard	...	

Work No. 362.

[continued

ASHFORD DUTY No. 361—continued.

Ashford Men.

(1) M.O.—No. 1 P. and D. men prepare.

(2) 1st set (M.O.) on duty 3.45 a.m., change with No. 91 at Canterbury West at 8.7 a.m., work and relieved at Ramsgate Loco. and home passenger per 10.29 a.m.

Ramsgate Men.

(3) 1st set (M.X.) on duty 2.5 a.m., change with No. 91 at Canterbury West at 8.7 a.m., work and relieved in depot.

Ashford Men.

(4) Off No. 91, change over at Canterbury West at 8.7 a.m., work and relieved at Ashford at 2.33 p.m.

(5) 3rd set on duty 2.3 p.m., relieve at Ashford 2.33 p.m., work and relieved in depot.

Bricklayers Arms Men.

(6) Off No. 421, dispose.

[continued

ASHFORD DUTY No. 362.
2 PT./2 FT. (Standard Class.)

M.O.—Stabled off No. 316 (Sunday).

MONDAYS ONLY.

**	Dover Loco.	... 4.25 a.m.	P
**	Dover Priory	... 4.45 a.m.	P
5.30 a.m.	Ashford...	... **	‖
**	Loco. Yard	... 8.45 a.m.	=

and as shewn for **Mondays excepted**.

MONDAYS EXCEPTED.

**	Ashford Loco.	... 8.45 a.m.	=
**	Ashford...	... 9.12 a.m.	P
9.55 a.m.	Hastings	... **	‖
**	St. Leonards Loco.	...11.35 a.m.	P
**	Hastings	...12. 9 p.m.	P
12.57 p.m.	Ashford...	... 1. 4 p.m.	P
1.43 p.m.	Maidstone East	—	

F—Shunting 2.0 p.m. to 3.0 p.m.

—	Maidstone East	... 2.35 p.m.	P
4.19 p.m.	Ashford...	... 4.35 p.m.	P
5.54 p.m.	Margate...	... 6.15 p.m.	P
	(Coupled to No. 485)		
6.35 p.m.	Ramsgate Loco.	—	

Stable for No. 361.

Dover Men.

(1) M.O.—Off No. 388 (Sunday), prepare ‖.

(2) 1st set (M.O.) on duty 4.10 a.m., work and dispose, prepare No. 366 for 7.30 a.m. ‖, work and relieved at Ashford 8.50 a.m., relieve No. 449 at 9.0 a.m., work and relieved at Dover Marine 12.30 p.m.

Ashford Men.

(3) 1st set on duty 8.0 a.m., change with No. 315 at Hastings at 10.0 a.m., work and commence requirements for 4.45 p.m. ‖, and home passenger per 2.38 p.m. Hastings.

St. Leonards Men.

(4) Off No. 315 change over at Hastings at 10.0 a.m., work and perform requirements for 11.35 a.m. ‖ and as ordered.

(5) 1st set on duty 11.20 a.m., change with No. 90 at Hastings at 11.50 a.m., work and dispose, relieve No. 377 (M.O.) 374 (M.X.) at 1.0 p.m., work 6.10 p.m., and home passenger.

[continued

ASHFORD DUTY No. 362—continued.

Ashford Men.

(6) Off No. 90, change over at Hastings at 11.50 a.m., work and relieved at Ashford at 12.55 p.m.

(7) 2nd set on duty 12.25 p.m., relieved at Ashford at 12.55 p.m., change with No. 485 at Margate at 6.10 p.m., work and relieved at Ashford at 8.31 p.m.

Ramsgate Men.

(8) Off No. 485 change over at Margate at 6.10 p.m., work and relieved in depot.

(9) Off No. 465 dispose.

No. 383—NOT USED.

Engine Workings—South Eastern Division E.R.10—Mondays to Fridays

RAMSGATE DUTY No. 496.
2 F. (C. Class.)

```
        Loco. Yard ...  ...   5.15 a.m.  ||
 **     Ramsgate ...    ...   ...
        C—Shunting 5.30 a.m. to 10.40 p.m.
               (Less 60 mins. Meals and E.R.)
 —      Ramsgate ...    ...  10.40 p.m.  ||
 **     Loco. Yard ...  ...
```

Ramsgate Men.

(1) 1st set on duty 3.30 a.m., prepare this duty, prepare No. 81, work this duty 5.15 a.m. ||, and relieved at 11.15 a.m.

(2) 2nd set on duty 11.0 a.m., relieve at 11.15 a.m., relieved at 4.20 p.m., relieve No. 485 at 4.29 p.m., change with No. 362 at Margate at 6.10 p.m., work relieved in depot.

(3) 3rd set on duty 4.5 p.m., relieve at 4.20 p.m., work and dispose.

No. 487—NOT USED.

Engine Workings—South Eastern Division E.R.10—Mondays to Fridays

RAMSGATE DUTY No. 494.
2 PT./2 FT. (Standard).

```
           Ramsgate Loco. ...  ...    6.40 a.m.  ||
 **        Margate... ...  ...
           C—Shunting 6.55 a.m. to 7.45 a.m.
 —         Margate... ...  ...    8.10 a.m.  P
 9.36 a.m. Ashford ... ...  ...
           C—Shunting (Up Side) 9.45 a.m. to 10.30 a.m.
11.43 a.m. Maidstone East ...  11. 3 a.m.
 1. 7 p.m. Ashford... ...  ...  12.28 p.m.  P
 2.18 p.m. Ashford... ...  ...   1.13 p.m.  P
 **        Ramsgate ...  ...   ...   ||
 **        Loco. Yard ...  ...   5.15 p.m.  P
 6.44 p.m. Ramsgate ...  ...   5.33 p.m.  P
           C—Shunting (Up Side) 7.5 p.m. to 7.50 p.m.
 —         Ashford ...  ...   7.50 p.m.  P
 7.53 p.m. Loco. Yard ...  ...  9.0 p.m.  P
 **        Ashford ...  ...   9.35 p.m.  P
10.54 p.m. Margate ...  ...   ...   **  ||
 —         Ramsgate Loco. ...  ...   ||
```

Ramsgate Men.

(1) No. 3 P. and D. men prepare.

(2) 1st set on duty 6.25 a.m., work and relieved in depot.

(3) Off No. 474, dispose.

(4) 2nd set on duty 4.30 p.m., work and dispose.

No. 495—NOT USED.

Engine Workings—South Eastern Division E.R.7—Mondays to Fridays

RAMSGATE DUTY No. 492.
2 FT. (Standard Class.)

```
           M.X.—Off No. 493.
           Loco. Yard ...  ...   4.40 a.m.  ||
 4.57 a.m. Margate... ...  ...   5.30 a.m.  P
 6.54 a.m. Ashford... ...  ...   7.14 a.m.  P
 7.50 a.m. Maidstone East ...   8.28 a.m.  P
 9. 7 a.m. Ashford... ...  ...   9.42 a.m.  P
11. 4 a.m. Margate... ...  ...   **  ||
 **        Ramsgate Loco. ...   2. 0 p.m.
                 (Coupled to No. 91)
 2.17 p.m. Margate... ...  ...   —
           C—Shunting 2.20 p.m. to 2.35 p.m.
 4.43 p.m. Margate... ...  ...   3.15 p.m.  P
 5.43 p.m. Maidstone East ...   5. 4 p.m.  P
 7.21 p.m. Ashford... ...  ...   6.36 p.m.  P
           C—Shunting (Up Side) 7.50 p.m. to 8.45 p.m.
 **        Ashford... ...  ...   **  ||
 —         Loco. Yard ...  ...   ||
           Stable for No. 493.
```

Ramsgate Men.

(1) 1st set on duty 3.55 a.m., work and relieved in depot.

(2) No. 6 P. and D. men dispose.

(3) Off No. 628, prepare for 2.0 p.m. ||.

(4) 2nd set on duty 1.45 p.m., relieved at Ashford at 7.21 p.m., relieve No. 468 at 7.40 p.m., work and relieved at Ramsgate at 9.25 p.m. depot.

Ashford Men.

(5) Off No. 290, relieve at Ashford at 7.21 p.m., work and dispose.

RAMSGATE DUTY No. 493.
2 PT./FT. (Standard Class.)

```
           Off No. 492.
           Loco. Yard ...  ...   6. 5 a.m.  ||
                 (Coupled to No. 347)
 **        Ashford... ...  ...
 7. 6 a.m. Maidstone East ...   6.28 a.m.  P
 8.19 a.m. Ashford ...  ...   7.36 a.m.  P
 9.51 a.m. Margate ...  ...   8.26 a.m.  P
           C—Shunting 10.0 a.m. to 12.40 p.m.
 **        Margate ...  ...  12.40 p.m.  ||
 **        Loco. Sidings ...   1.10 p.m.  P
 **        Margate ...  ...   1.18 p.m.  P
 1.23 p.m. Ramsgate ...  ...   **  ||
 2.37 p.m. Margate ...  ...   2.23 p.m.  P
           C—Shunting 3.0 p.m. to 6.30 p.m.
           C—Shunting 6.50 p.m. to 8.45 p.m.
 **        Margate ...  ...   9.20 p.m.  P
10. 5 p.m. Canterbury West...  10.52 p.m.  P
11.43 p.m. Margate ...  ...   ||
           C—Shunting 12.0 mdt. to 12.10 a.m.
12.25 a.m. Ramsgate ...  ...  12.10 a.m.  ||
12.50 a.m. Margate ...  ...  12.35 a.m.  E
 —         Ramsgate Loco.... ...
```

Ashford Men.

(1) ...

Ramsgate Men.

(2) Off No. 100, change over at Margate at 11.0 a.m., work, change with No. 475 at 12.5 p.m., work and relieved Ramsgate 12.50 p.m.

(3) Off No. 475, change over at Margate at 12.5 p.m., work and relieved in depot.

(4) Off No. 628, relieve in Ramsgate Depot at 1.40 p.m., change with No. 447 at Margate at 3.50 p.m., work and relieved Ramsgate 4.39 p.m.

(5) Off No. 447, change over at Margate at 3.50 p.m., relieved at Ramsgate 9.35 p.m.

(6) 1st set on duty 9.15 p.m., relieve at Ramsgate at 9.35 p.m., work and dispose and as ordered.

BRITISH RAILWAYS STANDARD STEAM LOCOMOTIVES

Volume 1 Background to Standardisation and the Pacific Classes

Immediately British Railways was formed in January 1948, the Railway Executive instructed Robert Riddles to design a series of standard locomotive designs. The intention was to gain material savings in running and maintenance costs by adopting as standard the best practices of the four independent companies. In this major new series, the Society presents for the first time the complete story of British locomotive standardisation from the days of the Robinson ROD 2-8-0s to the twelve BR Standard designs totalling 999 locomotives. This book, by Paul Chancellor and Peter Gilbert, presents the Standards' design history and for each of the 66 locomotives in the popular Britannia, Duke and Clan classes its complete construction, modification, allocation and operating history.
Larger page size 212 x 272mm, Casebound, 184 pages, 151 illustrations including 17 in colour.

LMS DIESELS

Locomotives and Railcars

Today's British motive power fleet is a tribute to the pioneering work of the LMS. Classes 56, 58, 60 and HST power cars use AC generators based on the 10800 Hawk development and Class 77 electrics used LMS designed bogies. Classes 40, 50 and DP2 used LMS designed engines and Peak Classes 44-46 used cab design from the famous 10000 and 10001. Our first generation diesel multiple units owe much to the 1938 80000-2 LMS railcars. And, of course, our Classes 08 and 11 bear testimony to the quality of their LMS design 60 years ago! Author Edgar Richards takes readers through the fascinating history of LMS diesel development. From the first steam conversion in 1932 to the rugged 0-6-0 shunters built in large numbers for war service at home and abroad, the revolutionary main line 10000, 10001, 10100 and 10800, and the Michelin, Coventry and LMS railcars, in total 208 locomotives, 15 railcars and 5 trolleys were operated by the LMS. Full details of their design, construction, modification, liveries, allocation and use are included. This book includes much new material and is highly recommended.
Casebound, 219 pages, 125 illustrations

LMS LOCOMOTIVE NAMES

The Named Locomotives of the London, Midland and Scottish Railway and its Constituent Companies

The LNWR had a vigorous naming policy and the Midland Railway an equally determined anti-naming stance. The 1923 grouping set the stage for an absorbing battle within the management teams over naming policy with Derby's early policy success followed by Crewe's ultimate victory. Author John Goodman's absorbing read presents the full story of the LMS and its constituent companies' naming policies and the history of each named engine owned by the LMS, a total of 812. The LNWR contributed 668 of these and a complete presentation of its complex re-naming system is an invaluable inclusion.
Casebound, 211 pages, 124 photographs, 25 drawings.

RCTS Publications List

Title of Book	ISBN No.	*Price
Locomotives of the LMS:		
The Jubilee 4-6-0s	0901115940	£24.95
LMS Diesels	0901115762	£19.95
LMS Locomotive Names	0901115797	£18.95

> OFFER★ BUY THIS BOOK FOR £10.00★ WHEN BOUGHT WITH LNWR LOCO NAMES

LNWR Locomotive Names	0901115908	£19.95
Locomotives of the LNWR Southern Division –		
L&BR, LNWR and Wolverton Locomotive Works	0901115894	£27.95
Raising Steam on the LMS	0901115851	£15.95

> SPECIAL OFFERS★
> | | | |
> |---|---|---|
> | Set of Highland Railway Locomotives (2 books) | | £23.50 (NETT PRICE) |
> | Set of Gt. Northern Locomotive History (4 books) | | £40.95 (NETT PRICE) |

BR Standard Steam Locomotives:		
Vol 1 Background and the Pacifics	0901115819	£19.95
Vol 2 The 4-6-0 and 2-6-0 Classes	0901115932	£24.95
Vol 3 The Tank Engine Classes	0901115770	£18.95

The Great Northern Railway in the East Midlands		
Nottingham-Grantham, Bottesford-Newark, Melton		
Mowbray, Leicester Line, Ironstone branches	0901115924	£18.95
Colwick Yards, London Rd-Gedling-Basford	0901115843	£13.95
The Erewash Valley lines, Pinxton Branch,		
Awsworth-Ilkeston, Heanor & Stanton Branches	0901115886	£15.95
Nottingham Vic, GC, Leen Valley Network	090111586X	£14.95

> *SPECIAL OFFER – FREE WHEN YOU BUY A GNinEM SERIES BOOK*
> | | | |
> |---|---|---|
> | A Travellers Guide to the Robin Hood Line | 0901115835 | £2.95 |

Plymouth's Railways in the 1930's	0901115916	£12.95

> | | | |
> |---|---|---|
> | The Railways of Keynsham | 0901115827 | £9.95 |
> OFFER BUY THIS BOOK FOR £5.00★ WHEN BOUGHT WITH PLYMOUTH'S RAILWAYS IN 1930s

The Birkenhead Railway (LNW & GW Joint)	0901115878	£14.95
Locomotives of the LNER:		
Part 1 Preliminary Survey	0901115118	£12.95
Part 2B Tender Engines Classes B1-B19	0901115738	£13.95
Part 9A Tank Engines Classes L1-L19	0901115401	£10.95
Part 9B Tank Engines Classes Q1-Z5	090111541X	£10.95
Part 10A Departmental Stock, Engine Sheds,		
Boiler and Tender Numbering	0901115657	£10.95

★UK Post free. Overseas add 40%

Available from:–
Assistant Publications Officer, Littlecote, 365 Old Bath Road, Leckhampton, Cheltenham, GL53 9AH
When ordering please quote reference STDS
We accept orders on our website www.rcts.org.uk We accept payment by credit card.

Correspondence on, ideas for, and volunteers to help on publications production are warmly invited by the Society. Please contact Reg Wood, 70 Heathfields, Downend, Bristol, BS16 6HS, England.

RCTS

The Railway Correspondence and Travel Society is Britain's leading organisation for people interested in all aspects of railways past, present and future. It is highly regarded by both professional railway people and enthusiasts, a position it has held since its formation over 75 years ago. A monthly journal, *The Railway Observer,* is sent to each member. In addition, there are indoor meetings at many centres throughout the country and visits to centres of railway interest.

Full details of the Society and how to become a member will gladly be supplied by Vron Cooke, 23 Haig Drive, Slough, SL1 9HA, England, or visit our website www.rcts.org.uk

Correspondence on this book and additional information are welcomed. This, together with ideas for future books, and volunteers to help on publications are keenly sought by the Publications Officer, A. Reg Wood, 70 Heathfields, Downend, Bristol BS16 6HS, England.